LANGUAGE IN SOCIETY   12

Observing and Analysing
Natural Language

Language in Society

GENERAL EDITOR
  Peter Trudgill, Professor of Linguistic Science,
  University of Reading

ADVISORY EDITORS
  Ralph Fasold, Professor of Linguistics,
  Georgetown University

  William Labov, Professor of Linguistics,
  University of Pennsylvania

Observing and Analysing Natural Language

A Critical Account of Sociolinguistic Method

LESLEY MILROY

BASIL BLACKWELL

First published 1987

Basil Blackwell Ltd
108 Cowley Road, Oxford, OX4 1JF, UK

Basil Blackwell Inc.
432 Park Avenue South, Suite 1503
New York, NY 10016, USA

British Library Cataloguing in Publication Data

Milroy, Lesley
Observing and analysing natural language:
a critical account of sociolinguistic method.
1. Sociolinguistics—Methodology
I. Title   III. Series
401'.9   P40.3

ISBN 0-631-13233-3
ISBN 0-631-13623-1 Pbk

Library of Congress Cataloging in Publication Data

Milroy, Lesley
Observing and analysing natural language.

(Language in society : 12)
Bibliography; p.000
Includes index.
1. Sociolinguistics—Methodology. I. Title.
II. Series: Language in society (Oxford, Oxfordshire); 12.
P40.3.M54 1987   401'.9'072   87–5202
ISBN 0-631-13233-3
ISBN 0-631-13623-1 (pbk.)

Typeset in 10/11½pt Times
by Alan Sutton Publishing Limited
Printed in Great Britain by
Page Bros (Norwich) Ltd

Contents

For Jim, David, Andrew and Richard

Editor's Preface

As is well known, William Labov, whose work was initially responsible for the development of research in those areas of sociolinguistics which are today sometimes referred to as *secular linguistics*, was initially not at all happy that the label *sociolinguistics* should be attached to work that in his view, and I believe in the view of all of us who are practitioners of this science, should really have been referred to simply as *linguistics*. This terminological battle has subsequently been lost, but the popularity of the term *sociolinguistics* does have the advantage of stressing the primary location of this form of research in the community rather than in the office or laboratory, and of indicating the somewhat independent traditions and objectives the subject has subsequently acquired within the wider field of linguistics.

Work of this type is, at its best, so insightful, productive and exciting that one might be surprised at how relatively little of it is actually performed, for all that it is by no means a totally minority activity. This should, however, really come as no surprise, since work in this paradigm, for all its importance, is most often difficult, complicated, time-consuming and expensive. It is no wonder that many of the weaker brethren confine themselves to the comfort of working with their own intuitions in the security of their own offices. With the publication of this book, however, work in secular linguistics will now be that little bit less daunting, because in *Observing and Analysing Natural Language* is distilled the collective wisdom of the first generations of sociolinguists, including not least Lesley Milroy herself, who is one of the best practitioners of this form of sociolinguistics there has ever been. Here, that is, is an author who really knows what she is talking about because in her own pioneering work she has confronted and overcome many of the thorniest practical and theoretical problems that this field has to offer.

The book itself deals not only with fieldwork methodology and data collection, and not only with the analysis and interpretation of this data, it also deals, crucially, with the interrelationships between these two aspects of secular linguistic work, and with the often neglected connections between methodology, interpretation and linguistic theory. With this book we have, for the first time, a work which focuses on the history, objectives and achievements of secular linguistics to date, as well as on its methodology. It will be of enormous value to anyone studying, teaching or working in any sociolinguistic aspect of language in the community. Lesley Milroy's *Observing and Analysing Natural Language* is a very important milestone in this field. Indeed, it represents a coming of age in the development of sociolinguistics as a discipline.

Peter Trudgill

Preface

This book cannot in any sense be said to be a handbook or inventory of techniques, although it is certainly intended to be of practical value to those interested in studying the way people use language in naturally occurring social contexts. Sociolinguistic method is discussed in terms of its relationship to theory, in the belief that if this link is not acknowledged *interpretation* of research results may ultimately be difficult and unsatisfying. This is because apparently innocuous methods which are in fact associated with a specific theoretical paradigm can conceal important underlying assumptions. Methodological problems and principles will therefore be discussed not only in practical terms, but in terms of both assumptions underlying the chosen method, and the theoretical goal of the research. An account of method divorced from theory is not considered to be helpful, desirable, or even possible.

Chapters 1 to 4 focus chiefly on methods of data collection and chapters 5 to 8 on various aspects of data analysis and interpretation. But there are at all points areas of overlap, and underlying theoretical issues frequently emerge. Although a good deal of the discussion is placed within the general framework of the methods first developed by William Labov for use in urban settings (and indeed assumes some knowledge of his work), I very much hope that a number of principles will emerge which are of value to people who, while not necessarily researching within this paradigm, are concerned for a number of different reasons with the study of language in its social context. These include not only linguists with an academic interest in (for example) the language choice patterns of ethnic minorities in industrialized societies, in conservative rural dialects, in pidgin and creole languages and in 'exotic' languages. There are also professionals such as teachers, educational psychologists and speech therapists, who work extensively with language and who sometimes need to collect, analyse and interpret samples of naturally occurring speech. These wider applications are discussed in chapter 9, where a number of practical issues are explored which can be illuminated by sociolinguistic methods of data collection and analysis.

As far as seems possible without sacrificing style and clarity, I have avoided using the controversial generic pronoun forms *he, him, his.* But where alternative means of expressing generic reference seem awkward I have used the traditional forms, and hope that readers will accept this purely stylistic decision in the spirit in which it was taken.

Acknowledgements

Many people over the years have helped me, directly and indirectly, to write this book. Their assistance and influence on my approach to sociolinguistics is gratefully acknowledged here.

Most importantly, James Milroy has shared the responsibility for planning and directing the Belfast research projects where we both obtained 'hands on' experience. Without him, I would certainly not have embarked upon the work at all. Thanks are also due to the people who worked on those projects, contributing to them in different ways; they are Rose Maclaran, Domini O'Kane, John Harris, Linda Policansky, Zena Molyneux, Brendan Gunn, Máire Burke, Thomas Vogel and Ann Pitts. The financial support provided for both projects (HR 3771; HR 5777) by the Social Science Research Council is acknowledged with thanks.

I have also profited greatly from discussing with other linguists various aspects of their work, as will often be apparent from references in the text. Warm thanks are due particularly to the linguists who treated me so hospitably during my visit to Australia during the spring of 1983. Our stimulating and often lengthy discussions of methods, goals and problems of field linguistics influenced considerably my approach to writing this book. But like many other sociolinguists, I have learnt more from William Labov than from anyone else, and am happy to acknowledge his support and continuing influence. Peter Trudgill's comments on an earlier version of this book were particularly appreciated, as was his tactful moral support throughout the entire task of producing it. Jack Chambers, Janice Kay, James Milroy and Kay Mogford also read and commented helpfully on parts of the manuscript.

An early draft of the first two chapters was written during my tenure of a Simon Senior Research Fellowship at the University of Manchester, during 1982–3. This financial support is gratefully acknowledged. At a much later stage of production, Anne Stals transformed an unprepossessing manuscript into an impeccable typescript for which she has my grateful thanks. Thanks are due also to Helen Moore, for help with proof reading.

I am grateful to publishers and authors for permission to adapt their original figures and maps, the sources of which are specified in the text. Further details are as follows:

Figure 1.1 is adapted from A.E. Kibrik's *The methodology of field investigations in linguistics* (Mouton, 1977, p.7). Map 1.1 is adapted from David De Camp's 'Social and geographical factors in Jamaican dialects', which appeared in R.B. Le Page (ed.) *Creole language studies II* (Macmillan, 1961, p. 78). Figure 4.1 is adapted from a figure in W. Labov's 'Field methods used by the project on linguistic change and variation', *Sociolinguistic working paper* 81 (1981). Map 4.2 is adapted from Ann Pitts' 'Urban influence on phonological variation in a Northern Irish speech community'; the original figure appeared in *English world wide* 6,1 (Benjamins, 1985, p.66). Figure 6.1 is adapted from Barbara Horvath's *Variation in Australian English* (Cambridge University Press, 1985, p.71). Figure 8.2 is adapted from Allen Bells' 'Language style as audience design'; the original figure appeared in *Language in society* 13,2 (Cambridge University Press, 1984, p.171). Figure 8.4 is adapted from a figure in S.N. Parasher's 'Mother-tongue-English diglossia: a case study of educated Indian bilinguals' language use', *Anthropological linguistics* 22 (1980), 4. Figure 8.5 is adapted from Joan Rubin's *National bilingualism in Paraguay* (Mouton, 1968, p.109).

Finally, the spouses and children of authors have to put up with a great deal of disruption to the smooth running of their daily lives, and mine are no exception. I thank Jim, David, Andrew and Richard for their continuing love and support.

Lesley Milroy
University of Newcastle upon Tyne

1

Field Linguistics: Some Models and Methods

1.1 Data and Theory

It is illuminating to begin a discussion of sociolinguistic method by considering two general issues which have implications for the field linguist at all stages of data collection, analysis and interpretation; these are the relationship of the investigator to data and the relationship between data and grammars.

There are a number of ways in which an investigator might proceed in carrying out a piece of synchronic linguistic description. The term 'description' is used rather widely here (following Kibrik (1977)) to cover either descriptions of languages unknown to the investigator or descriptions of the investigator's native language, both of which can be based either on introspection or on some sort of field investigation. By considering the task of linguistic description in this way, we can examine rather radically the relationship between investigator and object of study in terms of the type of data used, assuming that the output will always be (to a greater or lesser extent) an idealized model of a fragment of a language.

Models might be of many different kinds, examples being an account of some aspect of 'core' grammar (such as the English Noun Phrase); the grammatical categories of an entire language (such as Dixon's (1971) grammar of Dyirbal); or an account of the systematically variable use by members of a speech community of a portion of the linguistic system (such as Labov's (1966) study of the distribution of five sociolinguistic variables in the Lower East Side of New York City). Although the models produced by sociolinguists are often felt in some sense to be closer to the data base than those of other types of linguist, it is important to remember that a representation such as Labov's famous graph of the variable realization of /r/ in New York City is actually *an idealized model of sociolinguistic structure;* the figures upon which it is based are the product of a long process of sociological, mathematical and linguistic abstraction. Idealized models of any kind, whatever the differences in method, theoretical goal and assumption which underlie them, bear an indirect relationship to data.

Gumperz has discussed Labov's methods and theoretical goals in such a way as to make the abstract character of his models very clear. He points out that although Labov rejects Saussurian and Chomskyan assumptions of uniformity in grammatical systems, he shares with other linguists an interest in understanding the general character of *grammars,* believing these to be affected by the social characteristics of human groups. Gumperz then goes on to argue that the relatively abstract approach associated with this theoretical goal entails a neglect of the *speaker as participant in interaction,* and that quite different methods are needed to investigate issues arising from the ability of speakers to interact, such as the co-occurrence (or otherwise) of their judgements in the interpretation of discourse: 'A speaker-oriented approach to conversation . . . focuses directly on the strategies that govern the actor's use of lexical, grammatical, sociolinguistic and other knowledge in the production and interpretation of messages in context' (Gumperz 1982: 35).

Labov himself has contrasted in a similar way two alternative approaches to linguistic variation: one can start by examining linguistic forms (variables) and their distribution, or by examining speakers and the kind of behaviour appropriate to different situations. Labov prefers the first type of framework because it gives a better idea of the *system* as a whole, although it is not capable of yielding optimal information about *speakers* (Labov 1966: 209).

Labov's focus on system rather than speaker leads to consideration of a widely accepted principle of scientific linguistics: the language itself is an abstract object not amenable to direct observation. However, as Kibrik notes, 'the concrete utterances which represent the realisation of the linguistic competence of speakers who know the language can be observed' (1977: 2). Such an emphasis seems uncontroversial, and is useful in that it helps us to remember the relative abstractness of (for example) the variable language patterns which are of interest to urban dialectologists. Nor does Kibrik's remark imply acceptance of Chomsky's controversial competence/performance distinction, which has not proved to be a useful one for sociolinguistics (see further L. Milroy 1985).

Labov has observed that the general programme of all linguists – not only those who are writing competence grammars – begins with a search for *invariance* (Labov 1975: 7). The context of this remark was an attempt to focus on precisely how one kind of linguistic enterprise differs from another, and Labov argued that good methods and theories could best be developed by considering the important assumptions which linguists shared before examining those which divided them. Commenting on the theory/ data relationship in a manner which also tends to emphasize the similarities between different types of linguistic enterprise, Kibrik lists what he considers to be three crucial concepts in any conceivable descriptive linguistic activity (but compare the comments of Gumperz, quoted above):

1 The *subject* of investigation (the language or part of the language).
2 The *object* of the investigation (written texts or tape-recorded data).
3 The *product* of the investigation. This is the *model* of the subject of the investigation which is usually called the *grammar*. Thus, Labov's graphic representations, which model patterns of language variation in New York City, may reasonably be described as grammars.

By using the term 'grammar' in this extension of its usual sense, we can begin to compare and contrast coherently the aims, methods and procedures of, for example, a descriptive linguist and an urban sociolinguist both working on a portion of the verb phrase (see Cheshire 1982a and J. Harris 1984 as examples of sociolinguists with those interests). It is not profitable to see these differences (as Chomsky apparently has done; Chomsky 1980: 248) in terms of differences in the amount of idealization of the data base; models are always abstract and indirectly related to data. But using Kibrik's framework, and assuming with Labov (1975) that co-operation is essential if linguists are to benefit from each other's insights, differences between descriptive linguists and sociolinguists may be analysed as differences in the relationship between the investigator, the subject of study and the object of study in the process of arriving at the final product (or model). Differences in the character of these relationships also give rise to methods which differ in their potential to achieve particular goals.

Following this general line of thinking, we can present in graphic form (figure 1.1) three different models of the process by which an investigator arrives at a product:

Figure 1.1(a) models an investigator/data/grammar relationship whereby the investigator directly accesses the target language by means of his or her own linguistic competence. Since the description is based on introspective self-observation (sometimes checked against the introspections of others), a body of data (the object of the investigation) is absent. One point which might be made is that this method cannot be used to study any language or language variety not known to the investigator, and since academic linguists are seldom competent speakers of non-standard dialects or uncodified languages, can in practice be used for describing only fully codified standard languages. This is not of course to deny that those who have grown up as native speakers of a dialect (for example, Peter Trudgill in Norwich) may have intuitions about its structure; so also might non-native speakers who have developed an intimate knowledge of the structure of a dialect (see J. Milroy 1981 for an example). But descriptions of non-standard dialects generally use intuition as an aid to focusing the

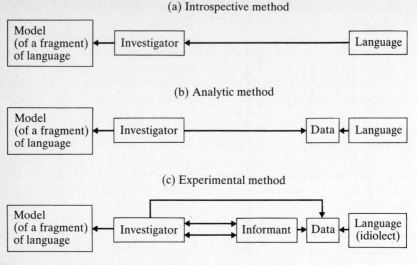

Figure 1.1   Modelling the methods of descriptive linguistics
(adapted from Kibrik 1977: 3)

investigation, rather than as a basic method; for although important facts about linguistic structure and organization are accessible to introspection, its applicability is sharply limited.

The method modelled in figure 1.1(b) also involves knowledge of the target language by the investigator. But rather than accessing intuitions directly, he or she bases generalizations upon a corpus of independently collected data. The clearest example of this method is modern work on discourse analysis and stylistics (see for example Stubbs 1983). The kinds of generalizations made by discourse analysts and stylisticians do not in fact appear to be accessible to intuition.

Much methodological discussion in the writings of the American structuralists (see further 1.2.1 below) implies that the structure of an *unknown* language can be recovered by analysing a corpus, without recourse to any other method; but as Bowman (1959) shows, this does not seem to be feasible. In practice, generalizations based on analyses of corpuses are usually derived using an additional method – either introspection or some kind of experimental procedure. Thus for example the substantial grammar of English written by Quirk and his associates (1972) is based upon both analytic and introspective methods of accessing information about linguistic structure, no clear distinction being drawn between information drawn from a corpus and information drawn from introspection.

In practice then, entirely corpus-based linguistic description of the kind attacked by Chomsky (1957: 15; 1965: 2) is extremely rare and probably represents a concept whose value is largely polemic. Since most linguists would probably agree that an adequate grammar cannot be derived solely from a corpus, the disagreement does not appear to be about the validity of a corpus-based analysis. Rather, it is about finding a principled way of supplementing or replacing a corpus-based approach. Labov (1975) provides an extended critique of the difficulties associated with introspection as an *alternative* method.

The term 'experimental', which describes the method modelled in figure 1.1(c), refers to the investigator's *control* over the data accessed. This method is used in conjunction with data independent of the investigator's own introspective observations, but does not involve inductively deriving linguistic generalizations from that data source. Rather, a native speaker is used to provide specified types of fact about the target language or variety, and most sociolinguists or dialectologists investigating a known language use a combination of this method with (a) and (b). Characteristically, linguists who investigate *unknown* languages use a combination of the experimental and analytic methods; sometimes an interpreter mediates between investigator and native speaker.

The term 'experimental' is used broadly to describe any method which entails the direct manipulation of an informant's responses. Within it is included a heterogeneous collection of procedures ranging from the minimal pair and commutation tests developed by the American structuralists to the formidable battery used by Labov (1966; 1975; 1981) for various purposes. Also included are the matched guise techniques developed by social psychologists (Giles and Powesland 1975) and standard methods used in psycholinguistics (Garnham 1985).

The three models shown in figure 1.1 of the interrelationship between investigator, data and grammar provide a general frame of reference in this book whenever there is a need to explore issues arising from them. At various points, for example, we shall have reason to consider the implications of using model (c). This is because the use of an informant for obtaining linguistic information raises a large number of problems with which sociolinguists are centrally concerned. In fact, some of them emerge as a natural consequence of observation whether or not informant responses are deliberately manipulated by the investigator (see further chapter 3).

1.2 Earlier Approaches to Linguistic Description

1.2.1 The American descriptivists

The American linguists commonly known as 'structuralists' or 'descriptivists' placed a high premium on the development and practice of a rigorous and accountable set of field methods. I shall outline here the characteristics of their approach and philosophy only in so far as they are relevant to the central concerns of this book. For a fuller account, the reader is referred to Lepschy (1982), and Hymes and Fought (1980).

The concern with field methods in mainstream American linguistics from about the 1920s until the emergence of Chomsky may be partly attributed to a desire to describe as rapidly and efficiently as possible a large number of dying American Indian languages. Gumperz (1982: 12) contrasts the atmosphere of empiricism at that time in America, where scholars were concerned with working in the field, with that in Europe, where they worked in offices. Many American linguists, following the line of reasoning exemplified by Bloomfield (1926; 1935), associated the development of rigorous methods of description with the accreditation of a *scientific* status to linguistics. They strove to obtain objectivity by developing accountable procedures for inductively deriving linguistic generalizations from observable data, and an important methodological principle springing from this concern was that the phonological, morphological, syntactic and semantic patterns of a language should be analysed separately. They should moreover be analysed in that order, so that the analyst could remain in touch with the 'observable' part of language – the sequence of sound segments which he always began by describing.

This concern with *accountability to the data* (the object of description, in Kibrik's terms) has subsequently been the hallmark of Labov's work; the *principle of accountability* extends the general philosophy of accountability to a specifiable pocedure which is the cornerstone of quantitative method (see further 6.1). In this respect Labov's views resemble those of earlier American linguists but differ sharply from those of Chomsky and others working within his paradigm. Replacing induction with a hypothetico-deductive mode of reasoning, the generativists argue that no corpus of data, however large, can usefully serve as a basis for linguistic generalizations since any corpus is a partial and accidental collection of utterances (Chomsky 1975: 15). Although Chomsky's general point about the inadequacy of corpuses as the *only* source of information is surely correct (if in practice uncontroversial – see 1.1) one effect of his remarks has been to remove the sense of accountability to an independently collected body of data which was once much more widespread in linguistics than it is now. Field linguists generally – not only those working in the Labovian tradition – have reservations about the consequences of heavy reliance upon introspection: 'whatever may be the difficulties in studying and evaluating human behaviour in relation to language, behaviour is nevertheless more objective and observable than intuition or introspection. We can observe behaviour; we can only affirm intuition' (Longacre 1964: 13). There is no doubt that the revolution in linguistic thinking pioneered by Chomsky has affected the way field linguists go about constructing *models* (see G. Sankoff 1980c: 65 for a discussion). But American descriptivist methods still provide the basis for many contemporary techniques of *data collection* and *data analysis*. The extensive studies of Australian languages by Robert Dixon and his associates are obvious examples. Rather less obviously, structuralist methods, the most influential of which are outlined below, have been developed in various ways for use in quantitative sociolinguistic work (see particularly Labov 1981).

The descriptivists considered that establishing which sounds were contrastive was the major task of a phonological analysis, and proceeded as follows:

> We take an utterance recorded as DEF. We now consult an utterance composed of the segments of DA'F where A' is a repetition of a segment A in an utterance which we had represented as ABC. If our informant accepts DA'F as a repetition of DEF . . . and if we are similarly able to obtain E'BC (E' being a repetition of E) as equivalent to ABC, then we say that A and E . . . are mutually substitutable (or equivalent) as free varients of each other . . . If we fail in these tests we say that A is different from E and not substitutable for it. *The test of segment substitutability is the action of the native speaker: his use of it or his acceptance of our use of it* [my italics]. (Z. Harris 1951: 31)

In the absence of any alternative framework capable of application to a substantial body of data, linguists studying exotic languages still need to establish contrastivity in a similar way (see Healey 1974: 8 for a New Guinea example). So also do sociolinguists; but one respect in which quantitative sociolinguists have in recent years advanced the substitution method is by querying the assumption of objectivity in pair testing and showing that native speaker judgements of 'same' and 'different' do not necessarily accord in any straightforward way with independently observed phonological patterns (see 3.3.1: 8.2.1). Harris's painstaking account gives an idea of the care with which the descriptivists formulated their 'discovery procedures' as they were called, this basic method of substituting one element for another being viewed as the equivalent in linguistics to the controlled experiment of the physical sciences. Most importantly, it permitted replicability (see Moore and Carling 1982: 19ff for a discussion of the relationship betwen method and contemporary linguistic theory and meta-theory).

The descriptivists attempted to use the results of their phonological (and morphological) analyses as a basis for describing the *syntactic* patterns of an unknown language. The main aim was to assign words to word classes on purely distributional grounds, using syntactic frames (parallel to Harris's phonological frame DEF) to present a range of items which were candidates for membership of a particular category. Although this technique is not relevant to contemporary sociolinguistic methods of studying syntax (see chapter 7), it is still widely used for the analysis of unknown languages. Detailed accounts may be found in Samarin (1967) and Healey (1974) where it is outlined with particular reference to Teleéfoól, a New Guinea language. Sutton and Walsh (1979: 23) list the grammatical categories likely to be relevant to contemporary work on Australian languages.

The criterion for determining membership of a syntactic category is again the willingness of a native speaker to accept a string as grammatical. As in the case of phonological pairs tests, sociolinguists have reported that speaker judgements do not accord well with the results of independent observation, and are more likley to reflect *stereotypical attitudes* to linguistic forms than the facts of grammatical structure. Labov (1975) has cited the unreliability of speaker judgements as an argument against the uncontrolled use of introspection as a methodological tool; certainly the main difference between the procedure of the generative linguists and that of the descriptivists for establishing grammaticality seems to be the use of the linguist's own judgement rather than the judgement of others.

Although descriptivist methods are still widely used in field linguistics generally (particularly in describing exotic languages) the link between field procedure and theory which was so important to the descriptivists has disappeared. Consequently, contemporary applications of descriptivist method tend to be rather more relaxed than was once felt to be appropriate, following what Longacre (1964: 12) has described as a 'guess and check' procedure. In practice, it is likely that informed guesswork (or the investigator's intuition) rather than the application of strict procedures based on form and distribution has always been used initially in tentatively assigning class membership to an item (cf. the example of Bowman 1959, cited in 1.1).

1.2.2 Traditional dialectology

Many aspects of an approach to the observation and description of language which was developed during the nineteenth and twentieth centuries have been taken over and sometimes adapted by contemporary rural and urban dialectologists. Its main features are described by Petyt (1980) and Chambers and Trudgill (1980). Generally speaking, the aim of dialectological work is to produce a geographical account of linguistic differences, the product often taking the form of a series of maps showing the broad areal limits of the linguistic features (usually lexical or phonological) chosen for study. Boundaries (known as *isoglosses*) are plotted on the map, which show where form A gives way to form B; a *dialect boundary* is said to exist where a number of isoglosses more or less coincide. For example, Wakelin (1972: 102) illustrates the boundary between the Northern and North-Midland dialect areas of England by showing eight isoglosses which mark the approximate southern limit of eight phonological features characteristic of northern English dialect speech.

If we are to understand the field methods of traditional dialectology, it is important to remember that they were devised not in order to survey patterns of contemporary language use as an end in itself, but to offer a means of answering questions about the earlier history of the language. The main objective was to study contemporary reflexes of older linguistic forms in their natural setting, concentrating on speakers and locations which were relatively free from external influence. Associated with this theoretical model was a view of rural life strongly coloured by eighteenth- and nineteenth-century romanticism, as is evident from the following description:

> In Europe, the practice has been to confine the survey to the speechways of the folk, and to give prominence to the oldest living generation in rural communities. A predilection for historical problems, the hope of shedding light on processes of linguistic change by observing the linguistic behaviour of the folk, and admiration for the soil-bound 'ethos' or 'world-view' of 'natural' people have been the motives and justification offered for this practice. (Kurath 1972: 13)

With these motives, Gilliéron approached his linguistic survey of France by seeking out older male, uneducated speakers who lived in remote rural communities. Both Orton (1962: 15) and McIntosh (1952: 85) discuss the value to more recent surveys of this type of speaker on whom it does indeed seem sensible to concentrate if the goal is to to collect evidence which confirms hypothetical reconstructions of earlier forms. But the problem is that rather different sampling procedures are needed if the survey purports to make a more general statement about patterns of language variation. While nineteenth-century research is overwhelmingly historical in orientation, twentieth-century dialectologists working within the traditional paradigm frequently seem to have shifted their theoretical goal in the direction of an attempt to describe the contemporary language. Thus, the *Linguistic Atlas of the United States and Canada* attempts to adapt the traditional model by selecting informants at three educational levels, each notionally categorized as 'old-fashioned' and 'modern' types. Kurath comments: 'Until recently, large-scale surveys have been deliberately restricted to folk speech, especially to that of the countryside . . . In *The Linguistic Atlas of the United States* all population centers of any size were regularly included and, in principle, all social levels are represented' (1972: 11).

A similar tendency in more recent British studies to shift the theoretical goal is evident form McIntosh's comment that the Scottish survey will concentrate on older (or, as he calls them, 'resistant') speakers *'only in the first instance'* (1952: 86). Orton on the other hand, while aware of the sensitivity of patterns of language use to factors such as status, age, sex and situational context, is nevertheless quite clear in his view that these facts are irrelevant, since his objective is to locate for the *Survey of English Dialects* speakers who can provide samples of traditional dialect speech (Orton 1962: 15). One of the major points made by Labov in his early comments on the work of the dialectologists is that a realistic account of contemporary language variation necessitates radical alterations to the traditional method; minor adaptations are insufficient.

Moving on from the question of appropriate techniques of speaker selection to consider methods of *data collection* in traditional dialectology, we find that the two major techniques are *on the spot phonetic transcription* by a trained fieldworker and *the postal questionnaire*. It is the technique of on the spot transcription, adapted in various ways, which has provided the major model for later work. In recent times it has been supplemented or replaced by the tape-recorder, a development which has made possible the study of larger stretches of spontaneous spoken language rather than isolated lexical items (see chapter 3). However, twentieth-century dialectology (exemplified by the *Survey of English Dialects),* which works within an only slightly modified framework of the traditional paradigm, has generally not fully exploited in its methods those technological advances which facilitate the study of spontaneous speech. Characteristically, the tape-recorder is used simply as a support for the fieldworker, who proceeds otherwise in much the same way as his or her nineteenth-century equivalent.

The postal questionnaire is an older technique, pioneered in Germany by Georg Wenker, who published his work in 1876. More recently it has been used by McIntosh (1952) and Le Page (1954); see also Le Page and Tabouret-Keller (1985: 83). McIntosh notes the obvious advantage of the method, that it provides an economic means of collecting large volumes of data. Questionnaires are still quite widely used where there is a need to collect a large amount of easily processible data quickly; examples are the ALUS survey of the Linguistic Minorities Project (1985) and Amuda's (1986) study of Yoruba/English code-switching patterns in Nigeria. The main disadvantage of questionnaires is that data may be inaccurately reported by informants who are not trained in phonetic transcription. Thus, McIntosh proposes using a postal questionnaire whenever possible, supplemented by the observations of a trained fieldworker when 'a closer scrutiny of the exact form of the word is neccessary' (1952: 78).

A parallel but slightly different difficulty in using informant responses is noted by the creolist R. B. Le Page in his early work (1957, 1958). Le

Page's procedure in his *Linguistic Survey of the British Caribbean* was to send a questionnaire containing the following instructions to school-teachers, who were asked to locate suitable informants:

It is essential that the answers given to each question should not be those which the school teacher or other helper (whom we will call the *Interrogator*) can supply from his own vocabulary, which will have been considerably enlarged and influenced by his education and travel, but those which a local *Informant* supplies without undue prompting. You are therefore requested to select as an *Informant* somebody, preferably middle-aged and not too well educated, who has lived in your area for the greater part of his or her life, and has had comparatively little contact with other places. The *Informant* will have to be a person whom you know is willing to talk to you unaffectedly in the language he would use to his own family; somebody who will not be trying to impress you with his knowledge of white-talk all the time or of what is said by other people in other places. It would be useful to explain to the informant that you only want the words and phrases exactly as they would be used by the ordinary unsophisticated people of this community. Men or women who work or live in daily contact with people from other countries or other walks of life should not be used as informants. In an agricul-tural village, select an elderly labourer, in a fishing village a fisherman – but not somebody who goes to sell goods in a distant market or somebody who works as a domestic servant. (Le Page 1954: 2)

Le Page has identified here a number of problems which are not associated exclusively with the use of a questionnaire, but are quite general in linguistic fieldwork. First of all, the effect of social or occupational mobility on language use is noted; second, the natural effect of style-shifting in inhibiting the use of 'everyday' language as opposed to more formal varieties is hinted at; and finally the effect of 'white-talk' on attitudes to the vernacular is noted, together with the consequence that an informant will often claim to use forms considered to be of higher status than his or her normal usage. All of these problems of eliciting samples of low-status vernacular speech in contexts where negative social values are attached to it have subsequently received considerable attention from investigators working within Labov's framework. Indeed, Le Page himself has now for many years worked generally within this framework, although he has been critical of some aspects of it (see McEntegart and Le Page 1982: Le Page and Tabouret-Keller 1985).

1.3 The Traditional Model: Some Adaptations and Criticisms

Until the mid-1960s, the general framework offered by the traditional dialectological model was widely used for descriptions of language variation largely because at that time it was the only coherent one available. We look in this section at various attempts to adapt it for purposes other than those for which it was originally intended and the difficulties consequently encountered.

1.3.1 De Camp's survey of Jamaican dialects

De Camp, like Le Page, began by working within the traditional paradigm, but later abandoned it for a more sophisticated approach to the problems of describing variability in creole languages (De Camp 1971). In his early work, he used traditional dialect-mapping techniques to plot linguistic differences between Jamaican dialects (see Map 1.1), but was clearly unhappy with the implication of *discreteness* underlying the concept of isoglosses. Even though dialectologists have generally acknowledged that dialect boundaries are not in reality sharp divisions, a method of presentation such as map 1.1 is difficult to interpret as a satisfying model of contemporary language variation. De Camp comments:

> Many people, including some educated Jamaicans, say that there are two distinct kinds of English spoken in Jamaica: 'standard English' and 'the dialect', meaning the folk speech of the uneducated. This is a persistent myth, a dangerous misconception. Indeed there is a great deal of difference between the English one hears at a Parent-teacher Association meeting of a fashionable suburban prep. school and that which one hears at a pocomania street meeting. But one can also find examples of every intermediate variety of English. Nearly all speakers of English in Jamaica could be arranged in a sort of linguistic continuum, ranging from the speech of the most backward peasant or labourer all the way to that of a well educated urban professional. Each speaker represents not a single point but a span of this continuum, for he is usually able to adjust his speech upwards or downwards for some distance on it. The middle-class housewife will understand the informal speech of a market woman and, if sufficiently provoked, may even retort in kind, though she would probably have difficulty in maintaining an extended conversation on the market woman's level. Similarly the market woman may adapt her speech in the direction of the matron's. Each of them would probably describe the different levels in her own speech as 'standard English' and 'the dialect', yet the market woman's 'standard' might be further down the linguistic continuum than the matron's broadest

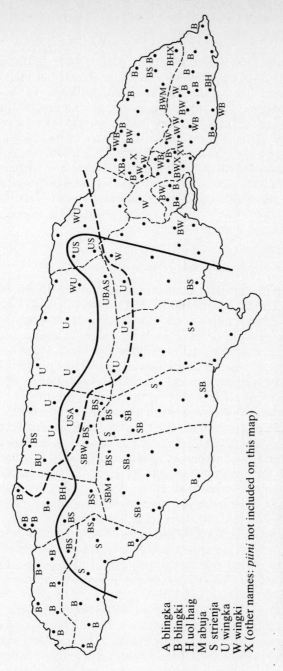

A blingka
B blingki
H uol haig
M abuja
S strienja
U wingka
W wingki
X (other names: *piini* not included on this map)

Map 1.1 Linguistic dialect differences in Jamaica for 'small firefly'
(adapted from De Camp 1961: 78)

'dialect'. Every speaker differs in the span of this continuum which he can command. (De Camp 1961: 81)

It is evident from these remarks that De Camp is interested in finding a way to model patterns of contemporary language use, rather than in applying his data in the manner of the traditional dialectologists to the solution of historical problems. His observations on the nature of the linguistic continuum in Jamaica use the example of creole data to raise objections to underlying assumptions of invariance and discreteness which have proved subsequently to be of considerable theoretical interest. Moreover, dialectological methods were simply not designed to deal with language variation associated with a range of social factors *within* a single geographical area. Nor could existing dialect-mapping techniques deal with the fact that individual speakers vary within a range which might overlap the range controlled by other speakers.

1.3.2 Between paradigms: some early urban studies

One of the most pervasive assumptions underlying traditional dialectological method is that a particular form of a dialect – usually represented by the speech of a conservative, socially marginal speaker – may in some sense be seen as the 'genuine' or 'pure' form. The main difference between early and more recent urban studies is that the latter examine *alternative* linguistic forms, seeing this alternation as a significant property of language rather than admitting the concept of the 'pure' or 'genuine' dialect. As we shall see, this difference in the conception of what constitutes a 'dialect' has important implications for informant selection procedures.

One example of a good traditional study of an urban dialect is Viereck's *Phonematische Analyse des Dialects von Gateshead-upon-Tyne* [sic] (1966), a substantial and clear synchronic phonological account which includes a discussion of the relation between Received Pronunciation and 'local standards' (an idea derived from H. C. Wyld). Viereck considers in some detail how dialect forms might interact with RP forms to produce such urban varieties as that of Gateshead. However, although Gateshead's population is given as 100,000 and consists of persons of both sexes, all ages and various social statuses, the description is based on the speech of twelve men, all retired manual workers, whose average age is seventy-six. This does not seem to be a reasonable basis for a systematic description of an urban dialect.

Gregg's work in Larne, Co. Antrim (1964) resembles Viereck's in that it contains substantial phonological information and shows a similar interest in the emergence of local urban standards. Gregg relates his findings in Larne to data on the local Ulster-Scots dialect, noting that while Larne speakers have a similiar phoneme inventory to rural hinterland speakers, they characteristically reorganize it in such a way that the available phonemic contrasts appear in different lexical sets. This kind of systematic difference is what Wells (1982) describes as an *incidential* difference in the distribution of phonemes. Although Gregg's account is sophisticated it is clearly traditional in orientation in so far as it is preoccupied with the 'genuine' speech of Larne as opposed to speech in which influence from nearby Belfast can be detected.

Similar comments might be made about Sivertsen's *Cockney Phonology* (1960). While recognizing that there are various kinds of Cockney which vary according to style and speaker, Sivertsen is explicitly interested in what she describes as 'rough Cockney', and her work is based mainly on the speech of four elderly female informants from Bethnal Green, selected for their relative social isolation, low social status, and lack of education. Although this is a substantial and clear description which includes a number of interesting observations (on, for example, sex-based differences in language) Sivertsen still reveals the traditional preoccupation with the 'pure' form of the dialect, in her view obtainable only from uneducated, old, low-status speakers.

The same preoccupation is revealed in a slightly different form in Weissmann's study of Bristol phonology (1970). Again we have a substantial and clear phonological account supplemented by both a phonemic and a phonetic transcription of spontaneous speech (recall the tendency of traditional dialectology to focus on single lexical items). Weissmann's selected informants were all young men, partly because he felt more comfortable with men, but more importantly because he felt (probably correctly) that men would modify their characteristic Bristol speech less than women. Thus we see again a *restriction* in the type of informant selected with a view to producing a static description of some kind of 'extreme' phonological system.

The best of these early urban studies, of which we have discussed only a few examples here, provide valuable sources of data on the phonologies of British urban dialects (see Kurath 1972: 184ff for a discussion of some similar American studies). But they present two main problems which are both exemplified in Sivertsen's study.

First, certain assumptions are inherent in the preoccupation with 'genuine' dialect, the most obvious being that young speakers, by virtue of access to education and modern communications networks, are more likely to be influenced by the standard. This assumption has not in general been borne out by empirical observation. For example, Hurford (1967), discussing the language of three generations of a London family, suggests that Cockney features are advancing among the youngest speakers at the expense of RP features.

Some recent quantitative studies suggest that the kind of age grading in language noted by Hurford in London is in fact rather general, to the extent that researchers now expect to find the most extreme form of an urban vernacular among adolescent speakers and may focus on that age group (see for example Cheshire 1982a). It is therefore dangerous to proceed in the manner of the older urban studies on the basis of apparently common-sense assumptions which may, when investigated, turn out to be false.

The second problem with these studies is their lack of *representativeness*. London is one of the largest cities in the world and has probably always been linguistically very heterogeneous. Even if we confine our interest to working-class speech from the East End, we are still talking about hundreds of thousands of people, and so it seems inappropriate, without explicit acknowledgement, to limit the description to a single type of informant. Some scholars have attempted to tackle this problem while still working broadly within the traditional framework, and a brief outline of two such attempts will help to place Labov's subsequent and much more influential work in perspective.

Houck's survey in Leeds was intended to provide a model for the study of urban dialects generally (Houck 1968). Using an extremely sophisticated two-stage sampling procedure, he ended up with a sample of 115, representing a 75 per cent success rate, which is very good for a linguistic survey (see further 2.1). Unfortunately, however, Houck gave little indication in his published work of how the speech of his 115 informants was handled; the intention seems to have been to set up a phonological system using minimal pairs elicited by means of sentence frames (cf. 1.2.1). Thus, although he succeeded in obtaining a large amount of representative data, he was not in the end able to find a way of handling it. Labov's methods of handling large amounts of data are discussed in chapter 5.

Heath's survey of the urban dialect of Cannock, Staffordshire, carried out in the late 1960s, is characterized by an equally rigorous approach to sampling (Heath 1980). The 80 informants are divided into five groups, in accordance with the amount of influence upon their speech of the 'extremes' of Received Pronunciation on the one hand and Cannock urban dialect on the other: the influence of traditional studies on Heath's approach, as on that of the other researchers whose urban dialectological work has been considered in this section, is shown by frequent references to the 'pure' Cannock speaker.

In subsequent chapters, we shall consider methods of data collection and analysis which do not oblige us to use the concept of the 'pure' dialect speaker but allow the contemporary language to be modelled in a somewhat more realistic way than was possible by adapting traditional methodology. For although there is much that is valuable and innovatory in Heath's work, which adapted traditional methods quite considerably, he was not able to model the *systematic* character of inter-speaker variation. The major contribution of Labov's methods was that in explicitly recognizing such patterns they provided a means of describing the language of *all* speakers of a dialect, without forcing the investigator to argue (or imply) that the language of one particular group was in some sense more 'genuine' than that of others.

2

Sampling

2.1 Introductory

While it is true that the traditional urban studies described in 1.3.2 are open to criticism on several counts, it is only realistic to concede that the task of describing the speech of *any* city is a daunting one. An investigator is immediately faced with such obvious and awkward facts as those noted by (for example) Sivertsen; individual informants vary in the extent to which they use a characteristic dialect feature (such as the glottal stop in Cockney), and speak noticeably differently according to situational context. In Cannock, Heath simply remarked that speakers dropped *h* 'inconsistently' (1980: 51). However, radically different methods have revealed a consistency in interpersonal and intrapersonal linguistic variability which is quite elusive if we search for it in the idiolect of the 'ideal' dialect speaker.

These methods were first developed by William Labov in his innovatory urban study *The social stratification of English in New York City* (1966). Since clear accounts of Labov's methods are available elsewhere (see for example Labov 1966, 1972b; Chambers and Trudgill 1980; Hudson 1980; Wardhaugh 1986), they are outlined only briefly here; the purpose of this chapter, taking Labov's procedure as a starting point, is to discuss the principles of *sampling* both *speakers* and *language* in such a way as to bring out the relationship between research design and research objectives. At the same time, it is important to be aware of the theoretical implications of adopting any given method and ultimately of the kind of claims which a given method entitles an investigator to make about results.

We begin by looking at the issues raised by an attempt to give a *representative* account of the language of a group of speakers – let us say the inhabitants of a city. By this we mean that we are describing the language of the citizens in general, without a bias towards any particular subgroup in the population. For example, the speakers described in the traditional studies discussed in chapter 1 could not be said to be representative of the community whose language was being studied, since they were characteristically of a particular type.

2.2 Random Sampling a Population

2.2.1   Some general principles

Labov attempted to attain representativeness in the Lower East Side of New York City by taking his informants from a previously constructed *random sample* of the population. A *sample frame* is any list which enumerates the relevant population, simple examples being electoral registers and telephone directories; the main principle of random sampling is that anyone within the sample frame has an equal chance of being selected. Any sample frame is, however, likely to be biased in some way; for example an electoral register excludes persons under eighteen years old, and telephone directories list only telephone subscribers. This will usually have the effect of excluding less wealthy sections of the population, and a higher proportion is likely to be excluded in Britain than in the United States. Assuming, however, that this kind of bias is taken into account, the general idea is that every *n*th individual enumerated on the frame will be selected by some mechanical procedure.

In fact, Labov was by no means the first urban dialectologist to be sensitive to the need to give a representative account of urban speech. We have already seen that Houck (who provided a model for Heath) devised a sophisticated sampling procedure. And it is plain from Kurath's discussion of dialectological method that the idea of sampling had been current for some time (Kurath 1972: 13). However, Labov's sampling methods are important and distinctive in that they were part of a larger, principled programme for the *quantitative* study of language variation, which itself was designed to address important theoretical problems in linguistics. Sampling procedure is one part of the general method associated with Labov's 'quantitative paradigm'; in fact, as we shall see, it is not necessarily central to it.

The New York City sample, itself a subsample derived from a larger sample constructed for sociological research, originally comprised 340 individuals. But as in all randomly selected sets of linguistic informants, many of these were not interviewed for reasons such as death, illness, change of residence, non-local origin or simply refusal to co-operate. Labov's ultimate description was based mainly on 88 speakers – just over one quarter of the original random sample. Difficulties of this kind have led some researchers to query both the wisdom and the validity of a complicated sampling procedure which in the end might not measure up to the standards demanded by disciplines outside linguistics; the main objections are discussed by Romaine (1980). Briefly, they are first that linguistic samples are usually too small to ensure that the set of persons interviewed is representative of the population as a whole, in the sense that findings can be extrapolated from the sample to the population *within measurable and statistically specifiable confidence limits* (Moser and Kalton 1971). A second (and related) problem is the difficulty of *replacing* members of the original sample who, for one reason or another, cannot be interviewed. We shall discuss this problem first.

Replacement of unavailable members of a sample is a time-consuming process, the general principle being to ensure that the replacements have characteristics similar to those of the randomly selectd persons whom they replace. If this is not done the remaining sample is likely to show bias of some kind. For example, McEntegart and Le Page point out that from a sample of 280 children in Belize, usable data was obtained only from 200. The researchers suspected that a large proportion of those who did not talk enough to provide adequate data were from a particular ethnic subgroup who reacted unfavourably to the Jamaican fieldworker. The non-random distribution of these absentees vitiated the randomness of the entire sample (McEntegart and Le Page 1982: 107).

Many of Labov's original sample were excluded from his final list because they were non-native speakers of the dialect (or indeed the language). Given his general research design, it is hard to see what strategy he might have adopted for replacing this group. But by *selecting* speakers in this way he was in fact introducing bias into his original sample (see further 2.2.4). On the basis of unrecorded telephone calls and short face-to-face conversations, he argued that the group of *native* speakers who refused to be interviewed did not need to be replaced bacause they did not differ linguistically from those who *were* interviewed. Although Labov may have been right in making this claim about *language,* it is clear that his ultimate sample is not statistically representative in the sense that its relationship to the population can be precisely specified (see Erickson and Nonsanchuk 1977 for a clear discussion of this statistical issue). However, this is not as severe a criticism as it might seem, and is spelt out here only to make the point that researchers need to be cautious in formulating claims about data. For although his sample was not strictly representative, Labov's procedure was undoubtedly a great advance on earlier methods in that it ensured representativeness in the non-technical but (for socio-linguists) very important sense that he neither concentrated on any particular group of speakers, nor claimed that any particular type of speech was 'typical' of New York City. These two effects of the method differentiate Labov's approach to urban dialectology sharply from that of the traditional studies reviewed in 1.3.2.

A realistic discussion of sociolinguistic sampling needs then to distinguish strict statistical representativeness from the rather weaker kind of representativeness attained in most urban surveys. Certainly, it is by no means clear that strict representativeness would necessarily give greater insights into sociolinguistic structure (but see 2.2.4 for an account of a recent study of the language of ethnic minorities in England where it *is* important). What seems to be critical is that researchers decide which type of representativeness is sufficient – or attainable – for them.

2.2.2 Sample size

Socially sensitive studies of language variation depend on good data. This entails the provision of sufficient types and quantitites of language, and also that the social context in which the language is gathered is taken into account. Thus, the notion of 'representativeness' needs to be broadened to include different types of language (used by the same speaker) as well as different types of speaker. In an excellent discussion of quantitative methodology, Gillian Sankoff (1980c) notes that the need for good data imposes on the researcher three different kinds of decision to make about sampling procedures. These are as follows:

1 To define the sampling universe. That is, to delineate, at least roughly, the boundaries of the group or community in which one is interested. An adequate sample frame which investigates group members may then be sought.
2 To assess the relevant dimensions of variation within the community – this involves constructing stratification for the sample. Thus, we must ask whether ethnic group, sex, or social class of speaker might affect the kind of language used. Most studies so far have shown that to a very great extent they do, as does situational context.
3 The sample size needs to be fixed.

Sankoff then goes on to remark that once decisions 1, 2 and 3 have been made, sampling may be through a social network approach or by the formal, random methods on which we are focusing in this section.

Depending on the kind of community studied, decisions 1, 2 and 3 can each conceal huge problems, and since it pertains to the general issue of representativeness, we shall look at 3 first. In fact Sankoff notes, as do many linguists, that large samples tend not to be as necessary for linguistic surveys as for other surveys. This is apparently because linguistic behaviour is more homogeneous than many other types of behaviour studied by surveys – such as, for example, dietary or television programme preferences:

> The literature, as well as our own experience, would suggest that even for quite complex communities samples of more than about 150 individuals tend to be redundant, bringing increasing data-handling problems with diminishing analytical returns. It is crucial, however, that the sample be well chosen, and representative of all social subsections about which one wishes to generalise. (Sankoff 1980c: 52)

It is probably true, for practical reasons, that the very demanding kind of data handling involved in any linguistic study limits the sample size in the way Sankoff describes. However, like the biased samples discussed in 2.2.1, these small samples cannot usually be said to be statistically representative. Once again, we need to accept that unless the characteristics of the sample can be extrapolated to the population within measurable and acceptable confidence limits (which are related to sample size), it is likely to be representative only in a non-technical sense. However, there seems to be little point in aiming for technical representativeness in the face of the diminishing analytic returns described by Sankoff. An extreme example of this effect is Houck's work (1968), where we find a meticulous account of a technically acceptable random sampling procedure but no subsequent linguistic analysis at all.

2.2.3 Stratifying a sample

Most researchers who have adopted a formal random sampling approach have done so because they want to be able to generalize securely – 'to ensure . . . as true a scale model as possible of the population which we want to say something about' (Nordberg 1980: 2). This brings us to decision 2 as outlined by Sankoff, that of assessing the relevant dimensions of variation. The problem is that if our 'scale model' is one of a society which contains persons of different social statuses, different ages and both sexes, we shall be obliged, if we want to make generalizations about any of these subgroups, to subdivide an already small sample (recall that Labov based his generalizations on 88 individuals in New York City). If we adopt a stratified type of sampling in order to be sure of picking up individuals representing (say) four status groups, both sexes and four age groups, we shall need to fill 32 cells. If we elect to fill each cell with four speakers, we shall need a sample of 128. This is already larger than many sociolinguistic samples, and will in itself create a very large amount of data and necessitate much time-consuming analysis; but if we add one other variable – such as ethnic group of speaker – we potentially double the number of cells. Alternatively, if we keep our original sample size of 128, we arrive at cells containing two speakers. This has the unfortunate consequence that generalizations on the language of (for example) working-class female speakers of a particular age and ethinc group are based rather insecurely on just two speakers.

In practice of course many surveys have fewer than four speakers in each cell and smaller samples than our notional 128. Labov's generalizations in New York City were based on 88 speakers; Trudgill's in Norwich on 60 (Trudgill 1974). Shuy, Wolfram and Riley (1968) carried out a total of 702 interviews from 254 families in Detroit, using a most carefully constructed random sampling procedure (based on schools) to attain strict statistical representativeness. However, the data-handling problems characteristic of linguistic work meant that in the end only a fraction of the data was selected for analysis (36 speakers, on the basis of their general suitability). Thus, there appears to be a point where careful sampling actually becomes counterproductive.

In conclusion, it seems that practical considerations partly dictate sample size, and although stratified samples such as Labov's and Trudgill's have been criticized because generalizations about a group such as 'upper-middle-class women' may be based on a very small number of speakers, no easy solution has yet been found to the problem. Perhaps because of this the practice of using random procedures to obtain stratified samples is now less popular than it was in the late sixties and early seventies.

2.2.4 Defining the sample universe

Delineating the boundaries of the community in which we are interested (decision 1 on Sankoff's list) has not usually been discussed as a problem; but it is worth examining the basis of Labov's rejection of a large number of randomly selected persons because they were not 'native speakers'.

In view of the number of immigrants in New York City, it seems reasonable to ask first whether it is desirable to exclude such speakers from the sample universe. Even if we allow that it is legitimate to confine our attention to native speakers, recent work by Payne (1980) and Trudgill (1983a; 1986) shows that the *definition* of a native speaker is problematic in a manner critical for sociolinguistic analysis; native speakers cannot be picked out easily just by listening to their accents. Payne's work suggests that children born of parents from different dialect groups may never acquire the structural patterns of the dialect spoken by the community into which they are born. Similarly, Trudgill (1983a: 10) points out that some people have lived all their lives in Norwich without acquiring a Norwich accent.

Horvath's (1985) study of the English spoken in Sydney raised the definition of the sample universe as an important issue, and does not exclude in advance persons for whom English is a second language. This decision turned out to be theoretically important, since ethnic minority speakers seem to be leading linguistic changes which are affecting the entire Sydney speech community. However, the decision was also methodologically very far-reaching, since the range of data obtained required methods of analysis radically different from Labov's. The Sydney study (which is discussed further in 2.5 and 6.8.6 below) is an excellent illustration of the principle that decisions made at the sampling stage have implications for data analysis and interpretation.

The Linguistic Minorities Project, based in London, was faced rather directly with problems of defining the sample universe. The general goal was to study various aspects of the language of non-English speakers in England and Wales, and one part of the Project was the Adult Language Use Survey, which attempted to describe the languages used by eleven linguistic minority groups in three cities. The objectives of the description were rather different from those of an urban dialect survey, involving the discovery of facts about which languages are in use in Britain and how they are used, rather than the provision of a linguistic description. But despite its particular objectives, the sampling problems faced by the survey are highly relevant to any sociolinguist working in a modern multi-cultural society. From the beginning the researchers were extremely anxious to avoid bias in the sample of the kinds described by Moser and Kalton, with which readers will now have some familiarity:

> Bias in the selection can arise (1) if the sampling is done by a non-random method, which generally means that the selection is influenced consciously or unconsciously by human choice; (2) if the sampling frame (list, index or other population record) which serves as the basis of seleciton does not cover the population adequately, completely or accurately; (3) if some sections of the population are impossible to find or refuse to co-operate. (Moser and Kalton 1971: 79; quoted by Smith 1984)

The major problem with which I am concerned in this section lay in the provision of a sample frame, since it was extremely difficult for the researchers to discover the location of minority speakers, or even to discover how many individuals constituted the sampling universe. Minority groups of immigrant origin in Britain, as in many other countries, are geographically and socially distributed amongst the population in a non-random way. This means that random selection from a sample frame such as an electoral register will be both inadequate and inefficient; the national census (which has avoided questions on ethnicity) cannot provide a sample frame. In the event, the researchers used two methods of constructing sample frames, neither of which was entirely satisfactory.

The first was the use of *ethnic name analysis*. A sample frame was constructed by enumerating distinctive ethnic names extracted from electoral registers, and various systematic and random methods of selecting speakers from the resulting list were then employed. The second was the use of *community lists* of minority language speakers, obtained from the communities themselves. This method was used, for example, to delineate a sampling universe of Italian speakers in Coventry and London, where exhaustive lists of minority community Italian speakers were available. Ethnic name analysis had proved to be unsuitable for this group for two reasons. First, since most Italian speakers are non-Commonwealth citizens and are not entitled to vote, their names do not appear on electoral registers. Second, most Italian names are in any case not especially distinctive indicators of ethnic origin.

Clearly, objections can be raised to both of these methods of constructing sample frames and readers are referred to Smith (1984), Morawska and Smith (1984) and the report of the Linguistic Minorities Project (1985) for a fuller account. But difficulties in delineating the sample universe are likely to be generally critical for researchers studying ethnic minorities. Despite these difficulties, the LMP researchers felt that since they did not know the size or the location of the target population, they should attempt to attain as far as possible the goal of statistically representative sampling. Paradoxically, this lack of background knowledge of the relevant populations means that representativeness, although hard to attain, is rather more important than it is for urban dialect studies of established populations. In his conclusion, Smith assesses the success of the Survey's sampling methods as follows:

It is not really possible to make a statistical assessment of our sampling methods in different linguistic minorities. Factors such as the rate of registration on electoral registers (which varies from neighbourhood to neighbourhood, from city to city and from language to language), the incompleteness or bias in the various 'community' lists and the differential response rates deriving from various sources, mean that we cannot claim a precise level of confidence in our results. We would be very cautious in extrapolating from any of our ALUS language groups to the linguistic minority as a whole, even within a single city. At the wider national level we would be reluctant to say that any of our samples are representative, especially since some of our findings suggest that members of the same linguistic minority in different cities exhibit very different patterns in their social background and in their linguistic behaviour. However, we believe that on the whole our samples are of the best quality that could be achieved, that the response rates are encouragingly high and that the main sources of systematic bias have been eliminated. Within each local setting they are probably somewhat more representative than simple quota samples of a given number of speakers of given languages.

In the final analysis, the contribution of LMP to the techniques of social survey research lies in the development and application of sampling and fieldwork techniques which are appropriate to the previously unresearched field of linguistic minorities. Future research in this and related fields will be able to benefit from our experience and refine our methods. (Smith 1984: 33)

2.3 Judgement Sampling

It was suggested in 2.1 that for a linguist the important feature of Labov's sampling procedure is not its statistical sophistication, but the fact that it provides a basis for a description of urban speech which does not concentrate on any particular group of speakers, or claim that any particular type of speech is 'genuine'. Macaulay's study of Glasgow speech, using 54 speakers, is an example of a city-wide survey which uses *judgement* sampling, rather than any kind of random procedure: 'On the judgement of a member of the Education Department a total of seventeen schools . . . was selected as being representative of the schools in Glasgow' (Macaulay 1977: 20). Although this sample can be criticized even within its own lights as a judgement sample, it is successful in revealing important patterns of variation in Glasgow and in providing the basis for a description which is not confined to a particular subgroup of the population. Thus, although one must be cautious of claiming representativeness, Macaulay's study shows that it is possible to make useful generalizations about linguistic variation in a city without becoming involved in the practical difficulties of combining strict random sampling with demanding linguistic analysis. Certainly, a distinction needs to be made between sampling methods such as those discussed in 2.2, which use some kind of random procedure, and those like Macaulay's which are based on the judgement of the investigator rather than on any principle of random selection.

The principle underlying judgement sampling is that the researcher identifies in advance the *types* of speakers to be studied and then seeks out a quota of speakers who fit the specified categories. A good judgement sample needs to be based on some kind of defensible theoretical framework; in other words, the researcher needs to be able to demonstrate that his or her judgement is rational and well-motivated.

Both Romaine (1978a) and Reid (1978) based their studies of the language of Edinburgh children on schools, which were selected on the basis of the social and demographic characteristics of the schools' catchment areas. This information was derived from the 1971 Census of Population. Since Romaine's aim was to examine aspects of the language of working-class children, she selected a school from an area which ranked low in terms of various demographic characteristics enumerated in the Census such as housing, education, employment and health. Reid, on the other hand, selected one school near the top of a rank-ordered list, one near the bottom, and a fee-paying school; the purpose of his study was to compare and contrast aspects of the language of children from different social groups.

Romaine's and Reid's methods seem to be quite appropriate to the purposes of their studies, which are essentially to focus on the linguistic characteristics of specifiable and well-defined social groups; indeed, it is hard to see that any kind of random procedure would have been of value in these cases. But what is important about the composition of these judgement samples is that they are defensible on the basis of specifiable sociological and demographic criteria – those underlying the design of the 1971 Census. Romaine herself remarks that Macaulay's judgement sample in Glasgow is not based on such objectively specifiable criteria but on the subjective assessment of an Inspector of Education (Romaine 1980: 170). It could indeed be the case that the subjective assessment of the expert whom Macaulay consulted corresponded closely to a rank-order of schools derived from the Census – but that is not the point. Precisely *because* it was based on subjective assessment, the composition of Macaulay's sample is open to legitimate challenge by any individual who feels prepared and qualified to make a rival assessment. The same problem does not arise with a judgement sample selected on the basis of objectively defensible criteria.

It seems appropriate at this point to summarize the main issues so far, and assess the advantages and disadvantages of different methods of informant selection. Smith has suggested that in a study like the Linguistic Minorities Project Adult Language Use Survey, where the composition and characteristics of the population to be surveyed are little known, it is important to observe principles of random selection as strictly as possible in order to ensure reasonable representativeness. But in cities with a well-established population whose characteristics are definable on objectively specifiable dimensions (as derived for example from the Census), judgement sampling may, for two main reasons, be more appropriate for linguistic work.

First, the samples used in linguistic surveys are in general demonstrably *not* technically representative, and to claim that they are leaves a researcher open to quite proper academic criticism. Second, relatively small samples (too small to be considered technically representative) appear to be sufficient for useful accounts of language variation in large cities. For example, despite criticisms which might be levelled at Macaulay's procedure, the rank-order of speakers arranged by social class (as defined by the Register General's categories) correlates impressively closely with the rank order of their *language* scores, as calculated using indices for four vowels (Macaulay 1977: 58). It is true that there may be a great many interesting facts about language in Glasgow that Macaulay's sampling methods have not revealed (see further 6.3.1) – but it has not been demonstrated that they could have been better revealed by random methods of speaker selection. It seems to be generally true that very consistent patterns emerge even with a very small sample, provided that it is *systematically selected*.

It could be argued that Labov's much attenuated sample was in the end as much a judgement sample as a random sample (although it followed procedures of random selection). For in order to construct a sample appropriate to his research objectives, he discarded as unsuitable large numbers of speakers, retaining only those who met specifiable criteria. Certainly, in view of the problems associated with strict representative sampling, it may be more realistic for researchers conducting, for example, an urban dialect survey, to judgement sample *on the basis of specifiable and defensible principles* than to aim for true representativeness.

2.4 Research Objectives and Informant Sampling

One principle which has already emerged from the discussion (see particularly the comments on Romaine 1978a and Reid 1978) is that the objectives of a piece of research to a very large extent dictate methods of speaker selection. This relationship between goal and method is even more clearly illustrated by Arvilla Payne's study of children's language in the Philadelphia suburb known as King of Prussia, designed to discover 'the extent to which children of various ages acquire the phonological system of a second dialect after moving from one dialect region to a new one' (Payne 1980: 143).

The first task was to select a community where speakers of the appropriate types might be found. King of Prussia was selected for the following reasons:

> The study required (a) an area where there was one dominant dialect and many families from other dialect areas; (b) an area where children moving in had the opportunity of learning new dialect forms; and (c) a situation in which the parents' dialect had a maximal opportunity of influencing a child's language acquisition. In King of Prussia (a) the local dialect details were well known; (b) at least 50% of the population was local; and (c) the non-local dialects were known to have high or neutral prestige. (Payne 1980: 144)

Speakers *within* this area were next selected according to the composition of the block (each block consisting of twenty to thirty residences). Three types of block were identified, each exhibiting different neighbourhood residential patterns described as *mobile, mixed* and *local,* and at least four families from each block were interviewed. In all, six blocks were located (two of each type) thus yielding 24 families with a total of 108 children.

Further criteria for selecting types of family were introduced, as follows.

1   Families with local-born parents and children.
2   Families with local-born children and out-of-state parents.
3   Families with out-of-state-born children and parents.

One imagines that Payne's major problem was not in deciding which method of selection to use, but rather in identifying families in the various blocks which met these very specific requirements so that she could fill a quota which might be thought reasonable. She reports that initial contacts were made by approaching children in the streets; church and other community leaders helped to identify and contact suitable families.

These three relatively small-scale linguistic studies by Romaine, Reid and Payne show how methods of speaker selection need to be related to research objectives. In the case of Romaine's and Reid's studies, selection was relatively simple, involving the location of schools at appropriate points in a social and demographic scale. But the objectives of Payne's research narrowed down the choice, first of area of the city, then of residential neighbourhood within that area, and finally of speaker type. Indeed, as Labov and Sankoff have noted (1980: xi), sociolinguistic scholarship has in recent years tended generally to concentrate less on discussions of method than on finding suitable methods for the resolution of substantive issues.

2.5 The Variable of Social Class

I think it is true to say that *social class* of speaker has been seen by all urban sociolinguists as an important factor to take into account in sampling a population. It is a variable which is at first sight so obviously relevant to language variation in a modern western urban community that it is hard to see how it can be avoided; but paradoxically, it is a variable which has often created problems when researchers have attempted to replicate Labov's procedure in New York City of stratifying a sample by class. For that reason, an attempt will be made here to account for some of the practical sampling difficulties which have arisen; conceptual and inter-pretative problems associated with the social class variable are discussed further in 5.3.

Generally speaking, linguists do not worry much about the meaning of the social class variable, tending rather to use it as a means of imposing order on their complex linguistic data. Although they have been criticized for using the concept in this rather unreflecting way, it is not surprising that they have done so. The nature and definition of social class has for a long time been a controversial matter in the social sciences, and positions adopted by participants in the dispute usually reflect opposing ideological commitments.

When linguists declare an interest in the 'social class' of speakers, they are commenting on the position of those speakers relative to each other in a class-stratified society which has evolved as a consequence of unequal access to power and advantage. But despite the pervasiveness of class stratification, the social groups which emerge in a class-stratified society cannot readily be identified in the same way as, for example, social groups based on *caste,* as in India, where stratification is formally institutionalized (Trudgill 1983b: 10; Gumperz 1971; Bright 1964).

E. P. Thompson has commented both on the dynamic and complex nature of class, a much less definable notion than caste, and on its central role in western society:

> Class is not this or that part of the machine, but *the way the machine works* once it is set in motion – not this or that interest but the friction of interests – the movement itself, the heat, the thundering noise . . . When we speak of *a* class we are thinking of a very loosely defined body of people who share the same congeries of interests, social experiences, traditions and value-systems, who have a *disposition to behave* as a class, to define themselves in their actions and in their consciousness in relation to other groups of people in class ways. But class itself is not a thing, it is a happening. (Thompson 1963: 939)

It is this kind of grouping of persons into loosely defined bodies, intersubjectively perceived as occupying positions relative to each other, which linguists have tried to capture quantitatively by means of a *social class index score.*

Social class indexes are widely used in social research generally, and are constructed by selecting indicators of a person's position in the stratified system, such as occupation, housing, income or educational level, and assigning a numerical score in respect of each indicator which reflects his or her advantage. The index is usually a composite of two or more indicators, although sometimes investigators will use occupation alone, as did Macaulay in Glasgow, or education alone, like Jahangiri in Tehran (Jahangiri and Hudson 1982). If more than one indicator is used, they may be weighted to reflect the investigator's perception of their relative importance in indicating advantage.

In New York City, Labov used the three indicators of education, occupation and income to distinguish ten classes ranging from low-paid labourers with minimal education through to well-educated professionals and businessmen. For analytic purposes these were grouped into four strata – Lower class, Working class, Lower-middle class and Upper-middle class.

Trudgill in Norwich used a more complicated index composed of the following indicators: occupation, income, education, type of housing, locality, father's occupation. Speaker's positions on these scales were used to construct five social classes; Lower-working, Middle-working, Upper-working, Lower-middle, Middle-middle.

Shuy, Wolfram and Riley in Detroit distinguished four social classes

(Upper-middle, Lower-middle, Upper-working and Lower-working). Unlike Labov and Trudgill, they weighted their indicators; each speaker's score for occupation was multiplied by nine, for residence by six and for education by five. The resulting index reflected their view of the relative importance of these indicators in the system of stratification.

We can see immediately that different indicators are perceived as important by different investigators; moreover, perception of their *relative* importance seems to vary, not only from one culture to another but even within, for example, the United States. This arbitrariness is one of the principal problems in the use of a social class index, and the implications of attempting to transplant the procedure from one kind of society to another are not always clear. Sometimes its usefulness seems dubious, as in much of South America, which is characterized by a large difference in access to power and advantage between the elite and the majority of the population (Lloyd 1979). For such a society, a social class scale of the kind we have been discussing carries inappropriate implications of a gradient continuum.

At this point, we need to look more closely at our central term *social class,* which as Thompson's comments suggest, is extremely complex and important. Halsey's attempt to assemble a clear set of terms is helpful in locating the problem which many linguists find in using the concept; he begins by suggesting that *class* is best seen as an economic concept, distinct from *status* which pertains to *evaluation.* The stratification system can be viewed as having three *separate* (but interrelated) dimensions – class, status and party – through which power and advantage are distributed. It is the distinction between *class* and *status,* not normally made by linguists, on which we need to focus here:

Classes – for example professional people or factory workers – are formed socially out of the division of labour. They make up more or less cohesive and socially conscious groups from those occupational groups and their families which share similar work and market situations. Status is formed out of the no less fundamental tendency of human beings *to attach positive and negative values to human attributes, and to distribute respect or honour and contempt or derogation accordingly* [my italics]: status groups, for example peers of the realm or vagrants, form as social networks of those who share similar social prestige or lifestyle. Parties form out of the organised pursuit of social objectives . . . In short, classes belong to the economic, status groups to the social, and parties to the political structure of society. (Halsey 1978: 20)

This tripartite division of social organization derives from Max Weber, and the definition of class (when the term is used technically) in terms of occupation is widely accepted in European sociology. Its adoption need not imply commitment to any political orthodoxy, or any particular view of the historical or future role of class (but see further 5.3.2). If we restrict the reference of *class* in this way to the economic domain, it becomes clear that it is *status* rather than class with which linguists are concerned. That it is the *evaluative* domain which is most relevant to sociolinguistic differentiation is suggested by the interest accorded by linguists to the *evaluative* reactions of *hearers*. Some investigators have made this interest more explicit than others (see particularly Bell 1984b); but subjective reaction and self-evaluation tests as developed by Labov (1972b) have always been an important tool in interpreting variable linguistic data. It appears then that the important variable which sociolinguists usually characterize as *class* is more specifically an evaluative one – *status*. To the extent that occupational groups overlap with status groups sharing similar prestige and life-style, we can view the two variables as co-extensive and not worry too much about distinguishing them; that is precisely why *class* is frequently used as a general term. But the problem for linguists is that the interrelationship between status and class varies in different societies, with the result that attempts to transplant a stratification scale which was sufficent for its purpose in New York City may not always be successful.

The first point which needs to be made is that the proportion of the population which falls into a given *class* category (as defined in Britain by the Registrar-General's occupational scale) varies from one community to another. In modern Britain, where a disproportionate amount of the national wealth is concentrated in the south of England, comparison of the Census returns for a northern English, Northern Irish or Scottish city with those for a southern English city invariably shows that in southern England a very much higher proportion of the population falls into the higher classes. It is important to remember (as Thompson's comments suggest) that class is viewed more illuminatingly as a structural notion than as an aggregate of individuals; one consequence of local variation in class structure is likely to be a difference in the prestige accorded to the occupational elites in the two types of city, since a small occupational elite will be accorded relatively greater prestige. Thus, persons of the *same* class may have very different *statuses* if they live in cities with different class structures. This example is probably sufficient to give readers some idea of the reason for particular difficulties reported by investigators in Scotland and Northern Ireland who have tried to use as a model Labov's original New York City study. Invariably, it has either been adapted, criticized or circumvented in these places (see Romaine 1980) but, as Trudgill's work shows, has been more easily adaptable to conditions in southern England.

A second problem is that the amount of *mobility* between occupationally defined classes varies in different places. Mobility appears to be greater (for example) in the United States and Australia than in the United Kingdom and since migration in the British Isles has traditionally been into

England, is probably greater (historically at least) in England than in Scotland or Ireland (see MacAfee 1983: 26 for some relevant comments on mobility patterns in Glasgow).

Both of these factors affect the relationship between status and class, and make it important for sociolinguists to draw a distinction between them. Otherwise, problems can emerge with informants like the Belfast coal-merchant who fell into the lower-middle class group on the basis of his ownership of a business. Hence, he was classified occupationally along with a range of non-manual workers, clerks and technicians as 'lower-middle class' (cf. Halsey 1977: 24). But his origins, attitudes, values, life-style and language were characteristic of the working-class culture of the city, and on the basis of his language he was evaluated in this way by listeners.

Although a multiple indicator index like Trudgill's is designed to deal with such cases, it is the small size of many linguistic samples which can cause such difficulties to loom large in linguistic work; the general principle of a scale like the Registrar-General's, or indeed any kind of social class index, is that it is used to order very large numbers of people for the purpose of large-scale statistical analysis. In fact, in the Belfast sample of only 60 persons (see further 4.3.4) speakers like the coal-merchant were rare. But in some communities the mismatch between status and class can produce more radical difficulties. Particularly, in fast-developing modern cities with a high migrant population the interaction between the variables of status, class and ethnicity can create problems which result partly (but not entirely) from the characteristically non-random social and geographical distribution of immigrant ethnic groups. These difficulties, and the manner in which they were resolved, are exemplified by Horvath's recent study of the urban dialect of Sydney, a city which has received a massive influx of immigrants since World War II (Horvath 1985).

Horvath's original plan was to tap the variation existing in the community by obtaining a stratified sample which allowed observations to be made about the relationships between language on the one hand and age, sex, socio-economic class and ethnicity on the other. However, because of difficulties emerging from the non-random distribution of ethnic groups in Sydney, a judgement sample was taken to ensure a reasonable spread of speaker types, in preference to any kind of random selection. Initial contacts were asked if they could suggest anyone in thier friendship group who might be willing to participate in the survey, the aim being to interview a fixed quota of adults and teenagers, both male and female, belonging to different classes and ethnic groups. Using this general procedure, the researchers continued interviewing until all the social variables were represented by up to five speakers in each cell. Care was taken to ensure that the speakers were reasonably evenly distributed geographically around Sydney.

The problem which the researchers rapidly perceived was that the economic variable of class seemed to have quite a different relationship to the evaluative variable of status in Sydney and in New York City; in Australia, class differences are apparently less consistently translated into status differences (Horvath 1985: 4). Moreover, the social class index used by Labov was based on sociological classifications made within a theoretically defensible framework. But at the time of the research Horvath had available only a somewhat out-of-date classification by Congalton (1962; 1969) of 135 occupations. This scheme was not helpful in classifying informants in Sydney in the late seventies, and in fact many of the classification problems encountered by the survey were attributable to the mismatch between status and occupational class, a mismatch compounded by the effects of ethnicity which is particularly noticeable in a socially mobile urban community like Sydney.

Horvath's discussion of milk-bar owners exemplifies one aspect of the problem (1985: 46). Although this occupational group are classed as 'small business owners' by the Congalton system, milk-bar owners are probably of lower status than other small business owners. The fact that they are often of migrant origin is relevant, since in Australia as in many other places the relationship between *ethnicity* and *status* needs to be considered as related to but conceptually distinct from the relationship between *class* and *status:* frequently, two persons from different ethnic groups but with similar occupations are accorded different prestige evaluations.

Some milk-bar owners in Sydney run their businesses alone or with the help of their families; some live on the premises but pay assistants to work in the bar; yet others own several businesses and do not live on the premises at all. The Congalton system does not discriminate between these people, who are of very different statuses. So the problem here appears to be the mismatch between occupational scale and perceived status rankings.

However, even the availability of a more sophisticated scale (such as the Registrar-General's in this country) would not be of much help in dealing with problems in Sydney resulting from a widespread class mobility. Very frequently speakers had changed their class position since childhood or within their adult years – and Horvath notes that this in itself may be a fact with important sociolinguistic implications. Commonly, migrants have taken a downward step in both class and status on entering Australian society, but may reconstruct previous occupational positions after a period of about twenty years. The reverse happens in some communities when rural migrants enter the industrial economy, taking in the process what is probably regarded as a step *up* in status (see Gal 1979 on the opposition between 'peasants' and 'workers' in a rural community undergoing urbanization). In Sydney, however, the researchers assigned speakers to three categories – Middle Class, Upper-Working Class and Lower-Working Class; this adaptation of the Congalton system was probably the best they could achieve, given that there was no clear and reliable account of Australian demographic patterns available. The relationship between class and language was ultimately analysed using Principal Components Analysis (see 6.8.6), a technique which permits initial analysis of the linguistic data without prior aggregation of speakers into social classes. Consequently, the chances of a number of misconceived classificaltions seriously distorting sociolinguistic trends and patterns are much smaller than they might have been (Horvath 1985: 47).

2.6 Informant Sampling and Social Network

So far we have looked at studies which make some attempt to generalize about the language of a specifiable population, the goal of the large urban surveys being to select speakers in such a way as to give a 'scale model' of variation in the city as a whole. Smaller studies such as those of Romaine and Reid attempt to generalize about children, in a particular city, of a specific age, sex and social class. Payne's intention is to generalize on the dialect acquisition patterns of non-local Philadelphia children.

All of these studies, whether they involve random selection or judge-ment sampling, take as their starting point the isolated individual who is assumed to be linguistically typical of a particular age, class, or sex group. But a different approach to informant selection, referred to by Gillian Sankoff as the 'social network' approach, is also possible. Since the relationship between informant and fieldworker, the topic of the next chapter, is of crucial importance to the network approach, it will be outlined only very briefly here.

The chief characteristic of any kind of network procedure of speaker selection is that the unit of study is the *pre-existing social group,* rather than the individual as the representative of a more abstract social category. The main practical advantage is that the researcher is able to attach himself or herself to a group and, by making use of the group dynamics which influence patterns of language use, obtain very much larger amounts of spontaneous speech than is generally possible in interaction with a single individual who is isolated from his or her customary social network. Many network studies have involved attachment of the fieldworker for weeks or months to the target group.

It is important for the investigator to find a means of approaching a group with which he or she has no pre-existing personal ties; a method which can be used only for a circle of the investigator's friends is too limited to be useful. Examples of such studies are those of Labov in Harlem, who examined the language of young black males (Labov 1972b); Cheshire in Reading, who studied groups of working-class boys and girls who met in adventure playgrounds (Cheshire 1982a); the Milroys in in Belfast, who studied two generations in three Belfast working-class communities (Milroy and Milroy 1978) and Bortoni-Ricardo in Brasilia who studied the language of rural immigrants to Brazlandia, a satellite town of Brasilia (Bortoni-Ricardo 1985). A variety of techniques for approaching these groups, who were initially unknown to the investigator, was developed.

The relatively close relationship which often envolves over time between fieldworker and speakers in a network study is likely to influence the type of language obtained. For this reason, a network study may be capable of describing language variation in greater depth, tapping dimensions of variation which are not obtainable by a survey which samples isolated individuals across a whole city. Certainly, the two types of method are in general complementary rather than mutually exclusive, and major projects in Belfast, Harlem and Philadelphia have used both. But sometimes, for one reason or another, a broad survey is difficult to design or execute; or for the reasons discussed in 2.5, the crucial variable of class presents problems in constructing a stratified sample. In situations such as these it is likely that a network study might prove to be a practicable way of sampling speakers from a specified group.

2.7 Sampling Language in a Range of Situations

So far we have looked at methods of sampling *speakers* in a community; we look now briefly at one simple method of sampling speakers' *linguistic repertoires* - that is the totality of different types of language which they use in a range of situations.

It is a matter of common observation that on different occasions a speaker will use quite different types of language, dependent not only on his or her desire to convey meanings of (for example) irony, hostility, deference or intimacy, but also on a range of contextual factors. Of these the most important is probably the speaker's psycho-social orientation to his or her conversational partner(s) on the dimensions of *social distance* and *intimacy*. Some languages allow speakers to mark these relationships to interlocutors in a formal way, obvious examples being the various European languages where choice of second person pronoun appears to be conditioned specifically by these two variables. In other languages, including English, similar social meanings are conveyed by a range of strategies, and while it is intuitively clear to listeners that speakers are able to use linguistic means of marking out their orientation to others, they sometimes do so in ways that are not as clearly definable (in linguistic terms) as choice of second person pronoun. In other types of linguistic community, speakers might shift from one language to another to convey the same kinds of social meaning. Good accounts of this general area can be found in Brown and Levinson (1979), Fasold (1984) and Bell (1984b).

In view of the relationship between linguistic choice and aspects of the situational context it is clear that a principled study of this kind of variation needs to be related to a systematic analysis of the situational context and of various types of linguistic repertoire to which speakers have access (see chapter 8). But for the moment we confine ourselves to a brief discussion of Labov's relatively simple method of sampling a range of speech styles in a monolingual community.

His first procedure was to subdivide recordings of conversation gathered during linguistic interviews systematically into a careful and a casual style. Careful style was the label given to that large part of the interview where an isolated individual was answering questions put by a stranger. Casual style on the other hand referred to the speech produced when the constraints of the interview were overridden in a number of fairly clearly defined ways, such as when a stretch of speech was outside the structure of the interview proper, perhaps to a telephone caller or a third person entering the room. Sometimes the speaker became briefly involved in a personal narrative of some intense experience.

Labov additionally collected various types of reading style ordered on a linear scale in accordance with the amount of attention to his own speech being paid by a speaker. These consisted of a passage of continuous prose, followed by a word-list of single lexical items, and finally sets of minimal pairs (such as *god* and *guard* in New York City) which could be differentiated only if close attention was given to them by the speaker. Thus, five speech styles could be ordered in a single dimension in accordance with the amount of attention paid to speech, ranging from least formal (casual style) to most formal (minimal pair style).

Since Labov has often been criticized for his rather simplified analysis of style (which does not, for example, address the issues of how speakers use linguistic variation to mark out their psycho-social orientation to each other), it is important to note that he was not apparently attempting in the first place to make a general statement about the possible range of speech styles. The original reason for sampling different styles was to obtain a general view of the *norms* of a speech community, including information on the direction in which speakers shifted their language in relatively informal situations; for this purpose, a simple linear analysis of style seems to be quite appropriate. A fuller account of the methodological issues associated with the rather complex area of stylistic variation may be found in chapter 8. Meantime, we should note that there is no reason why researchers should not continue to use Labov's original methods of sampling styles, despite their limitations; they are useful and practicable where the objective is to examine contrastively the characteristics of two or more different types of language used by the same speaker. But if the purpose of the research is to model intra-speaker variation within a coherent theoretical framework, more sophisticated methods and models need to be considered.

2.8 Concluding Remarks

So far, we have examined methods originally developed by William Labov for sampling both inter-speaker and intra-speaker language variation in large urban communities. Because Labov worked out and described his procedure in sufficient detail for it to be generally replicable, it has been possible for a large number of researchers studying many different languages in different parts of the world to follow the general model which he provided. Although the discussion in this chapter has been confined largely to western communities, the model has been applied more widely – for example in pre-revolutionary Tehran, which had a social structure very different from New York City (Jahangiri and Hudson 1982).

Sometimes local conditions require some adaptation of the original sampling procedure. Examples of such adaptations have been considered along with more general problems associated with sampling for linguistic surveys and with the difficult notion of *class,* which invariably is important in any analysis of language in a western-type socially stratified urban community. Finally, Labov's relatively simple analysis of intra-speaker *stylistic* variation was briefly discussed.

The range of sampling methods used in recent work suggests that researchers are now more relaxed than they once were about methodo-logical issues such as whether or not their account should be technically representative or whether strict random sampling procedures should be used. This shift in attitude which comes with the maturing of sociolinguis-tics as a field of research enables researchers to select more freely than was once possible from a range of methods those which, within a defensible theoretical framework, will best enable them to achieve their goals. In the following chapter we shift our focus away from methods of selecting speakers, to concentrate on different ways of obtaining from those speakers good quality tape-recorded data.

3

Speakers: Some Issues in Data Collection

3.1 Introductory

Chapter 2 was concerned with locating linguistic informants in a manner sensitive to their social characteristics and appropriate to the aims of the research. The question then arises of how good data might be obtained from these speakers. This is an important issue, since the sensitivity of patterns of language use to various contextual factors means inevitably that the kind of approach which is made to a speaker will affect, in a number of specifiable ways, the data available for analysis. Discussion in this chapter is confined to *unscripted* speech styles; reading styles, which are also often elicited in sociolinguistic interviews, are considered in chapter 8.

It is convenient to begin by considering the now traditional one-to-one interviews. Labov has suggested that interviewers should obtain 'from one to two hours of speech from each speaker' (1981: 8). In fact, it is hard to be categorical about the appropriate length of an interview. Useful phonological data can often be obtained in a relatively short time – perhaps as short as twenty to thirty minutes. But a very different picture of a speaker's pattern of language use is liable to emerge over a longer period, and it will be this pattern which is of interest to an analyst who wants to get an idea of fluctuations in a speaker's use of key phonological variables. Thus, Douglas-Cowie (1978) suggests that, even when interviewed by a stranger, a speaker will settle down to a pattern approximating to his or her everyday interactional style after about the first hour. Speech produced before this period has elapsed tends to show radically different patterns. In Reading, however, Cheshire noted that for the purposes of *syntactic* analysis much greater quantities of data were required since the relevant structures were not likely to emerge as predictably or as frequently as phonological elements. Moreover, since gaps in the data might become apparent only after analysis was under way, it was important to build up a relationship with speakers of such a kind as to allow not only long periods of interaction, but also *subsequent* data-collection sessions. A modified participant observation technique was more appropriate for this purpose than any kind of interviewing (Cheshire 1982a: 13). The question of amount of data needed can therefore, like so many methodological questions, be answered primarily in terms of the goal of the research. Particularly important is the type of data required; for example, phonological, morphological, syntactic and lexical analyses will be very different from each other in this respect (see further chapters 6 and 7).

Labov partitioned his interview data into 'formal' and 'casual' style as systematically as possible by specifying as casual style those parts of the interaction where the constraints of the interview seemed to have been temporarily overridden. He listed a range of contexts in which this shift took place, additionally identifying it by the presence of what he called 'channel cues' (1972b: 94). These were various changes in speech rate and loudness, or in breathing.

Despite Labov's attempts to list systematically the contexts in which casual speech occurs (and by implication to give advice on obtaining casual speech) other researchers have not always found these contexts to be useful or relevant. For example, Trudgill in Norwich partitioned his data according to *topic* of conversation, while Macaulay in Glasgow and Shuy and his colleagues in Detroit did not present data from two contrasting speech styles at all.

Attempts to use the 'danger of death' question, specified by Labov as particularly successful in eliciting casual speech because of its tendency to re-engage the speaker in an event of great emotional crisis, have frequently backfired (see Labov 1972b: 93 for details and rationale of the technique). For example, Trudgill comments on its lack of success in Norwich, suggesting that perhaps Norwich people have led somewhat less eventful lives than New York City people. But in Belfast it was inappropriate for quite different reasons. During a conversation with a working-class family about the general hardships of life, it emerged that one nineteen-year-old man had already had a number of narrow escapes from death. First, as a merchant seaman he had almost drowned in the Baltic, his ship having been run down by a Russian vessel; then he had been held up by gunmen in a Belfast alley-way; arrested and beaten by troops as a Republican sympathizer; and two months before the period of the research he had been shot in the legs, during an inter-group Republican feud. His response to these alarming events was not at all the one predicted by Labov, but nevertheless accorded closely with Ulster norms of behaviour. It may be described as a rather world-weary cynicism at the duplicity of the authorities combined with a tendency to low-key black humour. On this occasion the danger of death question was not put explicitly; but on the two or three occasions when it was, the characteristic response of Belfast people was a matter-of-fact account of what were often quite unpleasant and dangerous experiences. No doubt some other question could in Ulster have fulfilled the function of engaging the speaker's attention in the way Labov describes; but this one did not.

The more general point which emerges from these difficulties in replicating Labov's interview technique in locations far removed from New York City is an important one. Labov is in effect attempting to manipulate contextual variables associated with participants, topic, type of speech event, which have a considerable and sometimes specifiable influence on variable patterns of language use, in order to control the type of language elicited. But the problem is that the effect of these interacting contextual factors is not well enough understood for them to be reliably manipulated. Thus, it is unlikely that Labov's formal criteria for obtaining and distinguishing stylistically diversified speech will be usable across a range of different types of community by fieldworkers of different ages, ethnic groups and personalities, and of both sexes. For this reason we will not proceed by looking at ways of manipulating contextual variables. The following section examines the *structure* of the interview as a speech event, and looks at the kind of language appropriate to that event which we might reasonably expect to elicit.

3.2 The Interview as a Speech Event

3.2.1 Some general comments

An interview in western society is a clearly defined and quite common speech event to which a formal speech style is appropriate. It generally involves dyadic interaction between strangers, with the roles of the two participants being quite clearly defined. *Turn-taking rights* are not equally distributed as they are in conversational interaction between peers. Rather, one participant (the interviewer) controls the discourse in the sense of both selecting topics and choosing the form of questions. The interviewee on the other hand, by agreeing to be interviewed, has contracted to answer these questions co-operatively. From the interviewee's point of view, a co-operative response is often one which is maximally brief and relevant (see Levinson 1983: 100 for a good discussion of work on this 'co-operative principle' in conversation). Once the interviewer has obtained a response, the obligation rests upon him to follow it up with a further question. People are generally quite well aware of the behaviour appropriate to these roles, and of their implications in terms of unequal distribution of rights to talk.

Labov has argued that the pattern of these power relations within the interview setting is one of the major problems which the fieldworker must tackle to achieve a 'favourable interactive position' (1981: 15), and suggests that the interviewer's social dominance 'stems from association with the dominating class'. While this may be partly true, the dominance deriving from asymmetrical *participant roles,* giving rise to a characteristic discourse structure, is also crucial. The relationship of these roles – that is of 'questioner' and 'respondent' – to the distribution of power and advantage in the world outside the interview setting is at best indirect; the example from Wolfson (1982), quoted in 3.2.2, is a striking instance of an attempt by an interviewee to redress a mismatch between dominance deriving from discourse roles, and real world dominance. Thus, it is perhaps fruitful to explore in the first instance the implications of these asymmetrical discourse roles, rather than to follow without further analysis Labov's suggestion of directly adjusting the relative social positions of interviewer and interviewee.

We may begin by noting that *direct* questions – that is, requests for information which are syntactically realized as interrogatives – are rather uncommon in everyday interactions between peers. The intrinsically threatening and challenging nature of direct questions is discussed in detail by Goody (1978), who argues that where interactants stand in a socially asymmetrical relationship to each other, a direct question will nearly always be viewed as a mechanism of social control, or as a command, and seldom as a simple request for information. As Goody shows, communities vary in their sensitivity to the implications of asking direct questions. She analyses a teaching situation in the African Gonja community where, because of the relative statuses of pupil and teacher, it is quite inappropriate for pupils to seem to challenge teachers by questioning them directly. D. Hymes (1972: 279) notes further instances of culturally determined interrogative behaviour.

In Britain, the clearest examples of settings where questions have a control function are police interrogation rooms, courtrooms and classrooms, and it is data collected in these settings which allow us to observe most clearly the asymmetrical patterns of control over the discourse associated with a question/answer structure. To illustrate this general point about discourse roles, we shall look at two exchanges, one from a courtroom and one from a classroom.

The following extract (A) is taken from a transcription of a recording of a case heard at the Arrears and Maintenance division of a magistrates court and cited by S. Harris (1984). The participants are a magistrate (M) and a defendant (KH).

(A) M: . . ./are you um/. . . are you going to *make* an offer
          /. . . uh. . . uh. . ./to discharge this debt?   (1)
     KH: /Would you in my position?/   (2)
     M: I/. . . I'm not here to answer questions/. . . you answer
          my question   (3)
     KH: One rule for one and one for another   (4)

M: /Can I have an answer to my question/. . . please/ the
     question is/are you prepared to make an offer to the
     Court/ to discharge/this debt?/   (5)
KH: /What sort of minimal offer would be required?/   (6)
M: It's not a bargaining situation/it's a *straight* question/ Mr
     H/can I have the answer?   (7)
KH: /Well I'll just pay the court a pound annually/   (8)
M: /That's not acceptable to us/   (9)
KH: /What would be acceptable to the Court?/   (10)
M: No we don't find/. . . uh. . . we want a sensible offer
     Mr H   (11)

Clearly, power and authority are here asymmetrically distributed between
the participants, this asymmetry being reflected in their discourse rights
and privileges, as comments by both clearly reveal. The magistrate several
times emphasizes his power to pose questions which compel a response – a
privilege not available to KH ((3), (5), (7)). The defendant for his part is
aware of this asymmetry and of the discourse role associated with his
powerless position (4). The various resistance strategies which he adopts
are not part of our concern here.

Extract (B) is taken from a stretch of classroom discourse. At this point
the teacher has just played to the class a tape of a man with an unfamiliar
accent with a view to discussing reactions to it with the children. The italics
are mine.

(B) Teacher: What kind of a person do you think he is? Do you –
               What are you laughing at?   (1)
     Pupil: Nothing   (2)
     Teacher: Pardon?   (3)
     Pupil: Nothing   (4)
     Teacher: You're laughing at nothing, nothing at all?   (5)
     Pupil: No   (6)
               It's funny really 'cos they don't think as though they
               were there they might not like it and it sounds rather
               a pompous attitude   (7)
                                        (Coulthard 1977: 108)

The interrogative 'what are you laughing at', can be interpreted either as
a request for information or as a directive to stop laughing. In the
classroom, because of the proscribed nature of the activity and the
teacher's power to enforce the proscription, it is often the latter, and the
pupil has interpreted it in this way. The teacher has to work quite hard to
convince him that (1) is, in fact, a request for information. A discussion of
the factors associated with mutual rights and obligations which lead a

participant to interpret an interrogative as a directive may be found in Labov and Fanshel (1977).

Continuing with our analysis of direct questions, we may note that the pupil's (and the teacher's) difficulty is part of a more general point that, depending on situational context, utterances can be interpreted in a wide range of ways. Thus, given certain rights and obligations holding between participants, and certain contextual conditions, a declarative such as

1   it's dinner time and I'm hungry

can be interpreted as a request/command to prepare dinner. Under other conditions it may be interpreted as a statement with no particular directive force (see Levinson 1983 for a clear account of these general principles). A clear one-to-one relationship between interrogatives and questions or declaratives and statements cannot be assumed to hold, so that an utterance like 1 which may be analysed syntactically as a declarative sentence may, in context, function as a request for action or for inform-ation. For example, a response such as

2   it'll be ready in twenty minutes

or a zero verbal response and a movement in the direction of the kitchen would be perfectly appropriate. So also would a non-compliant response like

3   would you stop nagging me

Following Brown and Levinson's (1978) argument that an important (and universal) function of indirect directives like 1 is to let both speakers and addressees off the hook thus offering some protection to their face, we can observe that the range of possible responses to 1 is much greater than, for example, those permitted by the magistrate in extract A. The addressee might acknowledge the directive force of the utterance with either a compliant or a non-compliant response as exemplified by 2 or 3. Alterna-tively, he may refuse to acknowledge any directive force by opting for a response such as 4, 5 or 6.

4   are you really?

5   yes, you do seem to need rather a lot of food

6   mmm

Assuming that his intention was to request dinner, the original speaker might similarly exploit the functional ambiguity of an indirect directive like 1. In the manner of all Machiavellian conversationalists, he can allow the directive force of 1 to stand if it meets with a compliant response like 2. If on the other hand it meets with a vigorously non-compliant response like 3 he might continue as follows:

7   I wasn't asking you to do anything. I was just saying I was hungry

The general point which springs from this discussion is that the direct questioning characteristic of interviews tends to leave little leeway for this kind of multiple interpretation (and manipulation) by the addressee. It is incumbent on him or her to respond, in a manner specified by the interviewer, to questions such as the following (taken from Labov 1981: 10):

8   Do you play the numbers around here?
9   Did you ever get blamed for something you didn't do?
10 What did (do) fights start about around here?

Although it is open to an interviewee to adopt resistance strategies of one sort or another (such as replying to 8 and 9 with a simple *yes* or *no*), s/he is nevertheless committed to formulating a relevant response to a question on a topic selected by the interviewer. Not to respond would involve committing himself/herself either to what might be called a 'noticeable absence' (i.e. a zero response) (cf. Sacks, Schegloff and Jefferson (1974)) or to an overtly non-compliant response such as

11 I don't really want to answer your question

Either option commits him/her to being openly unco operative. This lack of scope available to an addressee who has contracted an obligation to provide responses to direct questions helps to explain why they are so generally associated with the unequal distribution of power and, as we shall see, so frequently countered with brief responses. But it does not follow that direct questions do not occur in spontaneous speech during peer interactions; they plainly do; it seems, however, that they are asked and receive direct responses only under a sharply limited set of circumstances. Thus, Wilson (1981) argues that in conversations between peers, people do not normally answer questions directly if the reason for asking the question is not fairly clear. A question such as

12   What is the time please?

when addressed to a stranger in the street will normally receive a direct answer, as it is generally accepted as self-evident that persons have a number of good reasons for requesting this information. However, a question like

13   Have you got red underpants on?

addressed also to a stranger, is unlikely to elicit the information requested. Quite apart from the taboo nature of the subject matter, Wilson argues, such a question would not receive an answer unless a reason for asking it were given such as

14   I work for an underwear firm, and I'm carrying out a survey

Wilson suggests that in everyday conversation various strategies are used by conversationalists to locate a questioner's intention if the reason for the question is not clear. These involve (amongst others) responding with a request for further information as to questioner's intention, or answering the question and then requesting further information. Thus, we have the following sequences:

15   A: What age is your mother?
    B: Why?
16   A: Do you feel alright?
    B: Yes sure. Why do you ask?

(Wilson 1981: 67)

Wilson's work, taken along with Goody's arguments on the 'control' function of direct questions, suggests very strongly that a chain of question–answer sequences such as those which occur in interviews are very atypical of conversations between peers. Clearly, this point has a number of implications for the conduct of sociolinguistic interviews, which we shall examine below.

3.2.2 Sociolinguistic interviews and discourse roles

The first point which might be made is that individuals who are being questioned will seldom produce large volumes of speech in their replies. This may be in part a consequence of the 'co-operative principle', in the sense that they are attempting to comply by responding relevantly and briefly. But sometimes they may perceive questions as a 'test' of some sort, a perception springing from the common control function of questions in asymmetrical situations.

Second, the well-defined nature of the interview as a speech event along with the associated social and discourse roles of the participants can make it very difficult for an interviewer to 'fudge' the nature of the event in an attempt to encourage the interviewee to relax and produce larger volumes of speech. Wolfson (1982) has criticized Labov's suggestion that field-workers make interviews as informal as possible by adopting a position of 'lower authority and lesser consequence in the conversation' (Labov 1981: 15). She argues that this is likely to lead to confusion, embarrassment and even hostility, since interviewees *expect* interviewers to ask them a series of clear questions.

Third, if the interviewee perceives himself/herself as being of higher status than the interviewer, s/he might also perceive an allocation of discourse roles which assigns the role of questioner to the lower-status participant as strikingly inappropriate. This is what appears to have happened in the following exchange between a female student interviewer and a successful businessman – a restaurant owner. Both he and the waitress were a generation older than the student interviewer, and Wolfson reports the exchange as follows:

After answering a few questions about his birthplace, education and opinions about life in Philadelphia, the subject was led into the beginning of a conversation but suddenly he interrupted by saying:

Owner:	Let me ask you something. Are you from Philadelphia?
Int:	Yes
Owner:	Where were you born?
Waitress:	(laughs) Now he's gonna question you
Int:	Second and the Boulevard
Owner:	Second and the Boulevard. Uh huh. Do you find Philadelphia different?
Int:	Yeah
Owner:	You do? In what respect?
Int:	I think people used to be a lot friendlier
Owner:	Well, I think conditions have made it that way

(Wolfson 1982: 68)

The owner has reversed discourse roles, placing himself in control of the questions, while the waitress appears to be aware of the significance of this role-reversal, commenting on it as soon as it is apparent that the owner is embarking upon a series of questions. Moreover, although she does not make this point explicitly, Wolfson appears to view the owner's adoption of the role of interviewer as a violation of the fieldworker's discourse rights, as is suggested by her choice of the term 'interrupt' to characterize the role-reversal.

A parallel to the Wolfson interview may be found in Briggs (1984). After a series of disastrously uninformative interviews with the Lopezes, a wood carver and his wife in Cordóva, northern New Mexico, Briggs reports a successful set of interviews with another 'community elder'; 'He agreed to both the interviews and their tape-recording. When I returned from my car, Mr Cordóva asked me "Now what is it that you wanted to know?" I provided him with one of the questions that had fared so badly with the Lopezes. He then proceeded to produce a long, flowing narrative of the local carving industry' (Briggs 1984: 23). Although Briggs attributes his success with Mr Cordóva and his failure with the Lopezes to different factors altogether (cross-cultural differences in conversational structure), it may be significant that by addressing to Briggs the question 'Now what is it that you wanted to know?', Mr Cordóva has, to some extent, reversed the roles of interviewer and interviewee in such a way as to be congruent with the deference due to him as a knowledgeable older man. In this case, the role-reversal apparently worked to the fieldworker's advantage; but the Wolfson interview suggests not only that it sometimes will not, but also that such a role-reversal cannot easily be manipulated as a standard fieldwork technique.

A further implication of the interpersonal difficulties involved in direct questioning is that direct questions are sometimes not recognized by a community as an appropriate way of seeking information. A particularly clear example of this may be found in an account by Eades (1982) of attempts to obtain information in an Aboriginal community in South East Queensland. Eades found that when questions were presented as interrogatives, Aborigines were usually 'confused, dysfluent or non-compliant'. However, questions in the form of declaratives which could be marked by intonation or by tags were more successful. The following exchanges exemplify this point:

17   Fieldworker: Were you very young then?
      A: Eh?
      Fieldworker: You were very young?
      A: I was about 14
18   Fieldworker: Your husband was a Batjala man?
      A: He was a Batjala
      Fieldworker: And where was he from again?
      A: Beg pardon?
      Fieldworker: He was from further south, was he?
      A: He's, he's from here, not far from X station

                                          (Eades 1982: 65)

In the second sequence (18), the interviewer began with a culturally appropriate question type, reverting then inappropriately to the interrogative type which was acceptable in white middle-class society but not to the Aboriginal communities. The response 'beg pardon' reflected the inappropriate formulation of the question, while a subsequent rephrasing in a form acceptable to the addressee elicited an informative reply. Eades goes on to argue that the two types of question differ in more than their syntactic form, and that the strategy of presenting known or inferred information for verification or further elaboration reflects sociocultural aspects of Aboriginal society. Similar interactional patterns are reported by Hymes (1975) in her study of the Yakima-speaking American Indian community at Warm Springs, Central Oregon (V. Hymes 1975: 31). More generally, Briggs notes that his successful interview in Cordóva (see above) was with a bilingual speaker who 'had acquired not only the phonological, syntactic and semantic systems of American English, but . . . had mastered its conversational structure as well' (Briggs 1975: 25). The speaker's wife, who was monolingual, responded to questioning in the same uninformative fashion as the monolingual Lopezes, with whom Briggs had conducted a number of unsuccessful interviews.

While direct questioning in western societies does not present the same degree of difficulty as it does in Queensland Aboriginal society, or in Warm Springs, or in the Gonja society studied by Goody, it is nevertheless clear that it needs to be used generally with some care and circumspection. It is probably true that even within the British Isles communities vary in their tolerance of direct questioning; for example, I have the clear impression that direct questioning as a means of seeking information is less acceptable in Irish urban communities than in English ones, and less acceptable still in Irish rural communities (or possibly in rural communities generally). Certainly, we should not lose sight of the asymmetrical distribution of power suggested by the roles of questioner and respondent, which has far-reaching implication for the use of the interview as a linguistic fieldwork method. Bortoni-Ricardo (1975: 217) provides a good discussion of the issue.

Acknowledging the general problem, Labov has suggested that the 'basic counter-strategy of the sociolinguistic interview is to acknowledge the position of the interviewer as a learner, in a position of lower authority than the person he is talking to' (Labov 1981: 15). He does not discuss the role of the question–answer discourse structure in encoding the original asymmetrical relationship, but suggests various techniques for achieving a redress of balance. These range from adjustment of the interviewer's own (possibly somewhat bookish) speech style, to sensitive monitoring of the subject's level of interest. In practice, most sociolinguistic interviewers rely on fudging the speech event to the extent that speakers 'wander off the point' – i.e. select and initiate their own topics. And since it is plain that talkative speakers *are* frequently encountered who respond volubly even within an interview framework (particularly after some time has elapsed), the conduct of an interview is not always as frustrating as the discussion in this section might imply.

It is however assumed here that a good data-collection method is one which is usable not only with friends or acquaintances of the interviewer or persons with whom he or she proves to have a personal or social affinity. It is important, methodologically, to arrive at as reliable a specification as we can of the factors which favour or inhibit the collection of a large amount of data from as broad a social base as possible. We must not lose sight of the fact that before Labov began to publish accounts of his innovatory fieldwork techniques which embodied this principle (Labov 1966; Labov et al. 1968) the data bases of many studies of language in use were characterized by a very narrow range of speaker types. For example, the dialect surveys discussed in chapter 1 tapped only a small, unrepresentative subgroup, while the survey of English usage discussed by Greenbaum and Quirk (1970) appears to be based mainly on the language of university students. We can broaden our own data base successfully only by discovering how different groups respond to our information-seeking activities.

Although many successful face-to-face interviews have been recorded, it is the unreliability of intuitive, *ad hoc* methods of breaking down the social and discourse asymmetries associated with them which constitutes the problem. For where they *are* broken down and satisfactory amounts and types of data obtained, a range of factors which are outside the interviewer's control are often implicated. These may depend on his/her own temperament and that of the interviewee, as well as the degree of affinity (of age, sex, interest, status, ethnicity for example) which the pair have with each other. Further unpredictable events such as the entry of a third person into the conversation, an interruption like a telephone call or a knock at the door can of course all be helpful and, as Labov has noted (1981: 16), can be exploited by the interviewer.

External factors of a wider political type might also be relevant. For example, Hudson and Jahangiri (1982: 51) report that in Tehran the interviewer had to allay suspicions that the informants' political inclinations were under investigation. Similarly, Asian communities in Britain are often fearful of being spied upon by immigration authorities, and are very unhappy with questions which probe into ethnicity or family background. This narrows the interviewer's scope considerably, and Romaine's response to these problems was to base her work on Asian communities in Birmingham mainly on the speech of adolescents (Romaine 1984: 8). In the Clonard area of Belfast an altercation with a military patrol who were suspicious of the interviewer's recording equipment was the crucial event which led to a highly successful interview with one middle-aged man; previously he had been replying to questions in a friendly but guarded amnner. But again, the interruption was quite fortuitous, and it is the chance character of this event and others like it that makes even an 'informal' interview a relatively uncertain means of obtaining good data.

3.3 Some Structural Limitations of Interview Data

A further problem with the interview as a field technique is that even where reasonable amounts of data are collected, their structural characteristics may be limited in various ways. Examples may be cited at all levels of analysis – phonological, morphological, syntactic and discourse, and since this matter has a bearing on the kind of linguistic generalization the analyst ultimately feels able to make, it is useful to look at some examples.

3.3.1 Phonological examples

A limited subgroup of lexical items consisting of words such as *meat, beat, beast, heat, leave, cheap, beak* (and an unspecified number of others) alternate in Belfast inner-city speech between a high front vowel and a lower realization. I shall refer to this as the MEAT class. The first pronunciation involves assigning items to the /i/ class – thus for example rendering the first two homophonous with *meet* and *beet*. The second pronunciation occurs rarely in recorded speech, is highly stigmatized and limited to low-status speakers; it approximates to (but is not identical with) items like *mate* and *bait*. I shall refer to these for convenience as MEET and MATE class pronunciations respectively.

The alternation is of considerable theoretical interest, as it sheds light on a notorious historical problem of an apparent merger in early Modern

Table 3.1   MEET/MATE alternation in Belfast I

	A	B
1	MEET	MEET
		MEAT
2	MEAT	MATE
	MATE	

English and subsequent reseparation between words of MEAT and MATE classes; later still, MEAT words merged with the MEET class, giving the modern standard pattern (see Milroy and Harris 1980 for details and historical references). It has generally been thought by Ulster dialectologists who commented on the alternation that Belfast speakers had access to two systems as shown in table 3.1, system A reflecting an historically prior state of the language.

There were two problems involved in using even extended interviews for collecting data which might shed light on the phonological patterns of these intersecting word classes. The first was that very many speakers did not use the A type system at all, and that when it was used MATE class pronunciations occurred only in spontaneous speech. They did not occur in informal interviews, and even on tapes collected using rather more radical methods of eliciting spontaneous speech (see 3.6 below), they occurred not much more than once per hour, on average.

The second problem was that the researchers were not convinced that system A as posited in table 3.1 was correct; for example, the fieldworker was invited to 'Come in and get some heat' by one speaker, who realized the vowel of the last word with a long high-mid monophthong [e:]. A few seconds later the item *hate* occurred with a centring glide [ɪə] which, far from being homophonous with *heat,* seemed to be phonetically rather distinct. Thus an alternative system A was postulated:

Table 3.2   MEET/MATE alternation in Belfast II

	A		B
1	MEET	1	MEET
			MEAT
2	MEAT		
3	MATE	2	MATE

Clearly, if the state of affairs described in table 3.2 is correct, considerable light is thrown on the historical problem of the apparently unmerged and subsequently remerged MEAT class; the answer is that the first merger as shown in table 3.1A may not have taken place at all. To follow through this hunch, attempts were made to elicit from a Belfast speaker a list of pronunciations of alternating MEAT class items 'the way they say them in Belfast' together with a list of non-alternating MATE class items. Although the speaker understood perfectly what was required, it was plain that he viewed the MEAT and MATE classes as having merged. This was in fact not surprising, as some punch lines of jokes depended on MEAT/ MATE homophony, and rhyming patterns of contemporary vernacular poetry seemed to confirm the reported merger:

> The roost is next and for the nest you can take a seat
> Before proceeding further to the good oul' Golden Gate
>
> (Hammond 1978: 48)

A full account of the structural and historical issues, and of the methods ultimately used to investigate the hypothesis that a merger of the MEET and MATE classes had not taken place in spontaneous speech, may be found in J. Milroy and Harris (1980). But the more general point argued here is that the data needed for resolution of a substantial theoretical problem could not be collected by interview methods. Those vernacular alternants which were recorded nearly all occurred in peer conversations and only very rarely in speech addressed directly to the fieldworker. Elicitation by means of minimal pair tests was totally unsuccessful; if such data *had* been used, any account of the subsystems available to speakers would have been the inaccurate one shown in table 3.1. Parallel accounts of similar fieldwork problems in eliciting data to investigate a number of other falsely reported mergers can be found in Labov, Yaeger and Steiner (1972: 229–54); Trudgill also discusses the similar cases of *fear/fair* and *toe/too* in Norwich (Trudgill 1974: 120–9). Similar to the MEAT/MATE example in Belfast is the alternation of a small number of items (for example, *pull, push, foot, took*) between the /ʉ/ and /ʌ/ classes. Tokens of the /ʌ/ class were almost entirely confined to informal interactions between peers, and were apparently not used at all by some speakers. The point of these examples – and many more could be cited – is that as in the MEET/MATE example the rare vernacular tokens are often vital to the resolution of quite substantial theoretical problems; unless careful fieldwork methods are used, an accurate characterization of phonological structure will simply not be possible. The historical issues associated with data such as these are fully discussed by J. Milroy (forthcoming).

A related problem particularly associated with data collected by means of interviews is that the effects of *speaker correction* of socially stigmatized items are often indirect, and can also give a misleading impression of phonological structure. In working-class West Belfast, tokens of /k/ are frequently heavily palatalised, with a palatal glide appearing between the initial consonant and a following front vowel. Pronunciations like [kjap, kjat, kjɪd] ('cap', 'cat', 'kid') are stigmatized and apparently recessive, being used mainly (but not entirely) by middle-aged and older men. During an interview, a middle-aged, West Belfast *woman* described a visit to a shop where she stood in a queue [kʉ:]. One possible explanation of this realization was that the Belfast urban dialect like many others (such as

Norwich, for example) deleted in some contexts the palatal approximant /j/. But only after vernacular pronunciations like [kjap] 'cap' had occurred in informal conversations did a clearer picture of the structure of the dialect emerge; the speaker had *hypercorrected* standard [kju:], classifying it along with non-standard /kj–/ items. Interestingly, this process revealed a misanalysis of phonological structure since the vernacular palatalization rule affects only items with a following front or low back unrounded vowel; a word like *cool*, for example, does not show [k]/[kj] alternation.

3.3.2 Syntactic and pragmatic examples

The structural limitations of interview data emerge also in relation to *syntactic* patterns where the problem is often rooted in the pragmatic constraints of the interview. An obvious example is interrogative constructions, which are plentiful in spontaneous speech in a range of discourse functions, but are likely to be inhibited in the speech of interviewees. One of the variables studied by Cheshire (using a participant observation method) in the speech of Reading adolescents was *tag questions*. Tag questions do not usually function in discourse as requests for information, but rather are conducive forms seeking confirmation of a previously stated proposition:

19   She's here already, isn't she?
20   This is your book, right?

Since their main function is to compel a (normally minimal) response from the addressee it is unlikely that they will often be used spontaneously by a speaker whose perceived social role is to respond to questions put by another.

A rather more subtle example of the interrelationship between elicitation method and structural characteristics of the data comes again from Belfast. One construction studied, the so called *hot-news perfect* (McCawley 1971) is unlikely to occur in question–answer sessions since it indicates an event in the immediate past:

21   A young man's only after getting shot out there
     [St. E. 'A young man has just got shot out there']

Commenting on these discourse and pragmatic constraints on higher-level syntactic variation, J. Harris (1984:316) makes the additional point that tokens of the hot-news perfect are absent from Irish rural data collected by formal interview methods in the Tape-Recorded Survey of Hiberno-English. Conversely, examples such as 21 turned up in some quantity in the

Belfast urban sociolinguistic projects, which utilized patrticipant-observation techniques to gain access to vernacular speech.

One syntactic variable sensitive to the discourse structure of the speech event, which has been studied explicitly with this kind of influence in mind, is the so-called conversational historic present (CHP). The following extract, recorded during a community action meeting on crime in a church auditorium in Philadelphia, shows very clearly how alternation between present and past tense is associated with *narrative* style. The speaker is a middle-aged man:

'Remember, if you're going to get better locks on your doors, that the price of labor is the same regardless of whether it's a, an inferior lock or a good lock. And again, let me digress for a just a moment and tell you another story that I think I told to the last group I attended – and Nellie's laughin' already. Aah -

A woman came to us and aah – after I gave her this scare tactic, you know, she went out and had a lock put on her door. She lived in an apartment. And when she came home that night, she goes to insert the key and the door goes open. Well, she's petrified now because she knows that this particular lock requires a key to open the door. So she calls the police. The local police came and checked over the apartment and found nothing. So the woman went to sleep – found nothing, nothing missing, so she went to sleep and locked the door and the next morning she gets up, same routine, comes back at the end of the day, the door's open again! So you know, twice is a little too much. Again she calls the police, the police go in, check, nothing is taken, nothing is disturbed. The lady is panicky. We come into the situation. We're talking to the woman and the door's closed. The door's closed and locked now, and the guy in the next apartment bangs his door – bang! – and as he bangs his door, the vertical tumblers – they're supposed to be put in with the vertical bolts going down – were put in by this enterprising locksmith, where the vertical bolts go up! (laughter from audience) Okay? Ordinarily in a good lock, a quality lock, the spring is sufficiently strong enough to keep the bolts in the up position. But because this was a howdy-doody lock, you know (laughter from the audience again) the spring wasn't strong enough to keep the bolt up there and then it, it fell down and this is what has – what had happened. Yes, sir?'

(Wolfson 1982: 73)

Wolfson (1982) has discussed the implications for sociolinguistic field methodology of the characteristic social and discourse patterning of the CHP construction. Her first point is that it seldom appears on tape at all unless some means are found of eliciting long stretches of discourse such as the one from which this extract is taken. Second, it very rarely appears in response to questions, even questions which elicit an elaborated response. This relates to the third point, namely that CHP is associated with *narratives,* which arise in conversation as a spontaneous response to the topic under descussion ('Let me digress for just a moment and tell you another story . . .'). The question–answer rule of the interview thus positively inhibits the subject from introducing topics of narratives. Yet, this is the way they occur in spontaneous conversation.

Wolfson's view of the consequences for fieldwork strategy which follow from the contrast between conversational structure and interview structure is as follows:

> First, the fact that the subject does not have the right to introduce topics during an interview severely restricts his opportunities for introducing narratives. Secondly, the subject of an interview knows that what he is expected to do is give answers to a series of questions. As a result, his narratives, when he does tell them are usually in the form of a summary – short and to the point with little detail as to the interaction of the participants. Conversational narratives, on the other hand, are usually full of such detail. This detail appears in a number of features – grammatical, phonologic, stylistic – which are absent from the summary. One such feature, the one which has been the object of this study, is the historical present tense, the use of the present tense to indicate past action. In collecting data for the study of this form, I found that its use is most fully developed in the performed narrative of everyday conversation, but almost entirely absent in summaries. (Wolfson 1982: 62)

Narratives *are* then found in interviews; but they are usually given in summary form and in accordance with the discourse norms discussed in 3.2.1. are directed firmly towards answering a question. Thus, they do not often include 'irrelevant' detail and structural patterns of the type Wolfson describes. If narratives produced in response to questions are structurally different from narratives produced in spontaneous conversation, it follows that any fieldwork method which involves a two-part discourse structure – even an informal interview – will be an inadequate means of collecting data on linguistic variables such as the conversational historic present which are responsive to discourse structure.

These phonological and syntactic examples all demonstrate the limitations of the interview – even the informal interview – as a means of collecting linguistic data. Sociolinguistic interviewers need at the very least to be alert to possible problems, since, particularly at the level of pragmatic and discourse constraints on syntactic structure, they are not always immediately obvious. Various techniques which have been developed for dealing with them by investigators into *syntactic* variation are discussed in 7.2.

The main *advantage* of interview data is allowing a broad general account of syntactic and phonological features to be compiled, and the general sociolinguistic norms of a community to be inferred from scrutiny of roughly *comparable* sets of data collected from large numbers of speakers. Breadth of focus is rather at the expense of depth and in chapter 4 we shall see how interview methods might be used to complement fieldwork methods which attain greater depth while conversely sacrificing breadth. The point is that, depending on our analytic purpose, we sometimes need to look at the wood and sometimes at the trees; and the weakness of one method can be complemented by the strength of another.

It is limitations of the interview method such as those discussed here which have led Labov over the years to emphasize the problems of gaining access to the *vernacular*; this he has described as the least monitored speech style of an individual – a style which tends to vanish under direct observation. The remainder of this chapter focuses on ways of gaining access to the vernacular – or at least of sampling language which is not always produced under the constraints of an interview discourse pattern. But first it is worth looking more closely at the notion of vernacular, a somewhat controversial concept considered by Labov to be of great practical and theoretical importance.

3.4 The Idea of the Vernacular

One of the best-known principles underlying Labov's data-collecting strategy is that the styles which he distinguished on his linear continuum are not all of equal interest. The array of five styles is not specified as an end in itself; rather it is a means of obtaining information on the linguistic norms of the (monolingual) community. These norms can be inferred by examining the direction in which speakers shift their speech in different situational contexts. But if the objective is to examine the processes and mechanisms of linguistic change, or the structural characteristics of a particular variety, the best data base is a speech style as close as possible to a speaker's spontaneous, everyday speech. In the previous section we demonstrated how a misleading picture of linguistic structure might emerge if no attempt was made to elicit a more spontaneous speech style than is characteristic of interviews.

The concept of the vernacular is, like other metalinguistic concepts such as *speech community, dialect, standard* or even *language*, not particularly well defined (see further Hudson 1980 and Milroy and Milroy 1985a). Labov has described the vernacular variously as the variety acquired in pre-adolescent years (1981: 3), and as the variety adopted by a speaker when he is monitoring his speech style least closely (1972b: 208). These two characterizations, according to Labov, are connected in that adolescent peer groups act as a mechanism for maintaining the vernacular, which is seen as the special property of the group. But as adolescents become older and involved in a wider range of social situations, they gradually acquire a range of superposed standard-influenced styles. Furthermore, they encounter more occasions for switching towards the standard, and consequently, the argument goes, use their original vernacular less and less (Labov 1972a: 257).

Although the relationship between the speech of adolescents and of adults is probably fairly accurately captured by this account (at least in American culture), there are difficulties in viewing a speaker's vernacular as the variety which he uses when he monitors his speech style least carefully. For it is clear that speakers can 'perform' in the vernacular under appropriate circumstances, demonstrating, for example, a wide range of vernacular phonological features in much the same way as they might, in different sets of circumstances, demonstrate their control over a set of features closer to the standard. Brendan Gunn (1983) reports encounters with 'experts' in the dialect during his fieldwork for a study of Cork city intonation, and it is likely that such individuals have recognized status in most speech communities. Moreover, many of the vernacular verbal arts described by Labov (1972a) such as 'toasting' or 'sounding' inevitably involve rather self-conscious performance and so can hardly be described as unmonitored speech styles. Yet, they constitute an important source of information on the structure of Black English Vernacular.

This brings us to a second and rather different sense of the term 'vernacular'. As exemplified in the last sentence of the previous paragraph, it is frequently used to refer to the low-status variety characteristic of a social group (such as American blacks) or of a geographical area. Hence we can refer to the vernacular of London, Liverpool, Belfast, Newcastle or Glasgow. Sometimes these vernaculars have names of their own, such as Scouse, Geordie or Cockney. Both this sense of the term, and the other sense (which relates to the speech of the individual) share an important underlying commonality of reference to publicly unrecognized and institutionally stigmatized language varieties. One sense refers to the dimension of personal style, the other to the larger-scale public dimension of standardization.

Despite these rather confusing differences in the way the term is used, there is little doubt that Labov is right in insisting on the primacy of the vernacular as a data base for structural analysis; this is particularly important in view of a general and pervasive tendency in the western world to view formal high-status varieties as in some sense the *real* language (Milroy and Milroy 1985a). But we have already seen that data collected under relatively formal conditions such as those of an interview have important limitations. Furthermore, the major theoretical interest of many sociolinguists is in inferring processes and developing theories of linguistic change from patterns of variation which are observable in synchronic data, and it has been found repeatedly that innovatory variants tend to appear in the most casual speech style. Conversely, as we have seen in 3.3.1, the sporadic and sometimes hypercorrect nature of a speaker's movement in the direction of the standard when an attempt is made to adopt a 'correct' style of speech often obscures important regularities. If, on the other hand, dialect or language *switching* is the focus of study, there is little chance of uncovering the organizational principles underlying code-switching behaviour unless a means can be found of penetrating the barrier of careful, publicly legitimized language use erected by most speakers (see further chapter 8).

Let us then accept that the principle of seeking access to the vernacular as a data base for sociolinguistic study is an important one, while at the same time conceding that, like many other metalinguistic concepts, the concept of the vernacular is not particularly well-defined. But this need not be a problem if we treat a speaker's or a community's vernacular as an abstract object, rather like its counterpart, the standard language. For then we shall not fall into the trap of attempting to record the vernacular of a given speaker, defining this as his most natural and unconstrained linguistic code. For it is clear that *any* speech varies considerably in response to situational context, not merely in response to self-monitoring on a single dimension of casual to formal. Stylistic variation has been described by one linguist as a type of 'audience design' – a special 'tailoring' of language to fit the requirements of various types of listener (Bell 1984b). Hence, the concept of an entirely natural speech event is, as several sociolinguists have pointed out, an untenable one. But the need to view the vernacular as an abstraction is not incompatible with the need to observe speech outside the discourse frame of the interview. If we are to obtain any kind of insight into the structure of everyday spoken language, we need to look at speech where the speaker has selected his own topic which does not emerge as a result of direct questioning. But as soon as we acknowledge that this kind of spontaneous speech is the object of our investigation, we run into the problem that Labov has described as 'the observer's paradox'.

The observer's paradox, which springs from the effects of direct observation upon language, may be characterized as follows: the vernacular is the focus of the linguist's interest, and large volumes of high-quality recordings of speech are needed to describe it. However, since speakers will tend to shift away from their vernaculars in situations where they are being tape-recorded by a stranger, the very act of recording is likely to distort the object of observation. One of the major tasks of a fieldworker who wishes to obtain reasonable quantities of good data may be seen as that of moving towards a resolution of the observer's paradox (in principle, it can never be entirely resolved). Although interviews are capable of obtaining data which is valuable for some purposes, they are by virtue of the role relationships encoded in their discourse structure likely to exacerbate the central problem of the observer's paradox.

Despite its confusions and apparent contradictions, we must then accept as valid Labov's emphasis on the vernacular as the most appropriate subject of study. Provided it is viewed as an abstraction, occupying a structural slot which places it in gradual opposition to the standard or publicly legitimized code, we shall not chase the holy grail of a completely spontaneous and natural speech style. Assuming now that an attempt to collect data *not* constrained by the social conditions of the interview is well worthwhile, we proceed to examine various ways of addressing the observer's paradox.

3.5 Gaining Access to the Vernacular

Over the last decade or so, a number of studies have appeared which have, in part at least, been modelled on the methods of Labov, Cohen, Robins and Lewis (1968). This study, which was itself designed partly in response to the insights contained in an influential paper by Blom and Gumperz (reported most accessibly in Blom and Gumperz 1972), drastically modified the linguistic interview as a fieldwork tool.

Both studies owe much to the anthropological technique of *participant observation*, which involves, on the part of the observer, 'empathetic and analytic immersion into a social world' (Burton 1978: 165). The nature of the observer's participant role means that the method is the antithesis of formal interviewing or surveying, where the role of observer *as* observer is quite unambiguous. Readers are referred to Vidich (1971) for a classic and lucid account of the method and to Cohen (1982) for a number of studies which vividly illustrate what is meant by 'empathetic and analytic immersion into a social world'. Burton (1978) provides a good account of a participant observation study of Catholic political attitudes in Belfast, including in the Appendix an excellent critical account of the method.

There are several problems associated with participant observation, but the one which is particularly relevant here is the effect of the observer's presence on the behaviour (including the linguistic behaviour) of the persons studied. As Vidich makes clear, the researcher, by joining the group, disturbs what s/he would like to hold constant, and the kind of disturbance s/he creates will vary according to his or her degree of participation. However, Burton's remarks on his fieldwork experiences are worth quoting here at some length:

Initially, people may have been a little reticent because I was a researcher, but as relationships developed this problem receded. The quality of a relationship becomes dependent on the same factors as in any relationship: personality, time, situation and so on. I would argue this by pointing to those individuals in Anro who were precisely those to comment, often bitterly accurately, on my role as researcher:

'I hope you're not one of those making sociological capital out of our plight'.
'Hey Frank, you're good at picking people's brains, what do you make of this?'
'Look at him, you can just see him mentally taking notes.'
'We did participant observation last night in sociology; I thought of you.'
'Now this [piece of information] is for you, not your research.'
'This is Frank. He's experimenting on us.'

Such remarks made me want to creep into the nearest hole and bury myself. However, the point that I am making is that all the people who made the above remarks later talked freely to me, or in my company, about a whole range of issues. This was because *apart from the building of trust, participant observation's efficacy lies in the inability of respondents to be constantly aware that they are in the presence of a researcher.* [my italics] (Burton 1978: 168–9)

Linguists who adopt a modified participant observation method rely no less than anthropologists like Burton on the inability of persons to be constantly aware for a long period that they are being observed. For linguists, the main advantage of the method lies in its capacity to offset, in the manner Burton describes, the worst effects of the observer's paradox. We shall see now how participant observation techniques have been modified in the two important linguistic studies by Labov et al. and by Blom and Gumperz, and how they in turn have been adapted and refined by others.

The purpose of Labov et al. (see Labov 1972a for further discussion) was to obtain reliable information on the structure and use of Black English Vernacular, a relatively uniform variety widely used by black speakers in the United States. Since Black English is simultaneously heavily stigmatized and perceived as a symbol of ethnic identity by the black community, it is to be expected that normal code-switching mechanisms would make direct observation of the dialect particularly difficult. To overcome these problems Labov and his colleagues adopted several important and interrelated procedures, all of which involved quite radical departures from face-to-face interviewing, and approximated for the fieldworkers to Burton's 'immersion in a social world'.

First they focused on the speech of adolescents; we have already commented on Labov's argument that the closest approximation to the vernacular is to be found in the speech of this age band. In her study of the speech of Reading adolescents, Cheshire (1982a) enumerates other practical advantages of working with adolescents when the objective is to obtain data in sufficient quantity and structural variety to describe a dialect in some depth. First of all, adolescents tend to be interested in engaging in prolonged conversation, and have enough spare time to enable them to do so; hence long-term participant observation is a viable proposition. Also, unlike most adults, they gather in groups in public places such as parks or adventure playgrounds where they can readily be located. A further advantage of this availability is that if structural 'gaps' emerge in the data during subsequent analysis, speakers can generally be located again without much trouble.

This last point was very important for Cheshire, since the objective of her study was to describe *comprehensively* the syntactic features of Reading vernacular, *viz.* to include in the description an account of all features which differentiated Reading vernacular from standard English. It is highly unlikely that these objectives could have been achieved by collecting syntactic data from a necessarily limited period of interaction with adults in their own homes. The particular problems of carrying out a study of *syntactic* variation (to which Cheshire's methods are particularly relevant) are discussed in 7.2.

The second strategy used by Labov et al. was to break down systematically the social roles of interviewer/interviewee along with the asymmetrical relationships which they implicitly encoded. During recording sessions, the black researchers joined the group in eating, drinking, singing, card-playing and 'sounding' (exchanging ritual insults). Similarly, Cheshire behaved in a way not at all expected of an interviewer, turning up on a large motorbike and showing her willingness to hang about and talk for long periods, not necessarily on topics specified by herself.

One method of breaking down the interview structure which was adopted by Labov et al. was to study *groups* rather than *individuals*. As demonstrated in Labov's famous account of an interview with Leon, a black eight-year-old, and his friend Gregory (Labov 1972a: 210) this has the effect of 'outnumbering' the interviewer and decreasing the likelihood that speakers will simply wait for questions to which they articulate responses. In fact Leon and Gregory tended to talk to each other rather than to the interviewer. Often, the fieldworker can attach himself to the fringes of the group. Although Labov et al. used both individual recording sessions and group sessions, it was during the group sessions that the richest data were recorded on which a reliable structural account of Black English Vernacular could be based. The speech of each member was recorded on a lavaliere microphone (worn round the neck) on a separate track, and the atmosphere of the sessions was more like that of a party than an interview.

One critical point is that if a speech event can be defined as something other than an interview, it is very likely that group members will talk to each other rather than adopting the role of respondents. Hence it becomes possible to obtain spontaneous data on constructions which are unlikely to emerge in the question–answer format of an interview (see 3.3.2).

The effect of group dynamics seems also to be important, as Nordberg explains:

> . . . the stylistic level is controlled in quite a different way than in an interview, i.e. the members of the group themselves exercise social constraint on one another's language. It would be quite unacceptable for someone in the group to put on an act during the recording and use a form of language which was not normally used in that speech community or among the individual speakers. The more closed the social network of the discussion group is, the stronger the social pressure will be to speak in accordance with the group norm. But even in the case of discussion groups which must be described as open social networks we are on safer ground when it comes to the authenticity of the language used than we are in the case of an interview. (Nordberg 1980: 7)

In support of these remarks, Nordberg goes on to cite experimental evidence from Thelander's work in Burtrask, northern Sweden, where the linguistic effects of manipulating group composition in various ways were systematically examined. Other researchers have described episodes which illustrate the kind of control which a closeknit group in particular exercises on the language behaviour of its members (Labov 1972a; L. Milroy 1980).

The point at issue then is not whether or not the presence of the group in some way allows participants to 'forget' that they are being observed. This is unlikely since, for example, the groups studied by Labov et al. had been convened specifically for the purpose of recording, and the microphones worn by speakers must have constrained their physical movements considerably. But it does appear that the tendency of outside observation to encourage careful, standardized styles and inhibit the emergence of vernacular structures is to a considerable extent *counteracted* by the operation of the group dynamics described by Nordberg.

For these reasons, a number of researchers have adopted the strategy of studying groups rather than individuals; in some cases, the investigator was not present at all (Reid 1978; V. Edwards 1986). Hewitt's study of the use made of patois by London adolescents focused on groups (Hewitt 1982), while Edwards finds very great differences in the language of British black adolescents depending upon whether it is collected in a group session or in response to the questions of a single interviewer. Cheshire, like both Hewitt and Edwards, combined the strategies of studying groups and focusing on adolescent language; she was plainly very successful in obtaining large amounts of good-quality data.

The final fieldwork strategy adopted by Labov et al. which I shall discuss here was to use several fieldworkers. Both Robins and Lewis were black, while Labov and Cohen were white. This was significant, since code choice is highly symbolic; to borrow a term from Gumperz (1982), stigmatized varieties often function as an 'insider' code in opposition to varieties closer to the legitimized code which symbolize various kinds of social distance. Therefore, persons accepted as insiders are more likely to be able to participate in group activities and to have access to types of language different from those observable to outsiders. This principle is likely to be particularly important where ethnic groups with a strong sense of their own distinctiveness are the object of study.

Several researchers have followed this principle of using more than one fieldworker, in order to broaden the range of language available for study. Douglas-Cowie (1978) demonstrated quite clearly the differences betwen the language addressed to an Ulster-Scots insider and an English outsider; V. Edwards (1986) finds dramatically different patterns, depending on whether the fieldworker is black or white. It should be noted in this context that the provision of an insider as fieldworker will not in itself necessarily encourage large amounts of talk. For example, an attempt to use as a fieldworker an eighteen-year-old man in Ballymacarrett, East Belfast, failed completely. The reason was that (not being particularly skilled in elicitation techniques) he attempted to obtain data from family, friends and neighbours by means of face-to-face interview. Given his insider status, this was such an incongruous type of event that they either refused to talk or, while attempting to be compliant, said very little; he was much less successful than a competent outsider.

In conclusion, it is important to note that although various strategies for gaining access to the vernacular have been considered separately, they need to be used carefully and appropriately in conjunction with each other, and with local conditions very much in mind. The overall effect is that the linguistic investigator is a participant-observer rather than an interviewer.

This chapter concludes with an issue which has been implicit throughout the discussion: the kind of analysis of social norms which needs be attempted before appropriate decisions on fieldwork strategy can be made.

3.6 Social Norms and Patterns of Language Use

The major significance of Blom and Gumperz's work in Norway lies in their adoption of an 'ethnographic' approach to the observation of vernacular speech which entailed an explicit analysis of local cultural categories before any structured elicitation of language was even attempted. In this section, I shall discuss the implications of this concept of the fieldworker as analytically active and socially aware before outlining the way in which it was adapted in Belfast. There, the fieldworker (myself) was able to use a knowledge of local norms to construct a specifiable relationship with speakers.

First of all, note that Blom and Gumperz were not primarily interested in examining the structural patterns of the standard and non-standard dialect of Hemnesberget, the community which they were studying. Rather, their goal was to specify the situation in which the bidialectal speakers shifted from one code to another and to explain this code-switching behaviour in terms of its social function for *speakers* (cf. 1.1). In order to do this, they found it necessary to focus on the relationship between choice of code and the local systems of social values rather more explicitly than is usual in the work of Labov. The fieldworkers were consequently committed to a period of relatively unstructured observation, where they learnt the social symbolism of the two codes; otherwise, it is unlikely that they would have understood in any detail the opposition between local and non-local values in terms of which they subsequently explained alternation between the codes. As a result of this observation they were able to formulate the specific hypothesis that code choice for the locals was constrained by what they described as 'local team' membership of interlocutors (in effect insider status) rather then by the topic under discussion. Without such a period of observation, either hypothesis would have appeared equally reasonable.

The fact that the researchers had spent a period of time in the community and were well known there meant that they had a clearly defined role as outsiders but and also developed links with insiders; these roles and relationships were crucial to the design of the more structured part of their investigation. This was a series of field experiments constructed to test the hypothesis that insiders, when interacting with each other, would not switch at all from the dialect, no matter which topic was being discussed. The researchers' procedure was to observe and record the behaviour of a group of locals at a party given by a friend. They confined their role to introducing a wide range of topics into the conversation at periodic intervals and then retreating to the edges of the group. As they expected, once internal interaction was established between members of the group, topic type had no effect in triggering code-switching behaviour.

Further experiments in the series identified different code-switching behaviour by various subgroups within the Hemnesberget community of a very interesting kind. At all times Blom and Gumperz studied pre-existing, self-recruited groups, rather than individuals whom they themselves had selected by some kind of sampling method.

Several studies have depended upon careful prior observation of local norms and values in much the same way – particularly studies of code-switching patterns, which need to specify social context carefully and to be aware of the social symbolism of various kinds of language choice. These form a group which presents sufficiently difficult issues to require separate discussion (see chapter 8). However, work on the Belfast urban dialect also depended very heavily on an analysis of local norms and values of the type carried out by Blom and Gumperz. This analysis was used explicitly as a means of designing a principled fieldwork method.

The Belfast study built upon their notion of exploiting the different effects upon language use of 'outsider' and 'insider' participants. With the problems posed by the observer's paradox very much in mind, a systematic attempt was made to define, in terms of these two categories of participant, the character of the fieldworker's relationship to members of the group. Further details may be found in L. Milroy 1980; but the essential procedure which was adopted in this study of three closeknit working-class groups in Belfast is as follows.

I introduced myself initially in each community not in my formal capacity as a researcher, but as a 'friend of a friend' (see Boissevain 1974 for a discussion of the significance of this relationship) mentioning the name of a person categorized as an insider with whom I had previously made contact and who had given me the names of persons who might initially be approached. As a consequence of the reciprocal rights and obligation which members of closeknit groups contract with each other, the mention of the insider's name had the effect of guaranteeing my good faith; moreover, members of the group appeared to feel some obligation to help me in my capacity as a friend of their friend, so that I acquired some of the rights as well as some of the obligations of an insider. At any rate, my role was defined as rather different from that of a researcher.

The effects of being able to adopt this ambiguous, or even dual, role were very far-reaching. Not only was it possible to seek information by means of relatively structured interviews, but I could also attach myself to the group and record extended interaction in which I frequently participated only marginally. The data collected using the two methods differed considerably in quantity and type in the way that might be predicted from the principles outlined in this chapter.

Such a procedure would of course not have been possible without an extended study of group norms and values; categories of stranger and neighbour, insider and outsider, vary in their reference from one community to another (see Cohen 1982 for examples). Furthermore, knowledge of the interactional norms of extended visiting which was associated with locally defined boundaries between private and public space and with 'insider' status permitted very much lengthier observation and recording sessions than might otherwise have been thought reasonable. For in the small terraced houses in these communities the outer front door was usually left open even in the coldest weather. Unless it was shut, signalling that the occupants of the house did not want visitors, neighbours and friends were free to walk in. Frequently, large numbers of visitors walked in and out of houses without knocking, often giving no reason for their visit. During recording sessions, it was common for several people to arrive and either join in the conversation or remain silent. Extended visiting patterns of this kind appear to be rather common (in Ireland at least) in low-status communities, particularly rural ones (see R. Harris 1972).

Clearly the interactions which resulted from extended visiting were likely to provide excellent samples of vernacular speech. But I would not have had access to them if I had not attached myself to the group in a specifiable, recognized capacity (as a friend of X). Moreover, extended visiting is so different from the middle-class visiting norms familiar to many fieldworkers that a conscious effort needs to be made to observe the patterns of this group behaviour if they are to be used as a means of gaining access to vernacular speech. Community norms need to be studied if patterns of normal communicative behaviour are to be properly understood; it cannot be assumed that they are the same as the researcher's (see further 4.4.3).

This principle is of course likely to be of particular importance for research dealing with language behaviour of ethnic minorities and it is already well known to linguists who study 'exotic' languages (see for example Sutton and Walsh 1979). However, not all researchers appreciate as positively as Blom and Gumperz its relevance for the study of rural and low-status indigenous communities in developed countries.

Chaper 2 considered some problems and principles associated with selecting *speakers* for a sociolinguistic research project, while this chapter focused on methods of recording appropriate types and quantities of *language*. Chapter 4 describes and evaluates the way in which two large urban sociolinguistic research projects have dealt with the problems and implemented the general principles discussed so far.

4

Methodological Principles and Fieldwork Strategy: Two Case Studies

4.1 Introductory

Methodological principles need to be discussed at the rather abstract level at which they were presented in the preceding chapters; otherwise it is not always easy to assess the applicability of a set of methods to a new research context. But it is also helpful to see how such principles have been put into operation, and for this reason we look now at a discussion of two large urban sociolinguistic research projects, in Philadelphia and Belfast, which have utilized a range of different methods to attain different types of goal. The information on Philadelphia in the following sections is taken from Labov's own account of the field methods used in the Philadelphia project on Linguistic Change and Variation, where a detailed evaluation can also be found (Labov 1981).

4.2 The Project on Linguistic Change and Variation

Labov sees the methods of this research as deriving from two sources. The first is the early dialectological methods (see 1.2.2) from which the interviewing techniques used in New York City were developed; these in turn are refined yet further in the Philadelphia project. The second source of influence, discussed in 3.6, is the participant observation techniques developed by Blom and Gumperz and adapted by Labov and his colleagues in their study of black adolescents in Harlem. Labov comments as follows on both of these traditions of sociolinguistic research:

> The original sources for the two models for field methods . . . are both extreme in the ways that they fail as solutions to the observer's paradox. Survey methodology is a highly developed technique for obtaining a representative sample of opinions and attitudes from an enumerated population, but the interactive technique used in such

surveys is designed to keep rapport at a moderate level and filter out all information that cannot be coded in the scheme developed. Here the experimenter effect is maximal, and the correspondence of the attitudes expressed to those that operate in every-day life is not easily determined. On the other hand, the opposing approach used by social anthropologists and enthnographers fails as a solution in the opposite way. The participant-observer may gather data on interactive behavior with a minimum of observer effect, but very little linguistic data can be recorded accurately in journals several hours after the event. Many participant-observers feel quite limited in the extent that they can introduce recording apparatus; when they do record group interaction with a minimum of other observational effects, the data is limited in both quality and quantity.

Our basic goal is to modify both methods as far as we can to reduce these limitations, and then combine both approaches to converge on the linguistic system we hope to describe. There will be sources of error in participant-observation and in face-to-face interviews, but they are complementary; by combining both methods, we can estimate the degree and direction of error in our final statement of the rules of the vernacular. (Labov 1981: 4)

In pursuit of this 'basic goal', the Philadelphia project retained, in the form of a *telephone survey*, the advantages of the formal interview with its emphasis on collecting strictly schematized and comparable data from a systematically sampled population. But a much looser style of interviewing was developed for use in a series of *neighbourhood studies*. The intention here was to allow the interviewer to simulate a conversation and over a period move towards a more symmetrical interactive relationship so that this interviewing style came to resemble participant observation. Overall, the two types of study each had its own areas of strength and compensated for the weaknesses of the other; the neighbourhood studies were intended to obtain *depth* of linguistic and social information, while the telephone survey provided *breadth*. We shall look at them in turn.

4.2.1 The neighbourhood studies

Six major neighbourhood studies were carried out in Philadelphia between 1972 and 1976, utilizing a range of information-seeking techniques:

[The neighbourhood studies] are designed to obtain a large amount of linguistic and social data on the major social networks of the neighbourhoods. They include long-range participant-observation which permits unlimited access to the linguistic competence of the central figures of those networks, along with recordings of group interaction in which the vernacular is displayed with minimum interference from the effects of observation.

At the same time, the neighbourhood studies utilize systematic sociolinguistic interviews to obtain comparable data on all members of the social network. (Labov 1981: 5)

The six neighbourhoods were selected to give a broad coverage of the major class and ethnic groups in the city – working-class Italian, Irish and Puerto-Rican; middle-class Catholic; working- and middle-class black and white. No attempt was made to claim even a weak kind of representativeness.

Two basic fieldwork strategies were used to obtain entry to the neighbourhoods. The first was to approach groups of people gathered in public areas like parks or street corners; the second was through individuals such as priests, teachers or shopkeepers who, in the nature of their work, are 'brokers' and have contacts with large numbers of individuals. Labov notes that the first type of approach appears to work best in working-class neighbourhoods while the second is more successful in middle-class neighbourhoods. The fieldworker presented the research quite accurately as a study of the neighbourhood, including its language, without singling out language for particular comment. The study of change in American life and cities was truthfully specified as an important goal – for indeed socially sensitive sociolinguistic work always takes place within such a context.

Once the first contacts were made, the fieldworker attempted to fulfil certain goals which are outlined only briefly here (see Labov 1981: 8 for details). Some are concerned with eliciting comparable and highly schematized data such as word-lists or responses to subjective reaction tests; for the moment, these will not be discussed (but see chapter 8). The goals on which the comment in this section will concentrate are the major ones of (a) obtaining the range of social and demographic data which is needed to interpret the linguistic material and (b) stimulating large amounts of converstaion with as little interference as possible from the observer.

The fieldworker was not provided with a formal set of interview questions to work through systematically; a formal questionnaire is replaced with *modules* or sets of questions organized around specific topics. These modules may then be organized into what Labov describes as *conversational networks*. The topics of the modules are selected using two criteria. First, previous experience had shown some topics to be successful in engaging speakers in interaction (the danger of death question discussed in 3.1 is of this type). But also important is the information which a given topic can yield on neighbourhood norms and on general social and background information of value to the researchers. The fieldworker on

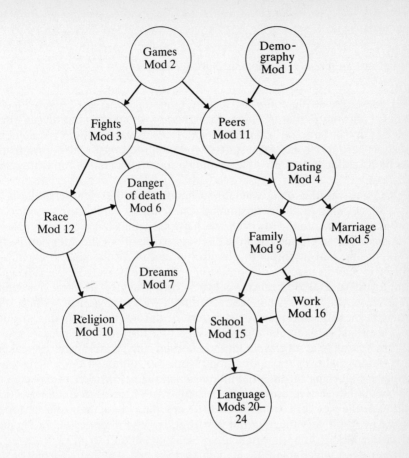

Figure 4.1   Characteristic network of modules for adolescent or young adult speaker (adapted from Labov 1981: Appendix)

any given occasion selects modules from a larger set in order to construct a conversational network appropriate to a given speaker; figure 4.1 shows a typical network selected for an adolescent or young adult in Philadelphia.

Question design is always given very careful attention in terms both of phrasing and ordering within modules; the initial and final questions from each module are designed to facilitate topic shifts to other modules in th system. Module 3, 'Fights', ends with the questions:

Do girls fight around here?
Did you ever get into a fight with a girl?

This can lead, for example, directly into the module dealing with dating patterns:

What are girls *really* like around here?

All questions, as illustrated by the three quoted here, are designed to be brief; Labov notes that questions formulated without preparation can often be lengthy and unclear, containing spontaneous conversation phenomena such as hesitations and false starts. Module questions are also formulated to be as colloquial as possible, avoiding any 'bookishness' in syntax and lexicon.

The general idea of this neighbourhood study interview schedule is to use interlocking modules to simulate the seamless topic-shift structure of normal conversation. However, we have seen that this approach can be criticized on the grounds that the discourse structure of the interview is still present and that attempts to obscure the nature of the speech event are likely to lead in practice to confusion and difficulty (see 3.2.2). Certainly there are several differences between the structure of these extended interviews and everyday conversation. Most obviously, since the asymmetrical question/answer structure of the interview remains, it does not seem plausible to claim that the topic-shifting techniques described by Labov resemble at all closely those in normal conversation where speakers have equal rights of topic initiation. Moreover, although there is no fixed order for working through the modules and the fieldworker is expected to allow the subject's interest in any particular set of topics to guide transition through the network from module to module, his or her role as topic-initiator is still very much in the forefront; it is the interviewer who makes decisions about how or when topics shall be shifted or closed down. A further point which might be made is that the concise, fluent *format* of the interviewer's questions is very unlike the format of normal conversation, where false starts, hesitations and ambiguities are the norm (Schegloff 1979). Perhaps more seriously, there is some evidence that in everyday interaction fluent, smooth speech by a conversational partner is viewed as a mark of social distance and of higher social status (Good 1979).

Labov apparently sees this interview format as extending over several sessions in meetings with individuals and pairs, the interview structure finally dissolving as greater familiarity with neighbourhood residents allows the fieldworker to conduct group sessions. Also included in the design is what Labov describes as 'continued interviews'. This is a second series, using as a conversational resource a different set of modules; these modules are designed to obtain information which can be used to plot out speakers' interpersonal network relationships both within and outside the neighbourhood. Again, the main technique is of modifying the structure of the face-to-face interview so that it comes to resemble, in certain respects, a conversation.

4.2.2 The telephone survey

The aim of the neighbourhood studies was to obtain in-depth information, both linguistic and social, from a number of selected communities. The telephone survey was designed to provide complementary information, on how the language of the community related to that of Philadelphia as a whole.

Informants were obtained by randomly selecting listed telephone numbers. They were then telephoned and asked to participate in a short interview (15 minutes long) presented as dealing with communication in Philadelphia. Permission to record the interview was sought after subjects had indicated willingness to participate.

Altogether, 109 persons were interviewed in this way – a relatively high number for an urban sociolinguistic survey. The original selection of telephone numbers totalled 238, out of which 196 were successfully contacted; of these, there were 87 refusals. These figures suggest that interviewing by telephone is not a particularly good way of cutting down the high refusal rate customary in sociolinguistic surveys; but interestingly, Nordberg (1980) reports a very much lower refusal rate in Sweden.

If claims of strict representativeness are made for a telephone survey such as Labov's in Philadelphia, the method is subject to exactly the same criticisms as those discussed in 2.2. But since interviews can be carried out from a single base, it is a very economical and efficient way of contacting a large number of speakers from a wide geographical and social sample. Since no particular attempt is being made to study spontaneous, informal conversation, the interview can be extremely short, focusing clearly on the linguistic features in which the investigator is interested. Although telephone speech is acoustically limited – the frequency range is sharply reduced at both ends – both Labov and Nordberg report that it is sufficiently clear even for instrumental analysis.

One obvious disadvantage of a telephone survey is that it does not represent people who are too poor to afford telephones. This would be a severe difficulty in the United Kingdom, where a larger proportion of the population would be excluded than in the United States; indeed the method is probably suitable only in countries where a very substantial number of people own telephones.

If we take the neighbourhood studies and the telephone survey together, we can see that two different sets of goals are pursued by means of two entirely different methods. In contrast with the design of the New York City interviews, no attempt is made to attain breadth of coverage (by sampling) and depth of linguistic information (by eliciting both formal and casual speech styles) in a single operation. Hence the design of the Philadelphia research acknowledges the problem of reconciling within a unitary study the need for both depth and breadth.

4.2.3 Rapid and anonymous surveys

The prototype of the rapid and anonymous sociolinguistic survey is of course the famous 'fourth floor' study in three New York City department stores. The basic idea is that in order to study a single linguistic feature, the investigator will elicit a set word or phrase in entirely naturalistic conditions from persons who happen to be in a given place at a given time. In New York City the population studied was department store assistants, and the linguistic feature was /r/ in both pre-consonantal and word final positon (as in the phrase *fourth floor*).

The procedure was for the investigator to ask for the location of any item already known in advance to be on the shop's fourth floor. He then obtained a repetition by pretending to mishear the response, thus eliciting four instances of the target feature in two separate phonetic environments. Pronunciations of the target feature were covertly marked down in a notebook on the spot, using a simple preset schema. The same principle was used in Philadelphia to investigate the alternation between [str] and [ʃtr] in *str* – clusters. This time, the data were obtained in the following way:

> We obtained data on (str) in a wide variety of Philadelphia neighbourhoods by asking for directions in the neighbourhood of a given street which had a name of a form *X Street*. However, we asked
>   'Can you tell me how to get to X Avenue?'
> In the great majority of cases, the informants would respond 'X Street?' with considerable emphasis on *Street*. (Labov 1981: 30)

Plainly, considerable ingenuity is needed to design rapid and anonymous survey questions which will reliably elicit the target feature, and the main advantages of the method are that a very clear view of the distribution of a single variant, geographically and sometimes socially, can be obtained extremely quickly. In fact, the [ʃtr] variant appears to represent an innovation in Philadelphia, and Labov was able to track its distribution through various types of residential area in the city. Nor is the observer's paradox an issue, since speakers are not tape-recorded and are not even aware that they are being observed. The method is, however, applicable only if the investigator has extremely clear goals in mind, already well worked out in advance, and a major disadvantage is the very limited nature of the data which it is capable of yielding. Not only is the investigator restricted to a single linguistic feature, but social information on the speaker is likely to be only approximate. A rapid and anonymous survey carried out in Birmingham, England, is described by Rimmer (1982).

4.3 The Belfast Projects

In the years 1975–81, two substantial sociolinguistic research projects were completed in Belfast, Northern Ireland, concerned with language variation and change in the city. The methods and findings of the first project, which was restricted to a study of vernacular phonology in three inner-city communties have been discussd elsewhere (Milroy and Milroy 1978; L. Milroy 1980; J. Milroy 1981a). However, we shall consider both projects together here, as they were designed as two phases of a single, integrated research programme.

As in Philadelphia, the Belfast study made use of two distinctly different methods to attain different goals. These are respectively a series of five *community studies* and a *doorstep survey*. In terms of what they seek to achieve, but not in details of their design, they are parallel to Labov's *neighbourhood studies* and *telephone survey*. In addition, the Belfast project incorporated a *rural hinterland* study of Lurgan, a small country town in the Lagan Valley, seventeen miles south-west of Belfast.

4.3.1 The community studies

Five of these were carried out altogether. Although Belfast has a much smaller and less socially and ethnically heterogeneous population than Philadelphia, the community studies resembled Labov's neighbourhood studies in that they were designed to give broad coverage of major geographical, status and ethnic divisions in the city. The first three, Ballymacarrett, the Clonard and the Hammer, are very low-status inner-city areas. Ballymacarrett is located east and the Clonard and the Hammer west of the River Lagan, which bisects Belfast and constitutes an important socio-geographical boundary. The other two, Braniel and Andersonstown, are both located on the outer edges of the city and might be described approximately as upper-working to lower-middle class. Braniel is east of the river and is exclusively Protestant, while Andersonstown is west of the river and is exclusively Catholic.

Ballymacarrett and the Clonard can be viewed as somewhat lower-status 'feeder' areas of Braniel and Andersonstown respectively. Many Andersonstown people originated from or had family ties with the Falls Road, the area where the Clonard is located; the Braniel population on the other hand are East Belfast people, many of whom have ties with the Newtownards Road where Ballymacarrett is located (see map 4.1). The identification of these interrelationships between the areas is well

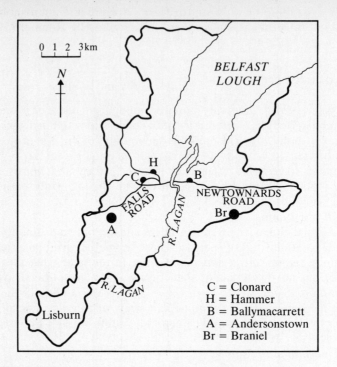

Map 4.1   Location of five speech communities in Belfast

motivated; for when Belfast people change their place of residence, for whatever reason, there is a strong likelihood that the new location will be selected in accordance with a highly predictable set of urban sectoral preferences. To some extent, these sectoral preferences are related to ethno-religious lines of demarcation (Boal and Poole 1976); certainly it is reasonable to view inner-city communities east and west of the river as each having a higher-status ethnic counterpart.

A comparison of the inner city and outer city informants' occupations gives a good idea of the relative status of the communities. Ballymacarrett and Clonard people were at the time of the research overwhelmingly unemployed or in unskilled and low-status occupations. Typical occupations were street sweepers, barrow boys, forklift-loader drivers, or labourers. The women were usually office cleaners or domestic helps; sometimes they worked in rather poor neighbourhood shops for low wages, being unable to get work in the better city centre stores like Boots or the British Home Stores, where labour was unionized. By way of contrast, we find in the outer areas skilled tradesmen (an electrician and a fitter), a school meals' supervisor, a bricklaying instructor at a government training centre, a shop assistant at Boots, a primary school teacher, students and unemployed ex-students and apprentices. Even these unemployed young people contrast with their counterparts in the inner-city areas in having potentially marketable skills and qualifications.

The general idea of selecting communities which were interrelated in this way on the dimensions of status and ethnicity was to 'match-up' linguistic data from the four areas, so as to obtain some fairly detailed information on the linguistic strategies which Belfast people employed as they moved from urban vernacular to slightly higher-status speech patterns. We were also curious as to whether east/west differences in the structure of the vernacular (see L. Milroy 1980) would be maintained by higher-status speakers. Thus, the choice of communities was constrained quite sharply by the analytical goals of the research.

An outline of the way field-workers gained entry to the communities, with particular reference to the thinking behind the method, may be found in 3.6; I shall look at the procedures in a little more detail here.

Recall that the fieldworkers were anxious to reach central community networks in each area in order to gain access to vernacular speech. Since contacts made through individuals with a clear institutional status – such as teachers, priests and community leaders – can often lead to rather standardized speakers, these contacts were avoided. Instead, communities were always approached initially through persons encountered directly or indirectly in the course of everyday living who had no institutional status in the communities, but were members of them. The Andersonstown fieldworker however, an anthropology graduate, was a local resident and was also one of the informants. It was in this community that the closest approximation to a traditional participant observation study was achieved, since the observer had for her entire life been part of the social setting which she was observing.

This guiding principle of participant observation – that the observer should be part of the setting which he or she is studying – was followed as closely as possible in the other communities. It was for this reason that the fieldworkers in the other areas, who were not local residents, adopted the role of 'a friend of a friend' which gave them a clear status of an informal kind. In all communities, but most particularly in the poorer inner-city areas (largely as a consequence of the denser, more multiplex structure of local networks) they were passed from one family to another, being received with warmth, friendliness and trust. The research was presented as an investigation of the way life and language in the community had changed, and general permission was sought to record interaction at which the fieldworker was present. Once people had agreed to participate, this permission was never refused. As a consequence of the local norm of extended visiting (which was commonest in the low-status inner-city areas and least common in Braniel) many of the recordings were of two, three or four people talking amongst themselves, often with minimal fieldworker participation.

The general idea, using these methods, was to carry on recording until a quota sample of sixteen people in each area had been filled. The target quota consisted of eight young adults (18–25 years) and eight middle-aged adults (40–55), equally divided between males and females. In practice of course very many speakers fell outside the target quota. The quality and quantity of data collectd during these community studies was excellent, including many group sessions with minimal (or even zero) linguistic participation by the fieldworker.

4.3.2 Participant observation methods: an evaluation

The very high quality of the data in terms of capacity to provide a good sample of everyday language is of course the major advantage of a participant observation method. Another major advantage is the insight it is capable of yielding into the social and communicative norms of the community. Under this head is included not only information on informal social ties and organization, but also the fields of study generally described as 'the ethnography of speaking' (Saville-Troike 1982) and 'interactional sociolinguistics' (Gumperz 1982; see further 8.4.1). A third advantage, pointed out by Labov (1981: 25), is that 'by emphasising deeper studies of groups and social networks, we gain in the possibility of explaining linguistic behaviour', in other words, we might derive insights into *why* a speaker's language occupies a particular position in a wider social structure. For example in Belfast, information collected during the community studies enabled us to attempt such an explanation in terms of group pressure to adopt vernacular norms exerted upon an individual whose interpersonal ties were largely local, dense and multiplex. It was argued that the strength of these pressures was roughly in proportion to the centrality of the speaker's position in the closeknit group. Conversely, persons occupying peripheral positions in such a group were more exposed to external standardizing pressures (L. Milroy 1980; Milroy and Milroy 1985b).

Although we may in this way gain in explanatory capacity, there are several important disadvantages associated with a participant observation study. The first, noted by Labov with respect to the Philadelphia neighbourhood studies, is that however good the data there is no way in the absence of a supplementary broader study of locating it in a wider sociolinguistic context. We simply do not know how it fits in to the system of sociolinguistic variation and stratification in the city as a whole. This has implications, for example, for the study of linguistic change in progress.

Such a study requires information on the language of a range of social groups and generation cohorts.

Second, for the fieldworker such studies are extremely demanding in tact, energy, persistence, time and emotional involvement. Strong and sometimes quite intense relationships with individuals are built up over a period of even a few weeks. Largely because of this level of involvement, it is often quite difficult to persevere with tape-recording during the observation period. It is perhaps worth commenting here that *informants* in this type of study are not usually unhappy about being tape-recorded; Peter Trudgill (1986b) has suggested that people are now generally familiar with recording equipment and relaxed about being recorded.

Third, the method is somewhat wasteful, being quite the converse of Labov's telephone survey in this respect. Many more speakers and many more hours of speech are usually recorded than can ultimately be analysed; a useful rule of thumb is that about ten hours will be needed to analyse each hour of recorded data. Another aspect of this extravagance is the large amount of *unanalysable* recorded data; this is presumably the point Labov is making when he remarks that the (technical) quality of participant-observation data is often poor (1981: 4). We do, however, need to modify the force of this comment by noting that in Belfast no problem was experienced in obtaining plenty of recordings of sufficient technical quality to be analysable. But wastage was also high because of interference from the normal background noise of day-to-day living; on one occasion, interference from electronic equipment in the room resulted in a whole blank tape. In short, this kind of work cannot be approached by examining its cost-effectiveness in terms of man-hours spent in the community.

A further problem emerges if, as in Belfast, the fieldworker is attempting to fill a quota of individuals divided into specified categories; this can often be frustratingly difficult. For example, in all the community studies the intention was to obtain recordings of eight males and eight females, dived into two age groups (18–25; 40–55). However, in the Braniel a young male fieldworker found (for rather obvious reasons) that he was not passed on to any young women of a similar age to himself. A different gap emerged in the Andersonstown data, which probably reflected the structure of the participant-observer's own social network; only one male in the older age group was contacted. It is clear that such gaps restrict methods of handling data (see chapters 5 and 6); for example data for age- and sex-groups could not easily be aggregated. The problem of filling quotas to specification is probably the most severe disadvantage of a participant-observation study; since the groups studied are self-recruited, the fieldworker by definition relinquishes control over choice of subject.

The problem of social role   One particular difficulty which is liable to beset participant observation studies was touched on in the previous paragraph; it concerns the social role allocated to the fieldworker as a consequence of his or her age, sex, ethnicity or other socially significant attributes. It was suggested in chapter 3 that social role can be varied to some extent by, for example, manipulating discourse patterns or by creating an acceptable category of identity such as that of 'friend of a friend'. However, attributes like those listed above clearly cannot easily be manipulated, a particular problem in Nordberg's view when an 'insider' is used as fieldworker:

> It is important to bear in mind that he/she has a defined social position in the local community, which in turn gives rise to a varying social role in relation to the interviewees. And I think this social position is more apparent to the informant and the variation in role relations more marked than if the interviewer is an outsider and not in a particular relation to the speakers from the outset. The same thing probably applies to smaller communities compared with larger ones. (Nordberg 1980: 5)

Certainly it is true that such difficulties emerge particularly with small-scale community studies. In Belfast, the first three of these (in the inner-city areas) were carried out by an outsider to Northern Ireland (myself) who as a consequence was not assigned a role in relation to local ethnic categories. Since English people are also stereotyped in Ulster in various (usually unfavourable) ways, it was probably equally important that my mixed, but mainly Scottish, accent made it extremely difficult for subjects to fit me into any clear popular category. However, the research assistant responsible for organizing fieldwork in the two outer-city community studies (John Harris) is an Ulsterman, and therefore, although in no sense associated with any of Ulster's political pressure groups, was very conscious that there were parts of the city which he could not visit freely and confidently. It was initially for this reason that fieldwork in Andersonstown was delegated to one of the informants, while Harris himself carried out the Braniel study.

Pursuing the issue of the fieldworker's social role, it is worth commenting on a very general and apparently reasonable assumption that the closer the fieldworker is matched to subjects in terms of various social attributes, the more successful he or she is likely to be. This is the position adopted, for example, by Nordberg (1980: 5), and is plainly correct up to a point. For example a bilingual fieldworker acceptable to an Asian community in Britain would probably need to be selected carefully for a range of characteristics such as religion, geographical provenance, or political affiliation, all of which are associated with a distinctive ethnicity. Similarly, Wolfson attributes her unsuccessful interview with the restaurant owner (see 3.2.2) to a mismatch of age, sex and status in addition perhaps to the particularly low social esteem accorded to a young woman. A female fieldworker certainly will not have access to some of the characteristically male speech events recorded by Labov et al. in 1968; none of these were recorded in the Belfast inner-city communities. By the same token a male fieldworker will not have easy access to conversations with adolescent girls, as John Harris found in Belfast.

But close matching in terms of age and sex and other attributes is not the only social factor which makes for choice of fieldworker; attitudes to males and females also need to be taken into account. While, as Wolfson implies, the generally low esteem in which women are held may create problems for a young female fieldworker, we have to note correspondingly that many communities find males – particularly young males – very threatening. For example, it is clear from work with an English- and Punjabi-speaking family in Newcastle upon Tyne, where a young white woman carried out modified participant observation sessions over a period of several months, that no male, regardless of age or ethnicity, would be allowed into the house (Scothern 1985). It may be the case rather generally that male fieldworkers find it difficult to gain access to a domestic setting – particularly if they are visiting women during the day when the man of the house is at work. This was certainly the case in Belfast, and may be the underlying reason for Labov's apparent preference for recording in public, non-domestic settings.

A further, apparently reasonable, assumption is that a male subject will adopt the more formal styles in his repertoire when addressing a woman (cf. Trudgill 1986a: 8). But in Belfast, quite sharp style-shifting in a *formal* direction was noted on one occasion when a young man addressed an older male researcher, after speaking to a woman. Age and perceived seniority were probably the cricial variables here. In summary, it is likely that the effect of the social role assigned to the fieldworker might be quite complex, with status, sex, age and ethnicity interacting in a manner which is not always initially obvious. The best solution is not necessarily the one proposed by Nordberg of socially matching fieldworkers to subjects.

4.3.3 Small group studies in Philadelphia and Belfast: a comparison

On the basis of experience in the Belfast community studies, the advantages and disadvantages of participant observation have been assessed. The main difference between the design of Labov's neighbourhood studies and the Belfast community studies is probably the extent to which they have endeavoured to adopt the major principle of this method – that the observer should be part of the setting being studied. Taking that principle as a starting point, an attempt was made in Belfast to assign to the fieldworker a clear social identity which allowed him or her to claim a role in the community. Consequently, no attempt was made to provide an interview schedule such as that developed by Labov; fieldworkers were simply briefed on the kind of social information (such as occupation, educational background, family connections and previous residence of speaker) which they would need to have acquired by the end of the observation period. The topics associated with this information – such as local attitudes and local networks of relationships – generally provided a more than adequate conversational resource.

Section 4.2.1 describes how, following quite a different method, Labov developed the traditional face-to-face interview into a series of interlocking modules with the intention of simulating the topic-shift patterns of conversation. In view of the interviewer's role in the discourse, it is not clear how far or how reliably such an extended interview really does resemble spontaneous conversation; but Labov's schema is likely to be less demanding of the fieldworker, more economical of time and resources, and so not subject to the same range of disadvantages as the participant observation methods of the Belfast community studies.

In general, it is probably fair to say that the Philadelphia neighbourhood studies provide a better *general* model for the in-depth study of communities located at various points in the class continuum. The Belfast methods, on the other hand, were developed primarily for the study of *closeknit* communities – and indeed it is likely that they are particularly and rather generally suitable for urban or rural communities of this type. Bortoni-Ricardo's (1985) work in Brasilia provides an example of a sociolinguistic 'network' study of a closeknit migrant community from a very different kind of society, using methods very similar to those described here.

We look now at the method adopted in Belfast (parallel to Labov's telephone survey) of complementing, by means of a rather wider but shallower study, the detailed information collected in the five communities.

4.3.4 The Belfast doorstep survey

When the doorstep survey was designed, intensive work on the three inner-city areas had already been completed. Consequently, it was in no sense intended to provide basic facts about sociolinguistic patterns in the city, but rather to obtain quite specific and limited linguistic information. In this respect also, its general goals differ from those of the community studies.

Altogether, 60 speakers were recorded, taken from a random sample of 120 households. This sample was provided for the project by the Northern Ireland Housing Executive and was in turn drawn from a larger sample of 500 households which the Executive had used for their own survey of housing patterns in the city (cf. Labov's subsampling procedure in New York City).

The original intention was to record about 80 speakers, divided more or less equally between males and females. The sample of 120 households was therefore divided into three matched lists of 40 addresses, A, B and C. Each provided a coverage of the major social and ethnic variations in residential pattern similar to that which could be found in the original list of 120. Fieldworkers used list A as a basis and the other two as a back-up resource; B and C were ordered in such a way that if researchers failed to record an interview at, for example, household number 4 on list A, household number 4 of lists B and C would be of a similar type in the same locale. This procedure was adopted in anticipation of difficulty in obtaining recordings from households on the basic list and was designed to ensure that for each household replacements with broadly similar social characteristics were available.

In the event, 73 speakers were interviewed at 38 addresses. An analysis was made of data from 60 speakers, 32 males and 28 females. In order to ensure comparability, the main effort in the interviews was focused on recording carefully designed word-lists, which sampled realizations of several phonological variables in a range of phonetic environments. Some spontaneous speech was also recorded. The interviews could be completed on the doorstep in as little as 10 minutes, but most lasted between 15 and 45 minutes and more often than not the fieldworker was invited into the house, offered tea and biscuits – and on one occasion two meat pies!

In view of the brevity of the basic interview, subjects were not contacted in advance; fieldworkers simply knocked on the door and requested interviews. It was hoped in this way to reduce the high refusal rate which is a hazard in sociolinguistic surveys, and indeed the method seemed in general to be successful in this respect; altogether, out of 40 addresses visited, only 8 refusals were recorded.

These refusals were mainly from relatively high-status households, and where they were not categorical (for example, people sometimes excused themselves on the grounds that they were too busy to be interviewed), were dealt with initially by a follow-up visit. Interestingly, these second visits were never successful, and interviewers then had recourse to the back-up lists.

There were two reasons for interview failure other than refusals; first, residents were sometimes too old or incapacitated to be interviewed, and second, many of the listed addresses in inner-city areas turned out to be demolished or boarded up. For practical reasons, fieldworkers adopted a policy in these cases of knocking at the door of the nearest house of a similar type; since the survey was based on geographical area and housing type, this seemed a reasonable way of obtaining data from a range of addresses while conserving time and resources. A formal letter of introduction from Queen's University, Belfast, was carried, to be produced on demand as accreditation; it proved however to be useful mainly for dealing with the security forces, since unwilling interviewees were not impressed by it and willing ones did not request it.

The purpose of the research was presented as an investigation of change in Belfast life and language. This rather vague account satisfied and stimulated the interest of most people; fieldworkers began asking interviewees how long they had lived in the area and moved on to discuss their general attitudes and background. The minimum social information required for each speaker was (approximate) age, sex, housing type and (where possible) occupation. Since the word-list (constructed to sample a range of linguistic environments) was considered particularly important, it was usually produced early in the proceedings. Where possible, fieldworkers attempted to record a male and a female at each address, and since very often both were not at home at the time of the first visit, a second and even a third visit was arranged to most addresses.

The general principle of the Belfast doorstep survey is quite similar to that of Labov's telephone survey in that neither are designed to attain any depth of insight into, for example, stylistic variation, or the structure of a speaker's vernacular. Rather, information is sought on broad patterns of variation across a wide social range in the urban community. As in Philadelphia the major effort of the Belfast research was focused on the community studies; the main function of both the doorstep survey and the telephone survey was to provide a context within which to place the findings of those studies. Although the data collected were quite adequate for this purpose, no attempt was made to claim representativeness for the doorstep survey. This was considered generally impractical (see 2.2) and in view of the particular difficulties of carrying out social research in Belfast, probably unattainable.

From the point of view of economy of effort and resources, a telephone survey is certainly preferable to a doorstep survey of the type described here. However, since the proportion of households owning telephones is much lower in Britain and Ireland than in the United States, a telephone survey in those countries is probably not feasible. The disadvantage of the method noted by Labov, *viz.*, that households from the lower end of the social range are not represented, would be very much greater.

A point which needs to be emphasized about brief, shallow surveys of the types exemplified in the Philadelphia and Belfast research is that they are most rewarding when they are designed to solve quite specifiable and well-understood problems. They are not suitable instruments for exploratory research, which is best carried out by in-depth investigation of a small number of speakers. In Belfast, for example, a great deal of well-documented linguistic information was used in designing the word-list, in order to examine the effect of specific phonetic environments on a range of vowels.

4.3.5 Evaluation of the Belfast doorstep survey

A linguistic survey such as this carried out in 1980 was able to benefit from the experience of earlier sociolinguistic work; many problems had already been anticipated. But it is worth drawing attention to two particular difficulties which stemmed from the disturbed condition of the city of Belfast, but are likely to occur rather generally in run-down industrial cities.

The civil disturbances had given rise to a number of population movements within the urban area, with the result that many randomly selected households were burnt down, boarded up, or derelict. Although there was a random procedure for replacing such houses with others of the same general type, interviewing was nevertheless a time-consuming, depressing and occasionally frightening experience. As inner cities in Britain continue to decay, it seems likely that this problem will be present, though perhaps in a less acute form, in a number of places.

A further difficulty arose from the departure of a large number of middle-class families from the Belfast area to neighbouring dormitory towns, a migratory pattern in line with changes in the demography of British cities generally for the last two decades or so. As a consequence, any random selection of households in such a city is likely to be skewed heavily in the direction of low-status groups. This is exactly what happened in Belfast, and the imbalance in the data is probably a fair reflection of the contemporary demographic structure of the city. Clearly, however, where the overall number of speakers is small as it is in many sociolinguistic surveys, the number of higher-status speakers turning up in a random selection procedure which samples from the entire urban area will be correspondingly small. In Belfast, this problem was in practice rather severe since most refusals came from higher-status households, so that a large amount of time and effort was expended in recording small numbers of such speakers.

Although this difficulty could be resolved by adopting some kind of stratified sampling procedure (Trudgill, for example, sampled four electoral wards of which the social characteristics were known), a more general question emerges of whether it is always reasonable to take the population of an urban area as a sampling universe, when in fact a high proportion of the higher-status people who work in that city actually reside in neighbouring towns. This is a question which should probably be considered by sociolinguists working in cities with a demographic structure of the kind described.

4.3.6 The rural hinterland study

This part of the Belfast project does not have an analogue in the

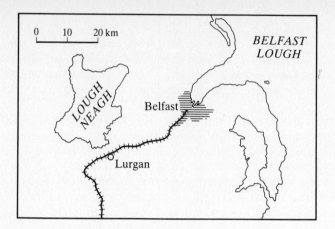

Map 4.2   Relative locations of Belfast and Lurgan
(after Pitts 1985: 66)

Philadelphia Project on Linguistic Change and Variation. Its design was motivated by a question of considerable sociolinguistic interest – the relationship between dialects of cities and those of surrounding areas. Since linguistic change and rapid dialect mixing appear to be a general characteristic of urban dialects (Labov 1972b: 300), it seems reasonable to assume that insight can be gained into the processes of their formation if a set of data from a city is compared with a set from a surrounding area. Belfast, being a relatively young industrial city, is an excellent site for such a investigation (see Milroy and Milroy 1978 for details).

The hinterland area selected for study (see Pitts 1983, 1985 for details) was Lurgan, a small rural town in the Lagan Valley, 17 miles south-west of Belfast and outside the urban overspill area (see map 4.2). It had been noted previously that certain phonological features characteristic of West Belfast where both Clonard and Andersonstown were located were also characteristic of the mid-Ulster dialect spoken in Lurgan (as opposed to the Ulster-Scots dialect of Belfast's northern and eastern hinterland). Hence, it seemed likely that information on similarities and differences between the five Belfast communities on the one hand and Lurgan on the other could be used for a variety of theoretical purposes. Apart from the investigation of linguistic change and the typology of urban dialects, a comparison of these sets of data might well have an important bearing on Labov's notion of a speech community as 'united by a common evaluation of the same variables which differentiate the speakers' (Labov 1966: 125). Could Belfast be said in this sense to be a single speech community separate from Lurgan? or do Lurgan speakers show sensitivity to the same sets of variables?

The participant observation techniques in this study were similar to those used in the urban community studies. The 'network' method was adopted as a general principle, and several Belfast University students who were Lurgan residents were located as initial contacts. On a number of occasions, the fieldworker arranged for subjects to self-record themselves and their friends, with excellent results. Altogether, 28 speakers were recorded, 16 men and 12 women. As in the community studies, they fell into two generation cohorts.

Altogether, the six studies which comprised the Belfast project, five from Belfast and one from Lurgan, allowed language variation to be analysed on the following dimensions: rural versus urban; high-status versus low-status (relatively speaking); east of the city versus west of the city. Methods of analysing this large amount of data are discussed in chapters 5 and 6.

4.4 A Note on Ethics

Some consideration of ethical issues is an important part of any attempt to provide an extensive discussion of sociolinguistic fieldwork methods. Increasingly, investigators have become aware of a rather heterogeneous range of problems (some of them not particularly easy to formulate) which may be characterized as ethical.

Although the American Anthropological Association's statement on ethics is of some relevance to sociolinguists and is easily accessible as an appendix to a book which deals specifically with ethical problems in fieldwork (Rynkiewich and Spradley 1971), linguists do not in general have recourse to a widely accepted ethical code. In this they are unlike medical researchers; for example the Ethical Committee of the University of Newcastle upon Tyne monitors research with human subjects from a medical ethical perspective. Linguistic work comes within its remit only if the subjects are National Health Service patients – for example, adult aphasics, or handicapped children. And the range of issues with which the Committee is concerned is quite different from those to be discussed here. Candid recording, for instance, is a troublesome issue for sociolinguists; but I have received the impression that medical researchers are generally less inclined to worry about audio-recording without the speaker's knowledge or permission, provided anonymity is maintained.

Despite linguists' lack of recourse to an agreed code of conduct, ethical issues in the linguistic sciences have sometimes been quite pressing. For example, in forensic contexts phoneticians and linguists have for some years now used their expertise to assist in voice identification; academically this is a highly controversial enterprise. A discussion of the issues may be found in Bolinger (1980: 111), and J. Milroy (1984) where a case of direct relevance to sociolinguists is documented in detail. In view of the absence of any clear ethical code for linguists working with human subjects, what follows should be interpreted as an attempt to air the major issues rather than to prescribe such a code. I shall begin by commenting on, and amplifying somewhat, Labov's discussion of sociolinguistic ethics which he organizes under three headings: candid recording, protection of anonymity and access to recordings.

4.4.1 Candid recording

In general the practice of Labov and his research team, adopted by most sociolinguists working within his general paradigm, has been to ban candid or surreptitious recording. A close parallel to the view that it is wrong to record speakers without their knowledge may be found in the controversy which has surrounded the use of telephoto lenses in photography; these 'spy' lenses are capable of taking photographs hundreds of yards away from the subject (Greenhill, Murray and Spence 1977: 18). The main reason for this caution is that since a magnetic tape or a photograph furnish a permanent record of behaviour, the subject is entitled to be aware that such a permanent record is being made. But there is another, perhaps rather less obvious, reason to avoid candid recording which is associated with the subject's self-image and is most easily understood by continuing to draw a parallel with photography.

Just as the sociolinguist prizes spontaneous, unmonitored speech, the professional photographer of human subjects prizes unposed photographs; but most people are very chary of allowing themselves to be photographed. Very few of us like to see pictures of ourselves looking tired, haggard or undignified, or with teeth missing. As a glance at most family photo albums will show, there are many aspects of their lives which people choose not to reveal to their friends.

The sound of his or her own voice is in a similar way an important part of a person's self-image. Labov reports (personal communication) that in his early work he once played back to a woman a tape-recording of her own casual speech to prove to her that her image of her accent was inaccurate. Her subsequent unhappy reaction caused him to regret that he had inadvertently damaged her self-esteem by destroying part of her image of self which she presented to the world. Because speakers view their voices as an important part of their self-images in this way, they are often unhappy about being recorded without their knowledge.

Linguists not working within Labov's general framework are often less careful than he is about candid recording. For example, Dixon (1984: 80) quite openly states that some interesting material was obtained from

Aboriginal speakers by candid recording. Crystal and Davy (1969) are happy to tape-record colleagues, friends and family surreptitiously, requesting permission only subsequently to use the material. One of the points which might be made here is that Labov sets out explicitly to provide a model for handling communities not known to the investigator. Crystal and Davy on the other hand are focusing on the language of a few speakers well known to them, and it may well be that in their case the nature of the personal ties between investigator and subject makes candid recording a less pressing ethical issue.

Obviously assuming that his readers will be dealing with subjects to whom they are relative strangers, Labov points out some *practical* disadvantages of candid recording; first of all, long-term access to a community is likely to be hindered if people think they are being spied on, and second, the quality of such recordings is often poor. As Labov remarks: 'A hidden tape-recorder and a hidden microphone produce data which is as dubious as the method itself' (Labov 1981: 32).

Although I personally endorse Labov's views on the matter of candid recording, it has to be admitted that the issues are not always as clear-cut as they seem. Particularly during successful long-term participant observation, the borderline between overt and covert recording can become blurred and quite difficult problems emerge.

During the Belfast community studies, for example – and no doubt this experience is quite general – conversations were often interrupted by several more people entering the room. Indeed, sometimes the original participants would leave in the course of a long recording session. Although the recording equipment was not concealed, and was monitored quite openly by the fieldworker, it was not always clear whether all participants were aware of being tape-recorded. In situations like this, it was not our practice or the practice of Labov's fieldworkers in Philadelphia to interrupt proceedings in order to renegotiate permission to record; in Belfast such permission was sought at the first contact with each household. There was moreover a standing agreement that the equipment would never be concealed and that the fieldworker would wipe from the tape before leaving the house any material which subjects or fieldworkers considered sensitive. In fact, more often than not the fieldworker took the initiative in this matter; investigators who build up long-term relationships with communities frequently hear and record material which they would prefer to remain ignorant about.

It was noted in 3.5 that long-term participant observation, as a consequence both of the relationship of trust which is built up and of a person's inability to remain vigilant for long periods, has the effect of blurring the distinction between covert and overt observation. Conversationalists do not operate with the idea that their remarks will find their way on to a permanent record and by definition it is usually *conversation* which a sociolinguist participant observer is studying, rather than some other more overtly structured kind of talk. As a natural consequence of the participant observation method, some situations which are highly successful recording sessions can leave the observer feeling unhappy that they have found their way on to a permanent record. I shall give just one example here.

In one of the Belfast inner-city communities, I built up a strong personal relationship with a very poor family. Most of the recording sessions, which took place in the evening, were pleasant and party-like; eating, drinking, smoking, chatting and card-playing often continued into the early hours of the morning. At the end of the observation period, it was extremely difficult to loosen these ties, which of course involved a considerable time commitment. Much of the conversation had focused on the disastrous and pathetic effect upon the family of the civil unrest in Belfast and its function was plainly cathartic; many recordings resembled therapy sessions more closely than sociolinguistic field tapes. I sometimes felt that I was taking unfair advantage of the family's need to talk through their problems with a sympathetic outsider.

The main point, however, is that in successful participant observation not only is the borderline blurred between covert and overt *observation;* so also is the borderline blurred between covert and overt *recording.* It must be stressed that after a certain time has elapsed, individuals will interact with the researcher just as they will with anyone else, notwithstanding the possible inhibiting effect of recording equipment. Photographers also take advantage of the inability of persons to remain constantly vigilant, often introducing themselves into a situation many hours before they attempt to take pictures (Greenhill et al. 1977: 18). As Burton remarks, 'Respondents who are aware of the researcher's interests do not constantly hold that awareness in mind' (1978: 169). The kind of information which a long-term participant observer receives must be treated with the greatest circumspection, for it depends ultimately not on whether he or she is carrying a tape-recorder, but on the degree of trust, mutual confiding and general affinity which has developed between researcher and subjects.

This discussion of candid recording may be concluded with a brief comment on a related but much less troublesome matter – recording in public places. Generally speaking, most researchers feel that there is no harm in tape-recording (or, for that matter, photographing) a politician on the hustings or any other obviously public person or event. But what of the customer in the shop who is talking loudly enough to be overheard? Or of the heated conversation in a pub or restaurant? There is little agreement on the ethics of recording without permission in situations like these, but Labov's general principle seems to offer a sensible guideline; it is that the researcher should 'avoid any act that would be embarrassing to explain if it became a public issue' (Labov 1981: 33).

4.4.2 Preservation of anonymity and access to recordings

There is amongst sociolinguists a general consensus that pseudonyms should be used for both personal and street names in order to preserve anonymity. Some anthropological researchers, such as for example Burton, and many of those whose work is collected by Cohen (1982), also identify neighbourhoods and even towns by pseudonyms. Participants should be assured of this anonymity at the outset of the research, and particularly in view of the kind of material which can emerge in the course of participant observation it should at all times be preserved absolutely.

For the same reason, sociolinguists need a firm policy with regard to access to tape-recordings. Both the Belfast and the Philadelphia projects restrict access to members of the research group or scholars who are temporarily affiliated for the purpose of carrying out a specified piece of work. If material is required for bona fide research by another scholar, or for public lectures, the Belfast group have available a composite tape, exemplifying various types of speech. This tape has been carefully vetted for sensitivity of content or for material which can lead to the identification of speakers. But tape-recordings are by no means freely available as a resource to all.

4.4.3 Some further problems

So far, section 4.4 has dealt with issues which are generally familiar to sociolinguists working in British, American or European urban communities. But in Britain at least, as more investigators study ethnic minority communities, it will become clear that much of what constitutes good ethical practice is highly culture-dependent. This point is of course relevant in any field situation where the researcher is studying persons in whose culture he or she does not participate, and the need to avoid offending established beliefs and values is taken for granted in anthropology texts such as that by Rynkiewich and Spradley.

Sometimes, the consequences of failing to attend to local cultural values can be drastic, as illustrated in this account by Dixon of an incident which took place in the early seventies in an Australian Aboriginal community:

> Richard Gould had published a book *Yiwara, foragers of the Australian desert* which unwisely included a photograph of sacred objects, knowledge of which is restricted to initiated men. An Aboriginal high school girl from a desert tribe had chanced to see this picture – and all hell had broken loose. She was to be ritually speared for having broken a taboo. AIAS [Australian Institute of Aboriginal Studies] tried to get in touch with Gould and his publishers to ask them to withdraw the book from sale, or at least remove this photo.

Meanwhile, Aboriginal communities in several parts of Australia, alerted by the wide media coverage, began banning anthropologists from entering Aboriginal reserves. (Dixon 1984: 38–9)

As a consequence of this incident (and no doubt others like it), the Australian Institute for Aboriginal Studies has laid down ethical guidelines and imposed strict conditions upon research grant applicants, including linguists. Several of these emphasize that researchers should attend carefully to the sacred and secret parts of Aboriginal life and language; publication of material whose widespread dissemination offends against Aboriginal religious practice is forbidden. These restrictions apply not only to the photographing of sacred objects but also, for example, to the recording of songs; many songs are exclusive to men or women, and must not be played to mixed audiences. Publication in print of certain items is also restricted.

Plainly such a set of guidelines as those drawn up by AIAS is entirely necessary, and to many readers the examples discussed here may seem rather extreme. But they are intended to illustrate the very general point that we cannot know in advance the belief systems of the communities we are studying; an important part of good fieldwork practice is to get to know them and take them into account at all stages of the research, up to and beyond the time of publication.

The AIAS guidelines deal also with the matter of the researcher's debt to the community which has enabled him or her to carry out research and, in many cases, advanced an academic career. This is a matter about which many sociolinguists feel sensitive, particularly since a large proportion of the communities which they study are repressed indigenous groups like the Aborigines, or underprivileged ethnic minorities like the American blacks or British Asians. Fundamentally, the low status of these groups is a consequence of their position in societies whose political systems do not attend to the equal and impartial distribution amongst all citizens of power and advantage. Generally speaking, academic researchers have no power to alter such a system, and can do little more than respond to their own feelings in a manner appropriate to the norms of the community and their own consciences. For example, in their linguistic 'salvage' work in Australia, many scholars feel that they are assisting by making available to Aboriginal communities a record of their languages which are under severe pressure from English (see for example, Dixon and Blake 1979). The AIAS guidelines codify this general principle, adding however that grant applicants must provide a summary and appraisal of their work *in a form appropriate for submission to an Aboriginal group* (AIAS 1980: 5).

The general issue of reconciling with his academic interests the feeling of social commitment to an underprivileged group with whom the researcher has built up a strong feeling of empathy is discussed by Labov (1982b); this discussion forms a preliminary to his account of the use made of linguistic evidence by the defendants in the famous Black English Trial in Michigan. Ultimately, the judge found in favour of the plaintiffs, who had argued that the educational authorities were illegally discriminating against their children by failing to take into account their distinctive language and culture. Labov's quite proper feelings of pleasure are evident to any reader of his article; he plainly views the episode as an example of the opportunities which may arise for linguists to repay a debt to the communities they have worked with. Readers are also referred to Smith (1985) for a full and very personal account of the broad ethical issues which he feels are raised when white academic researchers study poor non-white minority communities in Britain.

4.5 Conclusion

This chapter, together with chapters 2 and 3, has dealt rather selectively with a number of issues pertaining to fieldwork strategy, many of which are still the subject of controversy. The initial discussion was at a relatively abstract level, to help readers extrapolate principles relevant to their own particular piece of research. However – particularly in this chapter – I have also referred freely to the research strategies adopted in specific projects, so that readers might assess how they have been implemented in the field.

The following four chapters move away from fieldwork, to consider various aspects of data handling and analysis.

5

Analysing Variable Data:
Speaker Variables

5.1 Introductory

Once a large amount of data has been collected, the question arises of how
it should be analysed, and it is understandable if investigators faced with
many hours of tape-recorded conversation feel a little daunted. Traditional
dialectologists presented their data on maps – or, in the case of the Survey
of English dialects, more accessibly in four volumes of *Basic Material*
which listed informant responses. But these lists are not organized in any
way other than regionally; the methods of dialectology do not address
themselves to variation *within* a single region between the sexes, or
between status groups or generation cohorts (see 1.2.2). Nor can they
handle variation within the language of a single speaker. Because they
provided explicitly for the sampling of a wide range of speaker types and
speech styles, the data collection methods associated with Labov's model
allowed data to be analysed on all of these dimensions. The key to direct
analysis and systematic comparison of the very large amount of data
collected using these methods is the concept of the *linguistic variable*.

The variant realizations of a linguistic variable do not encode different
referential meanings. They co-vary with other units in the system and/or
with a range of *speaker* variables such as social class, ethnicity, age and sex.
The significance of the concept of the linguistic variable is that it allows
quantitative statements to be made about language use, so that Speaker A
might be said to use *more* or *less* of a particular variant than speaker B,
rather than categorically to use it or not to use it. Equally, speaker A may
be said to use more of variant X in situation Y than in situation Z, rather
than categorically to use X in either situation. This kind of statement
contrasts very sharply with the maps and lists of traditional dialectology,
where elements are generally treated *as if* they were categorical within a
given region. A small amount of data from two English cities, Bradford
and Norwich, shows how the concept of the linguistic variable can be used
to describe language patterns in these cities in relation to the social

characteristics of speakers. Since these social characteristics (or *speaker variables*) are our main concern in this chapter, we shall focus on the relationships between speaker variables and linguistic variables, deferring until chapter 6 any further discussion of *linguistic* variables.

The figures in table 5.1 refer to the variable (h), and list the percentages of zero realizations of word initial /h/ (in items like *hammer* and *heart*) recorded for five social class groups in these cities, ranging from Lower-working to Middle-middle class. It is clear that in both places, the higher the status group the greater the tendency to approximate to the spoken norm of Received Pronunciation, which retains [h]. However, each social group in Bradford uses the zero variant more than the corresponding group in Norwich.

Table 5.1   (h) in Bradford and Norwich: percentage of zero realization

Social class	Bradford	Norwich
Middle-middle	12	6
Lower-middle	28	14
Upper-working	67	40
Middle-working	89	60
Lower-working	93	60

Source: after Chambers and Trudgill (1980:69) and Petyt (1977)

The relationship between use of linguistic variables and various other speaker characteristics is illustrated in table 5.2, which summarizes patterns in the realization of the vowel variable (ai) by Belfast working-class speakers. The figures represent the amount of fronting and raising to [eɪ] of the vowel in words like *pipe* and *line*, the maximum score being 200, which represents a large proportion of extremely non-standard realizations. Figures are shown separately for Interview Style – the rather careful speech used in direct response to the fieldworker's questions – and for a more spontaneous style not used in response to questions and often not addressing the fieldworker (see 3.5; 8.2.2). There are also separate sets of figures for three age-groups and both sexes.

Several patterns are apparent from table 5.2. First, the tendency to use raised and fronted variants of (ai) decreases systematically with the age of the speaker. Second, within each age group women raise and front the vowel very much less than men; finally all speakers use raised and fronted variants very much more in spontaneous speech than in the relatively formal style of interaction appropriate to an interview. These findings along with those shown in table 5.1 are fairly typical of sociolinguistic surveys carried out in western, socially stratified cities. Generally speaking

Table 5.2   (ai) in Belfast: IS = interview style; SS = spontaneous style

Age	Scores out of 200		
	Men		Women
70+	173.0	IS	–
	194.0	SS	–
40–55	77.7	IS	62.7
	121.3	SS	126.0
18–25	74.0	IS	46.7
	133.7	SS	115.7

higher-status groups and women tend to approximate more closely to standardized varieties and all speakers shift away from non-standard forms in a situation such as a formal interview. Speakers of different age-groups frequently show different patterns of use, which do not necessarily represent a move either 'towards' or 'away from' a standard norm. Both patterns are reported in the literature.

5.2 Speaker Variables and Theories of Change

Labov's quantitative methods (and his interpretation of results) were not originally motivated to provide a statement of the relationship between linguistic structure and social structure. Although the pejorative term 'correlational sociolinguistics' is sometimes used by non-practitioners of the subject who appear to make this assumption, Labov himself has expressed the fear that his methods might give rise to a flood of replicated 'correlatory' studies of little theoretical value. As much of his work makes clear (see particularly Labov 1982b), the chief objective was not to describe relationships between speaker and linguistic variables, although this was certainly an interesting by-product of quantitative method which for some might comprise its main significance; it is certainly of great practical interest to a number of professions (see chapter 9). But Labov's main concern was to obtain insights into processes of linguistic change and to challenge linguistic theories which modelled language as a static entity, identifying *homogeneity* with *structure*. His views on this latter issue are set out in Labov 1975 (and elsewhere).

Evidence of change in progress is often provided by systematic differences in *apparent time* of the kind shown in table 5.2; that is, differences between generation cohorts. But a less obvious kind of evidence may, according to Labov, be provided by some kind of irregularity in the expected pattern of differentiation according to speech style, or sex or social class of speaker. A clear example of this kind of evidence of change might be found in Labov's famous analysis of the variable (r) in New York City. This variable shows a stable pattern of stratification according to social class except that one social group, the Lower-middle class, use in their more careful styles *more* rather than *less* of the high prestige variant than the status group immediately above them. Labov's interpretation of this irregularity is that it shows the Lower-middle class to be instrumental in diffusing a change throughout the speech community by adopting and emulating what is in fact an innovatory pattern introduced by a higher-status group (Labov 1972a: 122). Similar structural irregularities emerging from quantitative analysis might involve a social group unexpectedly using variants associated with *lower-status* values (see for example Trudgill 1974: 111). The same principle might apply to relationships between linguistic variables and other speaker variables such as sex (Milroy and Milroy 1985b) or ethnicity (Horvath 1985).

It is clear then that speaker variables are of considerable *theoretical* importance. At the *sampling* stage they are for practical reasons equally important, for it is hard to see how investigators could proceed without some recourse to demographic categories such as class, sex, or ethnicity. But despite their significance both at this practical level and in understanding processes of change, behind the apparent strength of relationships such as those shown in tables 5.1 and 5.2 lie pervasive difficulties in handling speaker variables. These difficulties are associated with both *definition* and *interpretation*. Variables which have been examined particularly frequently by sociolinguists are *social class, age, sex* and *ethnicity*. Good discussions of these and others may be found in various textbooks, notably Downes 1984 (chapter 6), and no attempt will be made here to duplicate this material. The purpose of the following sections is to explore the difficulties with reference to a number of rather awkward speaker variables, beginning with *social class*.

5.3 Social Class and Sociolinguistic Research

5.3.1 Some general comments

In chapter 2 this variable was discussed in relation to data collection and sampling procedures, rather than in relation to data analysis which is our concern here. It was noted that linguists tended to use the concept of social class rather unreflectingly, primarily as a means of imposing some order on variable linguistic data collected from a large number of (usually urban) speakers. But despite the obvious appeal of this rather pragmatic use of the social class concept, difficulties emerged in societies with social structures different from those in which it had been used apparently successfully (2.5). Intractable as these difficulties sometimes are at the sampling stage, they become much worse at the level of analysis and interpretation. To understand why this happens, we need to begin by looking at what is meant by the term 'social class'; its definition and application is subject to considerable debate within sociology. The discussion in the following paragraphs, which is confined to issues of particular importance for sociolinguistic research, draws heavily on Goldthorpe's (1985) balanced introductory account.

5.3.2 Competing analyses of social class

We are speaking here of an analytic construct which in a general way is concerned with the (unequal) distribution in societies of wealth, prestige and power, but is approached quite differently by Marxist and capitalist (functionalist) social theorists. According to the Marxist view, a class is a group of persons with a common relationship to the means of production and so is defined in all societies in economic terms. Although it may be possible in a capitalist society to distinguish several such classes – for example, farm workers, owners of small businesses and professionals, amongst others – there is a strong tendency for such boundaries to disappear, leaving a sharp distinction betwen the bourgeoisie who control wealth and the proletariat who produce it. This polarization results in conflict between the two large opposing groups which, according to Marxist sociohistorical theory, will lead to a crisis to be resolved ultimately by the workers seizing the means of production. Hence, class conflict is viewed as inevitable and indeed as the only major source of conflict in capitalist society.

Functionalist (or stratificational) sociologists disagree sharply in a number of respects with this Marxist analysis of social class. Most importantly they see the social structure of capitalist societies as being based not upon conflict but upon shared values. Nor do they look for evidence of sharp boundaries between the classes, preferring to operate with the notion of *social stratification* where clases are not sharply divided but form a continuum. The basis of social hierarchy is not contrasting relationships to the means of production, but different values which are placed upon different occupations. Evidence commonly cited in support of this analysis is the close agreement found between persons who are asked to rank-order according to prestige a list of occupations. As a consequence of this 'stratificationalist' approach, divisions between classes are seen as arbitrary and are drawn, usually on the basis of occupation, for analytic convenience. Thus, it is argued, people do not agree on the number and composition of classes, nor on the location of the boundaries between them, which are fuzzy and readily crossed by the socially mobile.

A class is thus said rather vaguely to consist of a group of persons sharing similar occupations and incomes, and as a consequence similar life-styles and beliefs. The emphasis in functionalist sociology is therefore on the values *shared* within and between classes, rather than on conflict as the basis of class structure. The fact of class conflict is not denied, but is seen as only one of several sources of conflict within society; and perhaps most crucially of all, the stratificationalist approach to class is unlike the Marxist approach in that it is used in a fairly *ad hoc* way as an analytic tool, rather than as part of an integrated sociohistorical theory.

It should be evident from this account that most sociolinguistic research which follows the paradigm established by Labov's *Social Stratification of English in New York City* is adopting, without explicit acknowledgement, a functionalist view of social class. It is the lack of awareness of the controversial nature and implications of this model which constitutes the problem, rather than any particular property of the model itself. Without such awareness, we cannot easily address the issue of what constitutes an appropriate social model for sociolinguistics.

A good example of the unacknowledged influence of the model may be found in the ready adoption by many sociolinguists of the notion of *prestige* to explain the patterns of sociolinguistic stratification which have become so familar; the persistence and spread of *low*-status forms is then accounted for by the notion of *covert prestige* (Trudgill 1983a, chapter 9). However iluminating such an analysis might be, the difficulty is that if the theory dependence of the whole notion of prestige is not explicitly acknowledged, patterns of linguistic differentiation are seen as emerging inevitably from a supposedly objective analysis of social structure. Highly theory-dependent explanations of these patterns then appear to be not much more than inspired common sense. But in fact the notion of class is not well defined, a stratificational analysis is not objective, and a sociolinguistic analysis which is heavily dependent upon the notion of prestige is part and parcel of a stratificational model.

At a slightly more abstract level, the unacknowledged influence of the functionalist model upon sociolinguistic theory is more pervasive even than the widespread use of the notion of prestige suggests; an interesting example is Labov's early definition of a speech community in terms of *shared norms and common evaluation* of the very linguistic variables which differentiate speakers (Labov 1966: 125); it is the emphasis on shared norms and values rather than on *conflict* which differentiates quite sharply Marxist and functionalist views of class.

One unfortunate consequence of this rather cavalier approach to the notion of class by sociolinguists is that meaningful debate on the question of how linguistic variability can most pertinently be related to social structure tends not to take place. For example, a Marxist perspective would be likely to view the individual's relation to the means of production as a more relevant determinant of attitude and behaviour (including linguistic behaviour) than his or her position in a stratified society. That in fact is the rationale underlying the concept of the *linguistic market* where linguistic differences between speakers are analysed in terms of 'the importance of the legitimized language in the socioeconomic life of the speaker' (D. Sankoff and Laberge 1978: 241). The groups which emerge are by no means identical to those yielded by an occupational index of the type associated with a stratificational model (see D. Sankoff and Laberge 1978 for details).

It is evident from the analysis of Sankoff and Laberge that the Marxist concept of class is less easily operationalized than the stratificational one. But this apparent methodological superiority does not necessarily spring from any intrinsic properties of the stratificational model. More probably it results (in part at least) from its general familiarity and widespread use as a descriptive tool in large-scale accounts of demographic structure; in Britain, the decennial Census of Population is an example. Conversely, because very little substantive empirical work has been based upon the Marxist model, it is not clear from a relatively small-scale study such as that by Sankoff and Laberge whether it offers a potentially more insightful way of analysing variation. The chief point at issue is not the competing merits of the models; more fundamentally the controversial nature of the social class concept needs to be acknowledged and discussed by sociolinguists in order to give researchers some purchase on the important question of how language relates to social structure.

5.3.3 Interpreting patterns of co-variation between language and social class

I have focused in this section so far on problems of *analysing* data which spring from the ill-defined nature of the social class variable. But further, related problems are associated with *interpreting* patterns of co-variation between language and social class which emerge from the stratificational analyses used in sociolinguistics. Since a very wide range of personal characteristics and behaviours have been found to co-vary with social class, this is a problem of social research generally, by no means unique to sociolinguistics.

Most descriptive studies in Britain base their classifications on the Registrar-General's ranking of occupations from I to V, according to their supposed prestige, with a major division between middle-class or white-collar workers (I, II, and III non-manual) and working-class or manual workers (III manual, IV and V). The most fundamental events in people's lives are strongly affected by their social class, ranging from their chances of surviving the first year of life through likely age of marriage and number of children to the kind of diseases they are most likely to die of (Reid 1977). Social class influences are particularly pervasive in education, showing an effect even at the nursery stage (Tizard and Hughes 1984).

It is not at all clear why a person's life-style, behaviour (both linguistic and non-linguistic) and opportunities should be so radically affected by his or her father's occupation. Although some differences appear to stem more or less directly from inequalities in wealth and power, others appear to be associated with attitudes and values which cannot be related directly to such inequalities; an example is the preference of British working-class mothers for bottle-feeding rather than breast-feeding their babies. We must therefore conclude that social class as it is used in stratificational studies is a *proxy* variable covering distinctions in life-style, attitude and belief, as well as differential access to wealth, power and prestige. The problem here is that unless some attempt is made by sociolinguists to 'unpack' the pertinent variables for which social class stands proxy, progress in formulating a satisfying explanation of the relationships between linguistic and social structure is likely to be slow. This book is not the place to undertake such a task; but one comment that might be made is that an initial distinction between *class* and *status* is likely to be important (cf. 2.5); for it is the evaluative rather than the economic dimension of stratification which seems to be relevant to linguistic variation.

Social class is not the only speaker variable which presents problems of definition and interpretation, but it has been singled out here for detailed discussion for two reasons. First, it interacts with other variables of interest to sociolinguists; and second, it illustrates in a particularly acute form the ill-defined character of speaker variables in comparison with *linguistic* variables. As we shall see in chapters 6 and 7, they present problems also; but these problems tend to be more generally acknowledged, and to be on the whole less intractable than the ones we are discussing here. Taking the case of social class as an example of a more general difficulty associated with speaker variables, I shall comment in the following sections in rather less detail on *sex* and *ethnicity*.

5.4 Sex of Speaker

All known societies appear to use language as one means amongst others of marking out gender differences (gender, strictly speaking, being a cultural and sex a biological category). The precise form this differentiation takes varies from community to community; for example it is likely to be manifested differently in pre- and post-industrial societies and to vary in accordance with culturally determined roles assigned by societies (see Coates 1986 for a general discussion of the issues). In bilingual communities undergoing a process of language shift, the sexes are likely to focus on the new monolingual norm at different rates (Gal 1979).

In westernized hierarchically stratified societies, the form this linguistic sex-marking has commonly been interpreted as taking is for women to approximate more closely than men of similar status to the prestige norm. But such an interpretation of the very salient sex differences which plainly do exist, and are moreover theoretically important, relies on the analyst's capacity to assign a comparable social class index score to both males and females. In fact one of the problems of a stratificational analysis is that it classifies women in a somewhat arbitrary manner, sometimes assigning to them the class of their husbands or fathers and sometimes determining their class by their own occupations. Because of this, it is hard to take seriously the various interpretations of linguistic sex-marking which are based upon the notion of *prestige*. Perhaps the commonest explanation of the patterns which emerge from a stratificational analysis is that in the absence of opportunities to mark status by occupation, women resort to language. A number of obvious objections might be made to explanations of this kind (Cameron and Coates 1985; Coates 1986). For example, it is not clear why, if they are motivated by a desire to mark prestige, wives of men in high-status occupations should not simply imitate the language of their husbands.

Once it has been acknowledged that linguistic differentiation is a particularly salient manifestation of the tendency of communities to mark out gender distinctions by a variety of means, it is difficult, given the general orientation of current sociolinguistics, to progress further in finding a convincing explanation of linguistic sex-marking. The most fruitful procedure might well be to seek lines of explanation other than those associated with the notion of prestige. Horvath's re-graphing of some of Labov's data in terms of 'natural' linguistic groupings even suggests that sex should *take precedence over* class as the major speaker variable; she remarks that 'if social class is seen to take precedence, then these other social dimensions might remain hidden or only dimly perceived' (Horvath 1985: 64). One implication of these comments is that it is perhaps more reasonable to explain class differences in terms of sex, than sex differences in terms of class.

In view of the current state of the art I can do no more here than suggest that alternative approaches are surely possible. For example, one might reasonably take as a starting point the observation that the characteristic occupations of men and of women are distinctly different, as are the kinds of relationships with co-employees associated with them. So also are the general patterns of informal social relationships contracted by men and by women (see further Milroy 1980). Cheshire (1982a) finds the same differences between male and female *adolescents*. Yet another avenue of explanation might develop from a comparison of certain properties of the language of care-takers of young children (who are usually women) with the language of women generally (Snow and Ferguson 1979; J. Milroy

1985). The point of these observations is not to argue the case for any particular line of explanation, but to emphasize that current approaches in sociolinguistics have not taken us very far in understanding linguistic sex-marking. Unquestioning acceptance of a functionalist model of social structure may even have hindered progress towards such an understanding (see further Milroy, in press).

5.5 Ethnicity

Ethnicity, like social class, presents problems of definition, but can reasonably be described as an individual's sense of belonging to a distinctive group whose members share a common history and culture. Although ethnicity is not coterminous with regional or racial origin, both may contribute to a more general sense of distinctiveness with which a sense of *linguistic* distinctiveness is often associated. This may not correspond to any major structural difference between languages; for example, the spoken forms of Urdu and Hindi are almost identical but are perceived as different apparently because of their strong association with Muslim and Hindu ethnicity (Linguistic Minorities Project 1985: 45). It is the subjective nature of ethnicity which can make it tricky to handle as a speaker variable.

Frequently ethnicity is maintained or even heightened by physical or political conditions; for example, ethnic minorities of Commonwealth origin in Britain are clearly marked out from the indigenous population by skin colour. Assimilation is consequently difficult, particularly as the minority groups experience considerable hostility. Their perceived status is usually low, because of the character of the relationship between Britain and their countries of origin which were once colonies. The heightened sense of distinctiveness which results from these conditions is likely to be marked by strenuous efforts to maintain linguistic distinctiveness.

Ethnicity is not, however, always marked by *linguistic* distinctiveness, Labov's work with Italian and Jewish speakers in New York City shows that such distinctiveness may persist for several generations, or conversely may disappear with the first generation of native-born speakers who nevertheless maintain a strong sense of ethnicity (Labov 1972b: 281). Similarly, political conditions in Northern Ireland serve to maintain a powerful sense of ethnic distinctiveness which is marked in a number of culturally codified ways (Larsen 1982: 135); but these do not appear to include systematic linguistic differences. Protestants and Catholics certainly see themselves as different peoples with different histories, and for the most part maintain different cultural traditions. But where the two groups live together, there appears to be no clear difference in language use, an example being the Protestants and Catholics of working-class East Belfast whose language was analysed during a pilot study designed to investigate possible effects of ethnicity (see 6.2.2). Systematic differences between Catholics and Protestants which *have* been observed are probably best characterized as *regional* differences, since for example East and West Belfast *Protestants* each perceive the accents of the other group as distinctive (L. Milroy 1980). However, in areas with a high level of Protestant/Catholic residential segregation, a clear distinction between regional and ethnic differences in language use is in practice difficult to maintain.

The Northern Ireland case illustrates a critical point hinted at at the beginning of this section which has important methodological implications for any researcher working with ethnicity as a speaker variable: ethnicity is a culturally created category, in no sense objectively 'given' or verifiable. Thus, it is quite possible in Northern Ireland for an ethnic Catholic to be a non-believer, or conversely for an (English) outsider who is an adherent of the Catholic religion to be categorized as non-Catholic. The point is that religion and ethnicity are not identical; but religion is a culturally accepted marker of ethnicity, and the terms 'Protestant' and 'Catholic' in Northern Ireland refer to ethnicity rather than religion. Similarly, region of origin is not always co-extensive with ethnicity. In countries like Australia with large immigrant populations, some groups for various reasons assimilate more readily than others, and lose their sense of distinctiveness (Clyne 1982). In Britain, the Polish community maintains its sense of distinc- tiveness through a well-organized network of cultural activities (Linguistic Minorities Project 1985: 68–76); but many individuals of Polish origin have assimilated readily and no longer have a sense of Polish ethnicity.

The final point which needs to be made about ethnicity is that as a speaker variable it cannot usually be isolated from social class. Because migrant populations are frequently recruited as low-paid workers, they tend in many countries to cluster in the poor areas of inner cities near to their workplaces, and to be concentrated in low-status occupations. Even members of ethnic minorities who were relatively prosperous in their country of origin and migrated originally as political refugees tend to become occupationally declassed, taking a step down in status relative to their former positions (Linguistic Minorities Project 1985: 74). It is worth noting that many of the most interesting studies of the language/ethnicity relationship are not quantitative at all, but focus qualitatively on the social meaning which bi- and multi-lingual speakers associate with the codes in their repertoire (see further 8.3).

5.6 Variables Associated with Speaker Identity

All three of the speaker variables discussed so far are associated in some way with the individual's place in intersecting social configurations. It was noted in 5.3.3 that the much-studied variable of social class appears to be a proxy variable, and in fact most linguists are probably not primarily interested in the correlation between occupation, educational level or any other social class indicator and language, but in a more general relationship between linguistic differentiation and social differentiation of which the stratification system is only a part. For this reason a number of researchers have attempted to work with speaker variables which are less abstract than social class, teasing out more specific aspects of the relationship between language and social structure. The general assumption is that in some sense speakers use language variation, consciously or unconsciously, to signal various kinds of social identity and social aspirations. This view of the relationship between linguistic and social structure has been articulated particularly forcefully by R. B. Le Page (see Le Page and Tabouret-Keller 1985).

A recent example of a study which attempts to single out a speaker variable of this general type is Holmquist's (1985) account of the influence of *political orientation* on patterns of language variation in a small, homogeneous Spanish-speaking community. As with speaker variables generally, there is despite the apparent specificity of this variable still a problem of interpretation; many other speaker variables are associated with political orientation such as, for example, an affinity for peasant rather than urban life. The difficulty is that in the absence of an explicit theory of sociolinguistic structure which attempts to account for these relationships, there is no principled way of deciding which variable offers the greater insight into patterns of variation.

Similar comments might be made about the speaker variable of *social ambition* used by Douglas-Cowie (1978) to account for linguistic variation in a Northern Irish village. Without an explicit theory, it is not clear whether the important underlying variable is indeed of a psycho-social kind, or whether it is (for example) associated with the looser social ties between the individual and the local group which are likely to be congruent with a high level of social ambition.

5.7 Social Network

5.7.1 General principles

One variable of this general 'identity' type is *social network*. An individual's social network is simply the sum of relationships which he or she has contracted with others, and in that rather obvious sense the concept is universally applicable. However, the structure and type of interpersonal relationships varies; most importantly, an individual's personal network might be relatively closeknit in the sense that the ties contracted with others are *dense* and *multiplex*. This means that a large proportion of contacts are also tied to each other, and that individuals are simultaneously linked in more than one capacity; for example X might know Y both as a neighbour and as a workmate.

The idea of using social network as a speaker variable was developed in Belfast in response to an explicit hypothesis concerning the capacity of closeknit networks to function in society as a norm enforcement mechanism. This means that if an individual is embedded in such a network, s/he is more liable than one whose network is relatively looseknit to be vulnerable to pressure exerted by everyday social contacts. This pressure may result in the maintenance of a set of norms – including linguistic norms – which then flourish in opposition to publicly legitimized norms. As this model would predict, individuals in Belfast whose personal networks were closeknit tended to approximate closely to the stigmatized vernacular norms characteristic of the locality, which like other 'in-group' norms powerfully symbolized values of solidarity, reciprocity and to some extent opposition to standardized norms along with *their* associated values. The capacity of closeknit networks to exert normative pressure formed a basis for using this speaker variable not only descriptively, but to explore more radically patterns of language maintenance and change.

5.7.2 Quantifying network structure

It is possible to assign to an individual a numerical score which reflects the structure of his or her personal network with reference to the key concepts of multiplexity and density. The measure used in inner-city Belfast to examine the relationship between language variation and network structure was a six-point scale which measured speaker scores on five *indicators* of multiplexity and density. These indicators were interpreted as conditions which, if fulfilled, suggested a relatively dense and multiplex personal network. Each individual was assigned a point for each condition s/he fulfilled, the *network strength score* being the sum of individual indicator scores (see L. Milroy 1980: 141 for details).

Although the theoretical motivation for positing social network as a speaker variable can be made relatively explicit, its use presents certain problems, the first of which concerns the measurement and quantification of network structure; for like social class and ethnicity, the ill-definedness of the network concept can make it difficult to operationalize. Fundamentally, it is a social rather than a psychological variable, its main purpose being to enable the researcher to compare individuals in such a way as to focus on differences between them with respect to *degree of integration* into a set of relationships which constitute a group capable of exerting normative pressure. The difficulty is that the *indicators* of this integration which are capable of being treated quantitatively (to enable such a comparison) are likely to be culturally determined and to vary from one community to another. This is best clarified by an example.

The indicators in Belfast were all concerned with relationships of kin, work and friendship, contracted within a defined territoral area where their influence was likely to be considerable. While it is quite possible that a different range of indicators might have served equally well in this setting as surface markers of an underlying variable of social integration, this particular set was selected in response to two methodological criteria. First, since the network variable was motivated by a more general social theory, they were intended to reflect conditions which, in a number of network studies, had seemed capable of predicting the extent to which an individual became subject to group pressures. For example, multiplex ties of *work* and *friendship* have emerged as powerful in this respect (see Cohen 1982 for examples and L. Milroy 1980 for further references). The second criterion adopted was that the measures should be recoverable from data collected in the field and easily verifiable. This ruled out (for example) affective measures of attitude which might well also be capable of yielding insight into the individual's degree of integration with the group. But since the data needed to construct such a measure is difficult to elicit and interpret, a more easily verifiable and simpler measure was preferred; for example a point was assigned for ties of kinship contracted in the neighbourhood.

It is clear that the indicators selected in Belfast are not necessarily relevant (or even usable) in all types of community where the language/ network relationship is of interest. This issue will be explored further in 5.7.4, where other sociolinguistic studies, which have selected different indicators, are considered. Meantime, the important principle which emerges is that the network measure is concerned with an underlying variable of *integration* to a social group; hence, selection of indicators is motivated by the need to characterize in a principled way differences between individuals with respect to degree of integration.

5.7.3 Looseknit networks

A further major problem associated with the use of the network variable is that it is most readily operationalized to study speakers whose networks are of a relatively closeknit type and cannot easily handle socially and geographically mobile speakers whose personal network ties are not predominantly dense or multiplex; yet, such persons make up a substantial proportion of the population in a post-industrial society. Looseknit networks are hard to deal with chiefly because a multi-valued speaker variable like social network involves comparing speakers who differ from each other in certain respects – let us say in respect of the multiplexity of the ties which they have contracted at the workplace – but are still similar enough to each other in other related respects to make such a comparison meaningful. Looking again at the case of the Belfast inner-city speakers whose network patterns were compared, it is evident that relative to a person who, for example, had changed jobs and houses several times, their networks were *all* closeknit. While we might make this general point and follow through its implications when we want to compare, for example, Braniel people with Ballymacarrett people, it is much less easy to see how the relatively looseknit network structures of Braniel people might meaningfully be compared with each other.

Many Braniel people owned cars and telephones, which they used as a means of maintaining important personal ties over long distances, and the capacity of these ties to influence their behaviour (linguistic or otherwise) is not clear. Other speakers seemed to be relatively exposed to standardizing mainstream influences, in that they had contracted few personal ties which were likely to exert normative pressure on their behaviour; but in any case the geographical spread of the ties contracted by most Braniel speakers made them difficult to investigate. While we might indeed readily hypothesize that these individuals were generally less likely than Ballymacarrett people to be subject to the pressures of their personal networks and more likely to be subject to a less localized outside influence, it is hard to suggest dimensions on which a number of looseknit networks, which differed greatly from each other, might be systematically compared (but see 5.7.4 for an account of Bortoni-Ricardo's study of rural immigrants to a Brazilian city).

Although looseknit networks are difficult to handle at the operational level, at the level of theory they are likely to be important. On the basis of evidence from a number of studies of small-scale societies, Mewett (1982) has suggested that class differences begin to emerge as the proportion of multiplex relationships declines, multiplexity being an important characteristic of a closeknit type of network structure. This observation suggests a framework for linking network studies with larger-scale class-based studies in formulating a more coherent multi-level sociolinguistic theory than we have at present. Furthermore, Granovetter (1973) has argued that 'weak' and uniplex interpersonal ties are important channels through which innovation and influence flow from one closeknit group to another. This rather larger-scale aspect of the social function of different types of network tie has important implications for a socially accountable theory of linguistic change and diffusion (Milroy and Milroy 1985b).

5.7.4 Applications of the network concept: a brief review

So far we have been concerned chiefly with the *limitations* of the network concept in sociolinguistic research; its *advantages* can be stated quite briefly. First, it forms the basis of a useful tool for studying relatively small, self-contained groups in more detail than is possible within a large-scale survey framework. Second, it provides a means of approaching an analysis where the concept of social class is difficult to apply; this is a problem commonly encountered by researchers studying minority ethnic groups, migrants, rural populations or populations in non-industrialized societies. Finally, network analysis offers a procedure for dealing with variation between speakers at the level of the individual rather than the group (see further 6.8.3). In the remainder of this section we shall compare the use made of the network variable in three very different studies. These are V. Edwards' (1986) account of the language of British black adolescents; Bortoni-Ricardo's (1985) account of changes in the language of rural migrants to a Brazilian city, and Schmidt's (1985) study of the language of bilingual Australian Aboriginal adolescent groups.

Since there is no enumerated list of British black persons (even assuming that this is a well-defined category), speakers from the British black community cannot be systematically sampled from a range of social classes (see 2.2.4). Even if the use of social class as a speaker variable *were* feasible in this rather fundamental practical sense, it would be unlikely to yield much insight into the interplay between social and linguistic differentiation (for the rather obvious reason that a social class index cannot distinguish in an illuminating way between members of a group who are mostly unemployed or concentrated in low-status occupations). But since it seems to be possible to analyse the black community as a whole as consisting of overlapping sets of relatively closeknit groups, the network variable is rather more helpful in describing the relationship between linguistic variability and non-linguistic differences between speakers.

It was suggested in 5.7.2 that the crucial variable (from a sociolinguist's point of view) underlying any measure of personal network structure is *degree of integration* into a closeknit group. It was also noted that the same indicators were not necessarily relevant to different groups; for example, membership of groups associated with religious institutions might well be irrelevant in a contemporary northern English coal-mining community, but highly relevant in a Midlands black community. In fact the indicators used by Edwards were chosen for their capacity to distinguish between individuals who associated themselves to varying degrees with the norms and values of the black community; of particular importance is the distinction between black and non-black ethnicity. For this reason, Edwards' indicators were designed to measure in various ways the extent to which speakers have contact with black friends and neighbours and participate in black social activities. Whether or not the speakers were employed at all was also taken into account, since employment will almost always involve fairly extended interaction with non-black individuals. In fact, the index of integration into the black community which was constructed using these indicators correlated well with the extent to which the individual speakers used the *patois* characteristic of that community.

Bortoni-Ricardo's account of the sociolinguistic adjustment of rural migrants to Brazlandia, a satellite city of Brasilia, is a particularly interesting and innovative application of the network concept. A survey based on a stratificational analysis is not appropriate or feasible for a sociolinguistic study carried out in Brazil; the chief objections are that the notion of a continuum is neither congruent with the sharp distinction between rich and poor, nor does it adequately discriminate between the individuals studied, all of whom were relatively poor. Bortoni-Ricardo did not posit a linguistic movement by the migrants in the direction of an urban standardized norm of the kind familiar in studies using the social class variable (see further 6.3.1); taking the group's own linguistic norms as a starting point, she examined the extent to which speakers had moved away from their stigmatized Caipira dialect.

Bortoni-Ricardo's main hypothesis about change in *social structure* associated with the change from rural to urban life is that it involves a move from an *insulated* network consisting largely of kinsfolk and neighbours to an *integrated* urban network where the links will be less multiplex and associated with a wider range of social contexts. The linguistic counterpart of this process is analysed as one of *dialect diffuseness* – a movement away from the norms of the Caipira dialect. Two separate network indices are used to measure the changing patterns of the migrants' social relationships; the first is the *integration index* and the second the *urbanization index*. The integration index expresses numerically certain relevant characteristics of the three persons with whom each migrant most frequently interacts – for example whether or not they are kinsfolk, or whether the ties have been contracted in the premigration period. The score assigned to each migrant is intended to characterize progress in the transition from an insulated to an integrated type of network, and as such is a tool capable of investigating *looseknit* types of personal network structure (see 5.7.3). As Bortoni-Ricardo shows, integration scores are correlated with a *linguistic* movement away from the norms of the Caipira dialect.

The *urbanization index* is designed to supplement this structural measure, representing the extent to which the members of each migrant's personal network are integrated into urban life. A number of indicators are used to compute this index, two of which are educational level and occupational mobility; the indicators are selected for their capacity to measure the extent to which the persons with whom a migrant customarily interacts is integrated into (i.e. participates in) urban life. From a methodological point of view, Bortoni-Ricardo's work is particularly interesting, because in developing these two types of index it extends the application of the network variable beyond an analysis of small closeknit groups to an analysis of the extent to which individuals have detached themselves from such groups.

Schmidt's study differs from those discussed so far in that it does not quantify network structure at all, but uses the concept to account for differences between speakers which emerge from a quantitative analysis of *linguistic* data. The language of two small, closeknit groups of young Aboriginal women from a Queensland community (the Rock n' Rollers and the Buckeroos) is studied against a background of societal bilingualism (Dyirbal and English) where Dyirbal is giving way, apparently fairly rapidly, to English. The young speakers mix the two languages in different ways and proportions and a number of creole-like charactristics are recorded, such as the Buckeroos' frequent use of *bin* as a past tense marker.

Schmidt's main interest is in a highly focused *peer group norm,* which is apparently a linguistically mixed code possessing characteristics both of Dyirbal and of English. This norm contrasts with that of the groups' careful speech which is very much closer to traditional Dyirbal (see Dixon 1971 for a description). There is for example more evidence of intrusion from English in peer-group speech, and relatively low frequency of traditional Dyirbal morphological features, such as ergative inflexions. Thus, speakers who have productive control of Dyirbal morphology tend not to use it in peer-group situations. Schmidt reports two particularly interesting findings which emerge from a quantitative analysis of this mixed-code peer-group norm. First, although there is considerable between-group variation, there is very little variation between the language of speakers *within* each group. Second, although the peer-group norm is characterized by speakers as Dyirbal rather than English, the extent of its Dyirbal admixture (sometimes only around 50 per cent) corresponds to the extent to which traditional Dyirbal features are controlled by the least fluent Dyirbal speaker in the group. Schmidt explains the group's ability to maintain this very homogeneous mixed code, the norms of which are apparently pragmatically determined, in terms of the capacity of closeknit networks to exert normative pressures upon individuals.

5.8 Concluding Remarks

This chapter has concentrated on exploring some problems of *definition* and *interpretation* which make speaker variables so difficult to handle, with particular reference to the variables of social class, sex, ethnicity and social network. The role of speaker variables in sociolinguistic theory was assessed, and the practical difficulties of putting into operation the social class and network variables in different types of community was explored.

Since Labov first developed his quantitative methods, a very wide range of different speaker variables has been examined in relation to patterns of variation, and indeed these methods can be used wherever a speaker characteristic is capable of being expressed numerically. But there is little point in relating speaker variables to patterns of language variation without also attempting to place the analysis within a coherent theoretical framework. As Labov and Sankoff point out (1980: xi), the emphasis in recent years arising naturally from the maturing of sociolinguistics as a research area has been less on purely methodological concerns such as measurement techniques and the presentation of correlational relationships between linguistic and social structure. Increasingly, researchers have attempted to conceptualize speaker variables in such a way as to solve a widening range of substantive problems. Assuming that this (rather than a purely descriptive correlational approach) characterizes our general orientation, we turn in chapters 6 and 7 to look at principles of handling *linguistic* variables.

6

Analysing Phonological Variation

6.1 Introductory

Labov's concept of the *linguistic variable* (see 5.1), was developed
originally to handle phonology rather than syntax. Of great methodological
importance is the *principle of accountability,* which in essence states that
analysts should not selectively pick out from a text those variants of a
variable which tend to confirm their argument, while ignoring others which
do not. It is the recognition of this principle and its implications which is
particularly characteristic of Labov's approach to data (cf. 1.2.1): 'for the
section of speech being examined all occurrences of a given variant are
noted, and where it has been possible to define the variables as a closed set
of variants, all non-occurrences in the relevant environments' (Labov
1982a: 30). There are, however, a number of problems underlying this
concise and apparently simple statement. As we shall see, it is often
difficult to specify 'relevant environments' and, even more fundamentally,
to define the input to a given variable; Labov's suggestion that it might
sometimes *not* be possible to define variables as a closed set of variants is
particularly relevant to *syntactic* variation (see chapter 7).

Tables 5.1 and 5.2 illustrate two different ways of *quantifying* variables,
once an accountable analysis has been completed. Both are modelled on
Labov's work in New York City. In table 5.1, (h) is treated as *binary,* that
is as having two variants, [h] and [ø]. Variants of binary variables (which
are implicitly assumed to be *discrete*) are most easily handled as *percentages;* table 5.1 for example lists zero realizations of (h) as a percentage
of the total number of occurrences of both variants.

As *vowel* realizations vary along relatively easily specifiable continuous
dimensions such as *height* or *backness,* and more than two variants can
often be identified, vowel variable scores are often (but not always – see
6.3.2) calculated in a rather different way, using a *vowel index* score. This
involves arranging variants (as many as the analyst is able and wishes to
distinguish) along a single phonetic dimension such as vowel height. It is
assumed that social values, which are also placed on a single linear

dimension, might be assigned to each variant. The index scores in table 5.2 show the amount of fronting and raising to [ɛɪ] on a three-point scale of the vowel in words such as *pipe* and *line*. The least non-standard variant is scored zero, an intermediate variant as 100 and the most non-standard as 200. Scores approaching 200 therefore represent a high proportion of very non-standard realizations.

Since very full accounts are available both in Labov's reports of his early work (Labov 1972b) and in many more recent sociolinguistics text books (see particularly Hudson 1980; Wardhaugh 1986), the original notion of the linguistic variable has been outlined only sketchily here. Assuming some acquaintance with the concept, this chapter focuses more specifically on a range of practical and theoretical issues associated with the use of the linguistic variable as an analytic tool. It is organized as follows: first the initial *identification* of variables is discussed, with attention to their embedding in linguistic structure (6.2); second, some problems (and proposed solutions) are explored, which arise from attempts to *analyse* data using the concept of the variable as it was originally developed (6.3–6.6); third, some difficulties in establishing *lexical input* to phonological variables (6.7) are described. The final section examines some issues associated with *quantification* of data.

6.2 Identifying Linguistic Variables

6.2.1 The problem

Initial identification of variables has not generally been discussed as a problem, presumably because linguistic elements of English which vary in a socially patterned manner are often very salient and sometimes rather general throughout the English-speaking world. Such an example is the alternation between [in] and [iŋ] on the *ing* form of verbs, which has been studied in a number of places. But more commonly variables are highly localized. For example although (h) is socially salient variable in Britain south of the River Tees (cf. table 5.1), it is not a variable north of this point, nor in Ireland or Australia or the United States. Since speakers do not alternate in a patterned way betwen [h] and [ø] in stressed syllables, the phonological unit /h/ is simply irrelevant to any account of variation in these areas.

In the case of another much-studied variable, (r), we find in England (but not in many parts of the United States) that absence of post-vocalic [r] is characteristic of high-status speech and is moreover categorical except in some (mainly) western areas. In Ireland and Scotland on the other hand most speakers categorically pronounce post-vocalic [r]. One particular change in this pattern which has been detected in Scotland is structurally quite different from the New York City change:

> Both males and females seem to be innovating in this Scottish instance and the females are quite clearly the innovators in a prestige [i.e. r-pronouncing] form. The males . . . are innovating in a direction away from the local Scottish prestige norm, but in accepting r-lessness their usage happens to coincide with a much larger national norm. This pattern of differentiation in fact suggests that r-lessness is a separate competing development in Scots and is *not* being adopted in imitation of a Southern English prestige model such as RP. (Romaine 1978a: 156)

It seems then that (r) is not the 'same' variable in Scotland as it is in England or the United States. Since variables pattern differently in different places, their initial identification is by no means automatic and might not even be particularly easy. Sometimes if the investigator is a native of the area s/he is studying and is also trained in techniques of phonetic and phonological analysis, s/he is likely to be able to articulate and use intuitions about relevant variables. But no general account of methodology can reasonably assume that the investigator is a native speaker or has native speaker-like intuitions, and for an outsider at least identification involves finding evidence that a linguistic unit varies in a systematic way between speakers, or between different speech styles of a single speaker. It also involves *identifying linguistic constraints* on variation; that is, specifying the manner in which variable elements are embedded in linguistic structure. The procedure for identifying variables initially adopted in Belfast illustrates some problems which are quite commonly encountered, and some solutions.

6.2.2 Pilot studies: an example

Although they need not be ambitious in scope or very systematically organized, pilot studies are in general a useful preliminary to large research projects as they help to identify unexpected difficulties of many kinds and offer guidelines to overall design. In Belfast, a small pilot study proved to be helpful in identifying relevant linguistic and speaker variables (see 5.5 for a discussion of *ethnicity* in Belfast). Interviews, word-lists and reading passages were recorded with twenty speakers of both sexes and various ages from communities associated with both major ethnic groups in the city. The investigators had already developed some quite strong linguistic hunches, and while these often turned out to be fairly accurate, pilot work sometimes revealed that they were a little wide of the mark. It also helped in identifying important variables which had not previously been thought to be particularly interesting. A number of hazards were revealed which had not been specifically predicted but which needed to be taken into account in designing the main research project. For example there were evident differences in lexical incidence between items which had been thought to belong to the same phonological set; *get* and *never* in contemporary Belfast vernacular did not pattern in the same way as items such as *wet* and *wedding*, and so could not be considered as tokens of the variable (ɛ) (see further 6.7).

The general value of a pilot study for helping to assess the importance of information gathered by relatively unsystematic observation and analysis may be demonstrated with reference to the variable (a) in Belfast. It had already been noted informally that vernacular speakers realized certain items of the /a/ class with a front-raised, lengthened, slightly diphthongized variant; [bɛˡg] is a stereotypical Belfast pronunciation of the item 'bag'. However, the initial hunch that Belfast, like New York City, might show innovatory patterns of *front* raising of this vowel turned out to be wrong. It became quite clear that the less immediately obvious tendency to *back* /a/, which had also been observed, was a much more regular process and was associated with young (chiefly male) speakers. On the other hand, the more immediately obvious stereotypical raising of /a/ to [ɛ] emerged as a *recessive* feature, confined in contemporary Belfast vernacular to syllables closed by a *velar* consonant. *Real time* evidence from more than a century back (Patterson 1860) confirmed that the pattern had once affected the /a/ system in many more linguistic environments, and *apparent time* evidence obtained during the pilot study reflected this change; for example one eighteen-year-old man normally produced the form [käp] 'cap', in contrast with his mother's habitual pronunciation [kɛp]. Backing was apparently spreading to items that had once been fronted, but had not yet affected syllables closed by a velar consonant, like *bag, back* and *bang*.

The methodological implications of this combination of historical and contemporary evidence were quite direct; syllables closed by a velar consonant, which were categorically non-back, could not be counted as tokens of a variable which varied on the dimension of backness. In fact, it turned out that adequate analysis of (a) in the main research projects required some adaptation of Labov's quantitative methods as they were originally formulated (see further 6.4).

There is one particular reason to be cautious of unsystematic observations (even by native speakers) as a basis for adequate identification of variables. Because most people's range of social experience has become quite limited by the time they have attained adulthood, such observations are nearly always selective and may be hard to interpret or simply misleading. For example, one local post graduate student involved in the Belfast research was firmly convinced that front-raised pronunciations by working-class speakers of items like *cap* and *rat* reflected attempts at correction in the direction of Received Pronunciation; but the more systematically collected pilot-study data confirmed that this variant was in fact a low-status and recessive feature.

One methodological point of considerable importance in pilot work concerns *transcription*. Transcription of any kind is invariably a selective process, reflecting underlying theoretical goals and assumptions (Ochs 1979: 44). It is therefore unwise at the pilot stage, when these goals and assumptions are still being formulated, to idealize away too much from the data. Moreover, an over-abstract representation can conceal important information. When the objectives of the analysis are clearer, a selective transcription will be more useful than a detailed one, which is at that later stage of the research likely to contain much unwanted information.

This principle is valid at all levels of analysis; but the implication for phonological work is that *phonemic* transcriptions are often unsuitable for pilot studies. The experience of the Belfast researchers was that a narrow transcription was needed to identify in the first place the range of vowel variation associated with different phonetic environments. The variable (a) (see above) illustrates this point; the speech of a number of persons was transcribed in some phonetic detail before it became clear that tokens of the vowel in a certain range of environments were *never* front-raised, and seemed moreover to be implicationally ordered with respect to their tolerance of *back-raising* (see J. Milroy 1981a for details). This information was used to construct highly selective word-lists, capable of yielding a great deal of specific information about phonological structure (see for example table 6.2); it was also helpful in determining the lexical input to variables (see 6.7).

As the discussion in this section has implied, a general *analysis of the phonological system* is a prerequisite to quantitative analysis. While pilot work is an important means of obtaining the information required for such an analysis, traditional 'guess and check' methods (see 1.2.1) which draw on the skill and intuition of the analyst are also important. James Milroy's (1976) phonological analysis, which provided an essential basis for subsequent quantitative phonological work, drew both on the analyst's intuition and on the pilot-study data.

6.3 The Measurement and Quantification of Variables

6.3.1 Criticisms of the standard method

Much of the value of the method outlined in 6.1 for converting into numbers the phonetic values associated with a variable lies in its simplicity and replicability in a wide range of cases. But behind the apparently straightforward process of assigning numbers to variants of a variable in such a way as to reflect, reasonably faithfully, their phonetic and social relationships with each other lies a great deal of linguistic, sociological and mathematical abstraction. Labov has commented that 'even the simplest type of counting raises a number of subtle and difficult problems. The final decision as to what to count is actually the solution to the problem in hand; this decision is taken only through a long series of complicated exploratory maneuvers' (Labov 1972a: 82). The form taken by some of these 'exploratory maneuvers' was outlined in section 6.2.1, and some of 'the subtle and difficult problems' associated with the quantification process have been discussed in various places, most thoroughly by Hudson (1980: 157–67). In the remainder of this chapter, I shall focus rather selectively on some major difficulties which have emerged and some (partial) solutions. A wider range of issues associated with quantitative analysis (not necessarily specific to sociolinguistic research) is explored in 6.8.

The notion of the sociolinguistic variable whose variants are assumed to lie on single co-extensive phonetic and social dimensions has been criticized by (amongst others) Hudson and Holloway (1977); Romaine (1978a) and Knowles (1978). One objection is the loss of potentially important phonological information when phonological elements which vary on more than one dimension (such as vowel height, in addition to presence or absence of diphthongization) are analysed as varying only on a single dimension. The implications of this problem are explored in detail in 6.5 with reference to the variables (ε) and (o) in Belfast. Phonological information of a slightly different kind might also be lost in the sense that the average score assigned to a speaker may reflect either consistent use of a median value or more variable use of extreme values; the phonetic locus of variation may actually be *concealed* by a single score on a linear scale.

A second, related objection has been advanced of the assumption that variants of a variable lie along a single *sociolinguistic* dimension of non-standard to standard, which in turn co-varies with a single phonetic dimension. Rather acute difficulties have arisen in cities like Liverpool, Glasgow, Edinburgh and Belfast (described by Johnston (1983) as 'divergent dialect' areas) where there is a sharp discontinuity between the local vernacular and any recognizable supra-local spoken norm. One consequence of this discontinuity is a difficulty in identifying the prestige forms which are to be placed at the 'standard' end of the continuum. While in Norwich (for example) the influence of Received Pronunciation is consistent and considerable, researchers in Scotland such as Romaine (1978a; see also 6.2 above) and Macaulay (1977) have encountered difficulties in applying the concept of a *single* prestige norm. Romaine (1978b) has cited the case in Edinburgh of two locally born upper-middle-class speakers who had attended the same private school but spoke with quite different accents. One used RP, and the other the local (rhotic) high-prestige accent known as 'Morningside'. The situation is similar in Belfast where a range of educated accents can be heard; some of these sound Scottish and some

Irish, while others are apparently modelled on RP. Educated speakers appear to have available a range of linguistic choices quite different from the range available, for example, to educated Londoners.

A further complication, sometimes leading to rather severe methodological problems, is introduced in some divergent dialect communities by radical differences in *phonological structure* between the supra-local and the local prestige norm(s). For example, the assumption of a single non-standard to standard continuum with RP located at the standard extremity led Macaulay in Glasgow to exclude from his analysis of the (a) variable items which belonged to the /ɑ/ class of RP. Thus *psalm* and *halve* would be excluded, but *Sam* and *have* counted as tokens of (a). This seems a rather arbitrary procedure since most Scottish speakers – including educated speakers – do not have in their phonological systems a contrast between front and back low vowels and so would not differentiate these pairs. In fact, only three speakers in Macaulay's sample differentiated *Sam* and *psalm* when reading a minimal pair list (Macaulay 1977: 29).

Researchers have responded to these complexities in different ways. Knowles (1978), who is particularly critical of Labov, argues that while the assumption that variants of a variable may be placed on a single social and phonetic continuum makes quantification relatively easy, it also oversimplifies the real range of choices open to speakers. The limitations of a single linear scale are demonstrated in relation to realizations of five phonological variables in the city of Liverpool, of which one is an optionally merged variable (uə) and (oə) as in *sure* and *shore*. Some speakers keep /uə/ and /oə/ classes distinct, while others merge both classes with the /o/ class (words such as *Shaw*). Knowles suggests that a Liverpool speaker first has to choose whether to merge these classes or not, before further deciding whether to apply a number of lower-level optional rules. He characterizes this range of choices in the following way, pointing out that the second, third and fourth rules operate mainly in working-class speech.

Table 6.1

		uə		oə
1	lax [u.o] before an unstressed vowel	ʊə		ɔə
	or			
2	(a) diphthongize [u.o.]	ɪuə	ɰɐə	ɔuə
	or			
	(b) front [u]		ɰə	
3	modify VVV to V + glide + V		ɪwə	ɔwə
4	front final [ə]	uɛ	?uɛ	oɛ
		ɪuɛ	ɪuɛ	uɛ
		ɰɐɛ	ɪwɛ	ɔwɛ

Source: adapted from Knowles (1978: 85)

It is evident that Labov's methods of characterizing social and linguistic variation on a single continuum are indeed quite inappropriate for someone who wants to describe the phonology of an urban dialect in this kind of detail. Further, some very salient Liverpool dialect phenomena such as syllable-final aspirated fricatives (e.g.[buʃh] 'bush') are probably best described not quantitatively, but qualitatively in terms of the *articulatory setting* peculiar to the dialect, which can account for a number of superficially quite diverse phonetic characteristics. But Knowles's criticisms of Labov's methods lose much of their cogency if we remember that Labov was not attempting to provide an accurate, detailed and variation-sensitive description of an urban dialect. Although advances in urban dialectology are certainly a by-product of his methods, his principal objectives were to use variable data as a means of elucidating processes of linguistic change and more generally to contribute to core linguistic theory (cf. 5.2.1). To criticize his methods for failing to characterize the dialect accurately is therefore to miss their point.

6.3.2 An adaptation to the standard method: (r) in Edinburgh

Although both Romaine and Knowles are critical of some aspects of Labov's method, there is an important difference in their underlying goals and assumptions. While Knowles is concerned mainly with accurate description, it is clear from Romaine's (1978a) acount of the variable (r) in the language of Edinburgh schoolchildren that she shares Labov's general theoretical objectives of elucidating processes of linguistic change (cf. 6.1). Rather than simply criticizing quantitative analysis as a whole, she adapts slightly the standard method of measuring linguistic variables, pointing out that the three variants of (r) which can be distinguished ([ɹ], [ɾ] and [ø] are difficult to place on any rationally motivated *social* continuum. The solution is to avoid any implication of a continuum by calculating a percentage score for each of the three variants separately (cf. Hudson and Holloway 1977). A further advantage of this method is that it allows the phonetic location of an incipient change to be identified rather precisely, and particular variants to be associated with particular groups of speakers: 'The main difference between the boys and the girls in the use of (r) is that the girls are almost always rhotic and most frequently use [ɹ], while the boys are less frequently rhotic and tend to use [ɾ] more frequently than the girls' (Romaine 1978a: 150).

Like Romaine's Edinburgh research, the Belfast projects worked within Labov's general theoretical paradigm, attempting to tackle difficulties as they emerged. Generally, these difficulties were associated with the related assumptions of a single non-standard to standard sociolinguistic continuum and a corresponding unidimensional phonetic continuum (see 6.3.1).

Adaptations to the basic method designed to deal with the Belfast data are illustrated in 6.4 and 6.5 by three examples: the variable (a) as analysed in the household survey, and the variables (ε) and (o) as analysed in the Braniel and Andersonstown community studies.

6.4 Problems in Quantifying Variables: (a) in Belfast

James Milroy (1982) shows that in Belfast the patterns of middle-class speech cannot satisfactorily be characterized in relation to vernacular speech in terms of phonetic distance on a unilinear continuum; rather, there is a tendency in middle-class speech to avoid the extreme phonetic values at *both* ends of that continuum. This pattern is demonstrated in tables 6.2 and 6.3, which compare tokens of the variable (a) on word-lists read by a working-class and a middle-class speaker respectively. The middle-class speaker converges on the low front area of vowel space in all phonetic environments, while the working-class speaker displays a far greater range of phonetically conditioned allophonic variation, realizing the vowel with back-raised, front-raised and diphthongized variants. The phonetic details have in fact been simplified in table 6.2; for example, since diphthongized tokens have not been shown separately, realizations such as [mɔən] 'man' appear in the [ɔ] column (see further 6.5). Nevertheless, the patterns characteristic of the speakers' respective social groups emerge quite clearly.

Table 6.2   (a) range for a working-class Belfast speaker: word-list style (from random sample survey)

	ε	æ	a	ä	ɑ	ɔ
bag	+					
back		+				
cap			+			
map				+		
passage				+		
cab					+	
grass					+	
bad					+	
man					+	
castle			+			
dabble			+			
passing					+	

Table 6.3 (a) range for a middle-class Belfast speaker: word-list style (random sample survey)

	ε	æ	a	ä	ɑ	ɔ
bag		+				
back		+				
cap		+				
map		+				
passage		+				
cab		+				
grass		+				
bad		+				
man		+				
castle		+				
dabble		+				
passing		+				

J. Milroy developed techniques for handling quantitatively data of this kind by assigning to each speaker a *range* score calculated simply by counting from left to right the number of columns through which the variants ranged, and subtracting 1. Thus, the speakers represented by tables 6.2 and 6.3 were assigned range scores of 5 and 0 respectively. This statistic was used in conjunction with a *bidimensional* weighted index where [a] was taken as the point most distant from the vernacular, and scores assigned for variants on the dimensions both of height and backness. Quantitative analysis revealed statistically significant differences between working-class and middle-class speakers with respect to both range and index scores; as we shall see, the general sociolinguistic pattern reflected in tables 6.2 and 6.3 is repeated in other vowel variables.

6.5 Problems in Quantifying Variables: (ε) and (o) in Belfast

6.5.1 Phonetically complex variation

The particular difficulty illustrated by (ε) and (o) in Braniel and Andersonstown is different from the one discussed in 6.4. It is not concerned with relationships between *vernacular* and *non-vernacular* phonological patterns, but with characterizing vowels as varying on a single *phonetic* dimension. In fact, both *length* and *quality* appear in these (and other) examples to operate as independent but intersecting phonological processes, and both dimensions are apparently of considerable sociolinguistic significance.

Tokens of (ε) show a spectacular realizational difference between high-mid variants and low, somewhat centralized variants. It had been assumed in the first phase of the research (in the inner-city areas) that considerable variation in *length* could be accommodated within the standard paradigm by assuming that the feature [+low] implied [-long] and vice versa. But since *short* high realizations turned up quite frequently, it became apparent that a more complex schema was required. Interestingly, the assumption of a correspondence between length and quality presented more of a problem in the outer-city areas than in the more strongly vernacular inner-city areas (see further 6.5.3). Parallel to (ε) in these respects is the variable (o). Tokens of this vowel varied on dimensions of *height, backness, rounding* and *length*. Again, the correspondence between the dimensions of quality and length was closer in the inner-city areas.

In response to these complexities, the original notion of the sociolinguistic variable with variants which were assigned values along a single phonetic dimension was considerably modified. The range of variation and the procedure adopted for handling it is illustrated by tables 6.4 and 6.5, where tokens of (o) and (ε) are shown, taken from recordings of two Andersonstown speakers. Tokens are listed under the phonetic variant which they realize, and additionally are assigned a label which describes the following environment; these labels are explained as follows:

Environments

T   = voiceless stop or affricate, or sonorant + voiceless obstruent.
TS = environment described in T + following syllable in same morpheme.
D   = voiceless fricative or any voiced consonant not immediately followed by a voiceless segment.
DS = environment described in D plus following syllable in the same morpheme.

The theoretical and practical issues associated with this kind of analysis of vowel variation is discussed by J. Milroy (1981a) and J. Harris (1985).

Even the small amount of data on tables 6.4 and 6.5 suggests that variants are partly, but not wholly, *phonetically conditioned;* in fact the method described here is designed to accommodate this aspect of variation also. A further point to note is that the extreme left-hand columns in both table 6.4 and table 6.5 are empty and additionally the extreme right-hand column in table 6.5 is empty; this is because these 'extreme' realizations occur only in the inner-city areas. In light of the discussion in 6.2.3, it seems likely that the tendency of higher-status speakers to converge on a narrower range is rather general. Speakers in the more prestigious outer-city areas show in their realizations of (ε) and (o) a distibutional pattern relative to lower-status speakers similar to that shown for (a) in table 6.3.

Table 6.4   (o) in Andersonstown

ä	ɑ	ɑ	ɑː	ɔ	ɔː
T got (2) DS Polytech T shop T pot		T shop			
	DS concentrated DS vodka			DS probably	D job (3) D of D God
				TS bottom	

Table 6.5   (ε) in Andersonstown

ä	ε	εː	ε̣	ε̣ː	eː
T set-up (2) T lent T went (2) DS specials (3) DS remember TS twenty		DS specials T went	D red D tell D ten		

    This analytic procedure embodies assumptions rather different from those underlying Labov's original method. Variants of (ε) and (o) do not form a continuum along a single linear scale, but each of them may be said to be part of one or more *subscales* which can be constructed on, for example, the continua of roundness, or backness or length. *Phonological features* were eventually assigned to variants in order to construct these subscales, but the first step was to quantify the data in order to compare the patterns which emerged in different data batches. Table 6.6 shows group scores for (o) in Braniel and Andersonstown, calculated for each variant according to following environment, using as input data of the kind shown in table 6.4. Insights into variation arising from methodological changes of this kind can be quite different from (but not necessarily contradictory to) those yielded by the standard method (see 6.5.3).

6.5.2 Phonetic constraints on variation

Since the variation in 6.4 and 6.5 is partly at least *phonetically* constrained, it is helpful at this stage to try and summarize these constraints:

Rule 1   (o) in Belfast

$$
\begin{bmatrix} - \text{ cons} \\ + \text{ voc} \\ + \text{ back} \\ + \text{ low} \\ - \text{ mid} \\ - \text{ long} \end{bmatrix} \rightarrow \begin{bmatrix} + \text{ mid} \\ + \text{ long} \end{bmatrix} \Big/ \left. \begin{array}{l} \begin{bmatrix} + \text{ cont} \\ - \text{ voice} \end{bmatrix} \text{(c)} \\ \\ ([+ \text{ voice}]) \, [+ \text{ voice}] \end{array} \right\} \begin{array}{l} \mathbf{a} \\ \# \\ \mathbf{b} \end{array}
$$

Rule 1 describes the constraints on variation in tokens of (o), using a conventional generative format. Subrules 1a and 1b specify that in monomorphemic monosyllables (o) will be realized as a raised and lengthened variant before a voiceless fricative occurring either alone or in a cluster; alternatively, it will be raised and lengthened before any voiced consonant either alone or in a cluster. In other environments the raising and lengthening rule does not apply. In fact the rule fails to show the full complexity of the morpheme boundary constraint; what appears to happen is that if another syllable intervenes raising and lengthening fails, unless that syllable is an *inflectional* morpheme. Thus, the rule predicts raising and lengthening in the following items: *John, moss, pod, frost, robbing;* it will however fail in items such as *mossy, pot, vodka, comic, Robby.*

Not surprisingly, realization of (o) is much more variable than this very idealized representation implies, although (as even the small amount of data in table 6.4 suggests) it is certainly constrained by the factors specified. But lengthened realizations often turn up in 'short' environments, and both long and short realizations often vary qualitatively, as is clear from the figures in table 6.6. However, these figures provide the basis for constructing a large number of variation-sensitive rules both in terms of segments and in terms of features. The rules should be interpreted as purely descriptive devices capable of revealing various kinds of pattern in the data, some of which are ilustrated by tables 6.7 and 6.8 a, b and c. Cumbersome as the formulation in table 6.7 may be, it provides useful information.

First, the predictions of rule 1 are to a certain extent confirmed; for example, environment D overwhelmingly favours lengthened variants in

Table 6.6   (o) in (I) Andersonstown and (II) Braniel: variant percentages shown by phonetic environment (see p. 123)

Environment	ɑ	ɒ	ɒ:	ɔ	ɔ:	Rowtot.
I						
T	35	45	2	16	2	100
TS	24	50	0	25	1	100
D	0	0	13	1	86	100
DS	24	53	3	12	8	100
II						
T	24	41	0	27	8	100
TS	14	53	7	26	0	100
D	0	2	5	3	90	100
DS	14	36	2	28	20	100

Table 6.7   Realization of (o) by phonetic environment in Andersonstown and Braniel

		(a) Andersonstown		(b) Braniel	
/ɔ/ →	⟨[ɑ]⟩	T	62	T	64
		/– DS	26	DS	29
		TS	11	TS	7
		D	1		
	⟨[ɒ]⟩	T	50	T	51
		/– DS	36	DS	34
		TS	14	TS	13
				D	2
	⟨[ɒ:]⟩	D	78	D	68
		/– DS	12	TS ⎫	32
		T	10	DS ⎭	
	⟨[ɔ]⟩	T	52	T	47
		/– DS	24	DS	38
		TS	22	TS	9
		D	2	D	6
	⟨[ɔ:]⟩	D	93	D	80
		/– DS	5	DS	13
		T	2	T	7

both communities, although the proportions differ a little. A long, low, back variant appears 78 per cent of the time in Andersonstown as opposed to 68 per cent of the time in Braniel. But it is also clear that contrary to the pattern implied by rule 1, lengthening and raising operate to some extent independently of each other. Note also that the *ordering* of constraints on the application of the rule is the same in both communities (cf. the predictions of Guy 1980).

Table 6.8   Realization of (o) by phonetic environment in Andersonstown, Braniel and Clonard

(a) Andersonstown	(b) Braniel	(c) Clonard
$\langle+ \text{low}\rangle$ 81 $\langle- \text{low}\rangle$ 19 $/-T$	$\langle+ \text{low}\rangle$ 64 $\langle- \text{low}\rangle$ 36 $/-T$	$[+ \text{low}]$ $\begin{array}{l}/-T\\-TS\end{array}$
$\langle+ \text{low}\rangle$ 74 $\langle- \text{low}\rangle$ 26 $/-TS$	$\langle+ \text{low}\rangle$ 74 $\langle- \text{low}\rangle$ 26 $/-TS$	$\langle+ \text{low}\rangle$ 87 $\langle- \text{low}\rangle$ 13 $/-D$
$\langle+ \text{low}\rangle$ 86 $\langle- \text{low}\rangle$ 14 $/-D$	$\langle+ \text{low}\rangle$ 93 $\langle- \text{low}\rangle$ 7 $/-D$	$\langle+ \text{low}\rangle$ 91 $\langle- \text{low}\rangle$ 9 $/-DS$
$\langle+ \text{low}\rangle$ 80 $\langle- \text{low}\rangle$ 20 $/-DS$	$\langle+ \text{low}\rangle$ 51 $\langle- \text{low}\rangle$ 49 $/-DS$	

$/ɔ/ \rightarrow$ (Andersonstown), $/ɔ/ \rightarrow$ (Braniel), $/ɔ/ \rightarrow$ (Clonard)

Further interesting insights into patterns of variation emerge if the rules are formulated more abstractly, a procedure motivated by the partial conflation in the Belfast phonological system of several separate but related phonological processes (chiefly those of backing, rounding and raising). Table 6.8 is an example of the many such rules which can be constructed; variants sharing the same specification with respect to the feature [low] are conflated, so that patterns of variation on this dimension may be examined in each community in a range of phonetic environments. Similar rules may be constructed to examine the operation of processes of lengthening and rounding so that it is possible (for example) to compare in the two communities the distribution of vowel length in four phonetic environments (see J. Milroy et al. 1983, and J. Harris 1985 for details).

6.5.3 Interpreting patterns of variation

An advantage of an analysis which accommodates phonetically detailed information is that it allows phonetically detailed *generalizations,* some of which are of considerable theoretical interest. For example, table 6.6

suggests that there is a greater tendency in Braniel than in Andersonstown for speakers to adopt raised, rounded realizations. This is probably best explained in terms of the different dialect backgrounds associated with the two areas (see map 4.1) and the progressive adoption in Belfast of a Scottish pattern which is apparently spreading across the city from east to west (see further Milroy and Milroy 1985b; J. Harris 1985). Representations of the type shown in table 6.8, interpreted in conjunction with evidence of change in progress, allow us to compare the embedding in linguistic structure of the change in East and West Belfast communities of roughly equal status. Specifically, it is evident that the main differences between the communities with respect to the process of *raising* may be located in the T and DS environments.

An insight of quite a different kind emerges from a comparison of table 6.8c with table 6.8a and b. It is evident that the basic rule constraining variation in realization of (o) is much closer to being categorical in the strongly vernacular, low-status Clonard area than in the outer-city areas; a static representation like rule 1 is apparently not too wide of the mark as a guide to phonological patterns in the Clonard. This supports Labov's claim that vernacular speech is more consistent and regular than corrected speech (see 3.4); but however reasonable the claim, the original methods were not designed to show up such patterns in the data (cf. 6.2.1).

The contrasting patterns shown in table 6.8 may be interpreted in conjunction with the tendency reported in 6.2.4 for phonological units in low-status speech to cover a wider phonetic *range*. It then becomes possible to formulate generalizations on what might be described as the *sociolinguistic typology* of low-status versus relatively standardized, higher-status phonological systems. While structural units such as / ɔ /, /ɛ/ and /a/ in low-status urban Belfast speech cover a wide phonetic range, variants are constrained by phonetic environment in a highly regular fashion. Conversely, they tend to converge in higher-status speech on a much narrower phonetic area, but are less responsive to environmental constraints. Since it is not at the moment clear how general this type of sociolinguistic pattern might be, any attempt at *explanation* is premature; however, it is probably possible to relate the narrow range characteristic of the higher-status speakers' pattern to parallel structural tendencies in languages which have undergone processes of *standardization* (Milroy and Milroy 1985a, chapters 1 and 2).

The more general applicability to sociolinguistic analysis of a method which is sensitive both to the phonetically complex and linguistically constrained character of variation is illustrated in tables 6.9 and 6.10. Realizations of (ɛ) by both male and female speakers are compared in the two outer-city communities and in the small country town of Lurgan, seventeen miles from Belfast (see 4.3.6). A number of inferences might be drawn from the patterns which emerge; but a particular advantage of this method of analysis is that it points up rather clearly the effect of linguistic environment on variation and allows the main phonetic locus of differences between the sexes in each of the communities to be specified. It is also evident, for example, that in all environments, variation in (ε) is controlled by sex of speaker much less in Lurgan than in the urban communities, while sex of speaker has a clearer effect in Andersonstown than in Braniel.

Table 6.9   Women's (ε) realizations by phonetic environment (%)

		Andersonstown	Braniel	Lurgan
[+ low]	T	24	35	67
	TS	25	32	71
	DS	26	26	50
	D	3	2	13

Table 6.10   Men's (ε) realizations by phonetic environment (%)

		Andersonstown	Braniel	Lurgan
[+ low]	T	89	74	78
	TS	90	77	86
	DS	64	57	61
	D	4	13	13

Interesting and illuminating as these specific sociolinguistic patterns are, the material discussed in this section illustrates a more general point of considerable importance which should not be submerged in the large amount of detailed linguistic material presented: radical adaptations to the standard method of the kind outlined here are capable of revealing different types of pattern in the data and so increasing both our understanding of change and variation and our potential for constructing accountable theories.

6.6 Types of Linguistic Variable

An adaptation to Labov's methods rather differently motivated from those discussed in the last three sections may be found in Paul Kerswill's recent work in Durham City (1984). Kerswill's interest is in distinguishing

different types of variable rather than in developing methods of quantification which give different kinds of insight into sociolinguistic patterns.
Following Dressler and Wodak (1982) he distinguishes phonological
variation resulting from *connected speech processes* from a more general
type of linguistic variation which correlates with speaker variables such as
sex or social status and which is not restricted to phonological systems.
Connected speech processes (CSP) are phenomena such as the deletions
and assimilations characteristic of allegro speech, which appear to be in
some way *phonetically motivated* rather than linguistically arbitrary variation. Examples from RP and some other varieties of English are the
alternation at syllable boundaries between alveolars and palatals
([dɪdju:]~[dɪʤu:], 'did you') and alternation in similar contexts between
alveolar and bilabial ([hɒp bi:nz]~[hɒt bi:nz], 'hot beans'). In both examples
the alveolar is assimilated to the place of articulation of the following
segment. Another example of the CSP is variable deletion of both voiced
and voiceless alveolar stops in certain contexts ([fas(t)nɪs], 'fastness';
[sen(d) mi:], 'send me').

Despite their apparent 'naturalness,' these proce̱ses are variety-specific.
For example, one common CSP in Durham English is *voicing* assimilation
at syllable boundaries ('scraped [bd] down') while the *place of articulation
assimilation* characteristic of RP is not found (Kerswill 1984: 19). Dressler
and Wodak (1982) argue from experimental evidence that the operation of
CSPs is dependent on 'attention' factors – that is, whether the speaker is
articulating slowly and carefully (see further 8.2.2). Hence, they list both
'fortition' rules and 'lenition' rules, the operation of which enhance
perceptibility and articulatory ease respectively.

As well as attempting to distinguish CSPs from a more general type of
phonological variable (such as that found in Durham in the long and short
/a/ classes), Kerswill examines a certain type of *lexical* variable,
exemplified by parts of two competing pronoun systems found in Durham
City (table 6.11).

Lexical variation of this type is widespread in Durham and is not
restricted to items belonging to any particular grammatical class; Kerswill
reports that it is particularly salient as a sociolinguistic marker sensitive
both to the *age* and *social class* of the speaker; but unlike either CSPs or
other phonological variables, it is affected very little by speech style. A
reasonable assumption is that the traditional dialect lexicon is at present in
Durham being replaced rather rapidly by standard lexical items, and the
same general pattern of variation is likely to be characteristic of regions
such as the Scottish Lowlands where the local vernacular is historically
distinct from any supra-local standard.

It is certainly possible that the distinctions between different types of
variable drawn by Dressler and Wodak and by Kerswill will turn out to be
methodologially important in as much as they yield new insights into the

Table 6.11   Lexical variables in Durham City

	Durham Standard	Durham Vernacular
me (unstressed)	miː, mɪ	ɒ s, ə s
my (unstressed)	maɪ	mɪ
you (sing.)	juː, jə	ðuː, ðə
your (sing.)	jɔː, jə	ðaɪ, ðɪ
you (pl.)	juː, jə	juːz

Source: after Kerswill (1984: 5)

principles underlying patterns of variation and processes of change. But because both CSPs and more general phonological variables are variety-specific, it is difficult to distinguish them clearly enough to apply the taxonomy more generally. Should we, for example, count the glottalization of /t/ found in many languages and dialects as a CSP? And what of the deletion of /ð/ in Belfast English, which can easily be argued to be phonetically motivated? A very large number of variables described in the literature may be presented as candidate CSPs. Drawing a line between different types of variable is extremely difficult, largely because of a more general problem of making much sense of the intuitively plausible notion of *phonological naturalness* (see Lass 1984). Even if it were possible to draw such a distinction satisfactorily, the advantages of doing so are at the moment not at all clear.

6.7 Determining the Lexical Input to Phonological Variables

There is a good deal to be added of methodological and theoretical importance to Kerswill's comments on *lexical* variation, or variation which affects specific lexical items rather than entire phonological or grammatical classes. Investigators in a number of places have reported sociolinguistically salient variation affecting word-classes which might be described as *phonolexical sets*. The composition of these sets is not phonologically predictable, but seems to reflect the existence in the past of distinct sets of items which have merged in modern speech communities (see J. Milroy, forthcoming). A very clear example is the Belfast variable (u) which alternates between [ʌ] and [ü]. In the urban dialect of Belfast, as in most varieties of English, there is a word-class of /ʌ/ consisting of items such as *cut, mud, fun.* There is also an /ü/ word-class consisting of items such as *good, food, cook, would.* There is no word-class corresponding to RP /ɒ/, so that, for example, the two lexical items in the phrase *good food* are assigned in Belfast to the same rather than to different classes as in RP /gɒd fu:d/.

There is however a small set of lexical items which alternates between the phonetically quite distinct classes /ü/ and /ʌ/. The total membership of this third class cannot be predicted on phonological grounds, nor reliably specified by appealing to the intuitions of native speakers. For example, *foot, took, shook, look* have all been attested as alternating between [ʌ] and [ü], while *soot, cook, book, hook* seem always to be pronounced with [ü]. The alternating set is sociolinguistically very salient, varying according to class, sex and speech style; all the items in it occur frequently and the [ʌ] variant is a stereotypical vernacular pronunciation carrying strong symbolic value.

Precisely because the composition of phonolexical sets cannot be specified on phonological grounds, it is difficult to find a principled way of specifying the lexical input to the variable (u); eventually eighteen words were assigned to the set simply on the basis of observation. Since speakers' intuitions cannot be easily accessed to define the membership of sets such as these (see further 8.2.1) it is difficult to see what alternative procedure might have been adopted.

The existence in Scots of many phonolexical sets of the same general type gives rise on a rather large scale to similar methodological problems in sociolinguistic work in Scotland. Macaulay outlines the difficulties encountered in analysing the variable (u) – initially assumed to have as its input the vowel in words such as *school, book, full, fool.* As his comments show, failure to specify with reasonable accuracy the input to any proposed variable is likely to obscure existing patterns of variation between speakers;

> Although Glasgow speakers, like most Scots, do not distinguish *fool* from *full,* for some speakers the word class is subdivided because some lexical items may occur with a front unrounded vowel, e.g. [skɪl] for *school,* and others a with low back unrounded vowel, e.g. [pʌl] for *pull* but *[skʌl] and *[pɪl] are not found. The situation is complicated by the fact that the variable (i) can occur with [ʌ] as a variant. The figures for (u) were calculated by treating the variation as a continuum with fronting as the sole dimension and this may have distorted the actual situation. However, a recalculation of the indices for a random sample of the speakers suggests that the same pattern of social stratification would be maintained even if the word class had been more clearly defined. (Macaulay 1978: 134)

Problems of this kind are likely to be particularly common in divergent dialect areas where two identifiable and radically different phonologies have in the past influenced each other, later to become an integrated part of the linguistic resources available to the speech community. But difficulties of the same general type which spring from the apparently idiosyncratic behaviour of lexical items are reported in the United States also. For example Neu's (1980) analysis of final stop deletion suggests that some lexical items are affected by the process more than others. Thus, for example, inclusion of the frequently occurring item *and,* which shows high frequency deletion, skews the data considerably; for this reason, Labov excluded *and* from his original study of final stop deletion (Labov 1980: xvi).

Although it is not particularly surprising that *and* patterns in an idiosyncratic fashion, Neu's comments reflect a rather general failure of items to behave reliably in a comparable way even when they appear to be tokens of the same phonological set. Also reporting on patterns of final stop deletion, Fasold (1978) has remarked on the idiosyncratic behaviour of the item *kept* where [t] is almost always deleted. Because of the frequent occurence of *kept,* this causes difficulties in quantitative analysis. The lexical norm described by Fasold is probably associated with a rather complicated situation in Scottish and Irish dialects where a set of verbs including *keep, sleep, sweep* have apparently been recategorized as irregular, without the alveolar suffix as a past tense marker. Since the normal past tense forms in, for example, Belfast vernacular are *kep, slep, swep,* deletion is categorical for many speakers. When the stop *is* realized in these items it is indistinguishable from the hypercorrect stop *insertion* attested in, for example, *gast,* 'gas'; *clift,* 'cliff'; *fold,* 'foal' (see J. Milroy 1981b: 11n).

Nor is the general difficulty confined to final stop deletion. Labov (1972b: 73) has noted that in New York City the subset of short *a* items which is liable to tensing and raising is not predictable on phonological grounds, while in Philadelphia the behaviour of the items *mad, bad, glad* is different from that of others in the *a* word-class. This fact is crucial to the thrust of Payne's analysis of dialect acquisition patterns by out-of-state children (Payne 1980: 165; see also 2.4). Trudgill (1983a: 88) reports similar cases in East Anglia.

Although difficulties in reliably specifying the appropriate lexical input to phonological variables are reasonably well documented, they may be more widespread and pose a greater methodological problem than these rather scattered observations in the literature suggest. Since by definition the composition of phonolexical subsets is not predictable by a general rule, one way of revealing their presence in a body of data is routinely to record as both a *lexical item* and a *phonetic value* each putative token of a variable (see tables 6.2, 6.3, 6.4, 6.5 for examples). The advantage of this rather simple procedure is that in a batch of (let us say) a thousand tokens the anomalous patterning of particular lexical items becomes evident. Thus, for example, the items *get, next, never* did not show the phonetic range of variation characteristic of the /ɛ/ class in Belfast and so were not counted as tokens of (ɛ); in fact, they varied between [ɛ] and [ʊ], forming a small phonolexical set of which the total membership cannot easily be specified.

In recent years sociolinguists have shown a fair amount of interest in models of variation and change which are based on the notion of *lexical diffusion* (Chen 1976; Wang 1969; Labov 1981; J. Milroy 1981b; Trudgill 1986a: 58). It is therefore likely that the issues discussed in this section are of theoretical as well as purely methodological importance.

6.8 More on Quantification

6.8.1 Some general comments

Much of this chapter has been concerned with specifically *linguistic* difficulties of quantifying variables. These 'subtle and difficult problems' (cf. 6.3.1) are all associated with deciding what should be counted. But there is a further, less specifically linguistic, type of problem which arises after these decisions have been taken and the counting process is under way. This concerns the *analysis, presentation* and *interpretation* of the resulting numbers, issues which pertain to the *descriptive* and *inferential* functions of *statistics*.

Sociolinguists who present their data using the simple graphs and frequency tables popularized by Labov in his early work have often been criticized for lack of statistical sophistication. And it is true that while it is easy to glean rapidly from a representation such as table 5.1 or 5.2 information on relationships between speaker and linguistic variables, the quantitative analysis and interpretation of such data is in fact a complicated matter. Since it is not possible to handle statistical issues in any detail in a general account of sociolinguistic methodology, I shall concentrate in this section on picking out general principles of particular relevance to sociolinguists, referring as appropriate to more specialist treatments. Of particular interest are Butler's (1985b) statistical textbook for linguists, and Erickson and Nosanchuk's (1977) presentation of John Tukey's 'exploratory' statistical methods. Before proceeding to discuss quantitative analysis at this more general level, we shall look in 6.8.2 and 6.8.3 at two specific issues which have received some attention in the sociolinguistic literature.

6.8.2 How many tokens of a variable are needed?

This question needs to be tackled if we are to be reasonably certain that

observed variation reflects a speaker's norm rather than random fluctuation in the data. By implication it is raised, but not dealt with, by Labov's
statement of the principle of accountability (6.1.1); simply to note all
occurrences of variants without further considering the size of 'the section
of speech being examined' is plainly insufficient. For example if we are
examining a rather impoverished little text containing only five tokens of
(h) of which four are realized as [h] and one as [ø], a speaker score of 20
per cent on this variable is hardly meaningful, even within a single social
context, as a characterization of normal language use. It is likely that if five
other tokens were considered from a different section of text gathered in a
comparable social context the score would turn out to be very different –
say 80 per cent. While this might seem to be stating the obvious, the fact is
that this issue has not received a great deal of systematic (as opposed to
post hoc) discussion in the literature. Exceptions to this generalization are
Guy (1980) and Romaine (1980: 190–3).

Using a detailed study of final stop deletion to exemplify a more general
principle, Guy suggests that 30 tokens per variable is a reasonable goal to
aim for. As he points out, N=30 is an important dividing line in statistics
generally between large and small samples. Different parametric tests of
significance are used for samples above and below this figure, which take
account of different relationships to the population from which they are
drawn (Butler 1985b: 79–97). In fact the data presented by Guy seem to
conform to general statistical laws; if the number of tokens is lower than
10, there is a strong likelihood of random fluctuation, while a figure higher
than 10 moves towards 90 per cent conformity with the predicted norm,
rising to 100 per cent with 35 tokens. These observations usefully demonstrate the hazards of working with fewer than 10 tokens; the ideal appears
to be around 30, but if this cannot be attained a figure as much as possible
in excess of 10 is a sensible goal. It is however assumed that the total N will
not be subdivided to examine the effect of (for example) linguistic
environment; in that case the ideal figure would be 30 tokens per
environment, bringing the total for the variable as a whole to a figure
proportionate to the number of environments examined. The same is true
of a total which is subdivided for any other purpose: for example to
examine the effects of style. In general, more tokens are needed if
relationships among several variables at once are to be examined (Erickson
and Nosanchuk 1977: 139).

Romaine (1980) has suggested that although Guy's generalizations are
very much in line with mainstream statistical theory, they might not be
entirely appropriate for sociolinguistics. Pointing out that his recommendations are based on the detailed study of a single variable, she cites the
work of Albó (1970), who concludes from his examination of several
different variables in Cochabamba Quechua that the sensitivity of variables
to sample size is not constant. Sometimes a very small N is capable of

revealing patterns quite reliably. But factors such as the frequency of a particular phonological class in the language (in English, for example, the vowel in words such as *house, out* turns up relatively rarely) have an effect on the size of the sample needed. So also does the linguistic complexity of the variable as characterized by the number of variants which can be discriminated.

6.8.3 Individual scores and group scores

Finding a sufficient number of tokens of a variable for each speaker did not apparently emerge as a problem in the early urban surveys which followed Labov's 1966 model. This is because figures were usually calculated for *groups* of speakers rather than for individuals, a practice which seemed to fit in neatly with Labov's theoretical position that the locus of systematic variation was the group rather than the individual. But following Macaulay's (1977) example, linguists have frequently presented figures for individuals, and a number of objections have been raised to the practice of grouping speakers (see particularly Hudson (1980: 163–7; Romaine (1980: 190).)

There are certainly a number of obvious difficulties which need to be acknowledged; first of all, some groups are extemely small, and where divisions are made on the basis of two speaker variables (such as social class and sex) it may seem a little unreal to label the persons who fall into one of the resulting categories as something along the lines of 'the upper-middle-class female group'. It is hard to see what kind of claims might reasonably be made about linguistic variation expressed as average scores of groups such as these (an additional difficulty being the abstract and contentious nature of social class labels).

A more general statistical point is that the *mean*, which is the type of average most often used by sociolinguists, is not always the most suitable measure of central tendency within a group; under some conditions the *median* or the *mode* are more appropriate. Measures of central tendency need to be interpreted along with measures of within-group variability – that is the clustering of individual scores around a typical value. The statistic most often used to measure within-group variability is the *standard deviation*, although there are other possibilities. Accessible discussions both of measures of central tendency and of variability can be found in Butler (1985b, chapter 3) and Erickson and Nosanchuk (1977, chapter 3). Since the linguistic homogeneity of groups can vary considerably, it is important for sociolinguists who aggregate individual scores to use these measures carefully. In particular, group means need to be used rather more circumspectly than was thought necessary in the early studies.

Another reason to be cautious of over-reliance on the mean is that there are certain important *between-group* differences which a simple comparison of group means cannot reveal. Sometimes there is little or no overlap between the scores of individuals in Group A and the individuals in Group B (see L. Milroy 1980: 161 for an example), but more often there is considerable overlap. This distribution, considered along with within-group variability, tells us quite a lot about the relationship of *group* scores to *individual* scores, a matter of some interest to sociolinguists.

Macaulay has concluded from his Glasgow study that individual scores do in fact fall into groups in such a way as to allow Glasgow speech to be characterized as three major social dialects (Macaulay 1978). Guy (1980) has concluded from his study of final stop deletion that the individual follows the group norm very closely; but since we know that scores for different linguistic variables are not distributed within or between groups in a comparable way, we cannot conclude that all variables will behave in the same way as the syllable-final alveolar stop. In Belfast, an analysis of variance technique highlighted differences in the distribution of eight different linguistic variables (L. Milroy 1980: 121–49).

6.8.4 Statistical analysis: some general principles

The traditional approach to statistical analysis is to use one of a range of tools to test for 'significance' as a means of indicating whether or not an explicitly formulated hypothesis can be upheld; Fasold (1984, chapter 4) discusses the application of this general method in sociolinguistics. The difficulty with standard significance tests is that their valid and effective use usually depends on *the way the data are approached* – for example whether the research has been designed with a specific hypothesis in mind or a less focused *post hoc* analysis is being carried out with a view to revealing underlying patterns. The logic of significance testing with respect to this type of issue is discussed by Erickson and Nosanchuk (1977, chapter 8) and Butler (1985b, chapter 6). The use of tests also depends upon certain assumptions about the *nature of the data*, such as whether or not it is normally distributed, is of roughly equal within-group variability and reflects independent observations. Some tests such as analysis of variance are fairly *robust* in that they permit violation of such assumptions, while others are not. Butler provides a clear account of the assumptions underlying a number of different tests.

It is relatively easy nowadays with a minimum of statistical or comput-ational knowledge to use the facilities of a statistical package for computer analysis (such as the Statistical Package for the Social Sciences or Minitab) to carry out a wide range of tests. But it is important for users of these powerful facilities to have adequate knowledge of the principles upon which statistical testing is based. The limitations and advantages of the selected procedure need to be understood, and the purpose of the analysis carefully specified. Exactly the same comments apply to powerful programs like David Sankoff's VARBRUL which are designed specifically for sociolinguistic analysis. Both the mathematical assumptions and the assumptions concerning the nature of the linguistic input which underlie the program need to be appreciated before the researcher can decide on its suitability for a particular analytic purpose. Guy (1980) gives a detailed account of the logic, limitations and applications of VARBRUL, while a number of papers in D. Sankoff (1978) discuss various details of its design and application. More recently, Horvath (1985: 59) has provided a useful critical account of the advantages and limitations of VARBRUL, and a comparison of the VARBRUL technique with Principal Components Analysis (see further 6.8.6). But in assessing the usefulness of VAR-BRUL, it is important to note that it is at present neither commercially available nor adequately documented for inexperienced users.

The capacity of modern computers to organize huge masses of data in many ways very speedily is, if used with care, as valuable to the sociolinguist as to anyone else. But computers can also overwhelm the user with numbers very quickly, and cannot give any more help with their interpretation than with the initial selection of an appropriate statistical procedure. Naive users sometimes assume that the computer can tell them anything that is worth knowing; to quote from Erickson and Nosanchuk, 'when we plug in the computer we often "unplug" our brains' (1977: 28). It is important not to allow a mechanical aid, however powerful, to interfere with the careful specification of analytic goals and the selection of appropriate means of attaining them.

6.8.5 Exploratory and confirmatory statistics

The various caveats expressed in 6.8.4 on the use of statistical techniques by sociolinguists are not as negative as they might seem, since recently the overuse of significance testing in social science research generally has come in for some criticism. Researchers have noted that many data-handling techniques depend upon assumptions which are hardly ever met in the social and behavioural sciences (see 6.8.4). Data are often *dirty*, containing errors and gaps, and sociolinguistic data have similar characteristics (see McEntegart and Le Page 1982 for an assessment of the difficulties of applying standard statistical techniques in sociolinguistics). The problem has arisen in the social sciences because classical statistics were originally developed to meet the requirements of the *natural* sciences and reflect a deductive style of hypothesis development which is not suitable for exploring dirty data in the context of amorphous and incomplete theories. It was to fill this need that John Tukey (1977) developed his *exploratory* statistics.

The general purpose of exploratory statistics, as the name suggests, is to help investigators to take a good look at patterns in data and to search around for ideas about the form these patterns take. The techniques are quick and simple to use and learn, intuitive and visually appealing, and resistant to errors and flukes. One feature of Tukey's techniques is the degree of insight they give into the data. By displaying numbers in a simple and visually revealing way such as, for example, the graph/table hybrid known as 'stem and leaf', it is possible to see obvious patterns quickly and focus harder on more puzzling aspects of the data (Erickson and Nosanchuk 1977: 20). Exploratory statistics might reasonably be described as highly systematized common sense.

Having used exploratory techniques to 'ransack' the data, the idea is then to generate hypotheses which can be tested using *confirmatory* statistics. These correspond to the data-analysis tools of classical statistics described in most statistics text-books, but are recommended by Tukey for use only when an *explicit hypothesis* has been formulated. This will emerge from extensive application of a range of exploratory techniques, and such a procedure is particularly important prior to using one of the computer packages designed for confirmatory statistics.

Exploratory techniques are extremely well fitted to sociolinguistic research. Since sociolinguistics is full of incomplete theories and unanswered questions, it is often more important to find ways of thoroughly searching the data for different types of pattern than to generate hypotheses which might well be premature. In fact, Labov's propensity to set out patterns in his data in a highly visual way is quite in the spirit of exploratory statistics; but the data are not presented as comprehensively nor analysed as thoroughly as they would be using Tukey's principles. A very wide range of techniques is available, which are capable of revealing different types of pattern in a set of data. The basic texts which explain them are Tukey (1977) and Erickson and Nosanchuk (1977), who supply an exploratory counterpart to every confirmatory technique. Chambers, Cleveland, Kleiner and Tukey (1983) deal specifically with *graphical* methods of exploring the structure of data (see particularly the various types of scatterplot illustrated in Chapter 4). They point out that well known *communication graphic* techniques such as pie charts often do a good job of *summarising* data but are of little use as *exploratory* tools since they reveal little about their structure. Hoaglin, Mosteller and Tukey (1985) provide a readable account of a range of useful and simple techniques such as 'stem and leaf' (chapter 1) and boxplots (chapter 3); Lovie (1985) contains a more advanced collection of papers representing recent developments in statistics for the social and behavioural sciences.

6.8.6 Choosing a suitable analytic method

If any benefit is to be derived from statistical analysis, it is important to define the nature of the problem and then set out to find the most appropriate way of solving it. Since defining the problem can implicate a whole range of linguistic and social issues such as those discussed in this chapter and in chapter 5, decisions about appropriate methods of statistical analysis cannot be made in isolation. This is perhaps best demonstrated by citing three specific and very different examples, which should also give some indication of the wide range of problems which can be illuminated by an appropriate statistical analysis.

One part of the Belfast analysis was concerned with the relationship between linguistic variable scores and social network scores, the hypothesis being that the two sets of scores were related. The statistical test which measures the strength of the relationship between paired sets of observations of this kind is a *correlation* test, and a large number of these tests were carried out to investigate the relationship (L. Milroy 1980: 149–166; Fasold 1984, chapter 4). The decision to investigate this relationship in the first place was bound up with theories of the social function of closeknit networks (see 5.7.1).

A completely different problem to which a different statistical analysis was appropriate is reported by J. Milroy and Harris (1980). Their hypothesis was that the apparent merger of words of the MEAT and the MATE classes (see 3.3.1) in contemporary Belfast vernacular had not in fact taken place. The chi square test was used to look for differences between tokens of the two word classes in two linguistic environments; but decisions concerning the environments and the type of differences to be examined depended on a great deal of phonological, sociolinguistic and historical linguistic information.

A different approach again was appropriate to a very different problem in the sociolinguistic survey of Sydney, Australia. Here, a computer-assisted technique known as *Principal Components Analysis* (Horvath 1985: 53) was used to examine the hypothesis that groups of speakers would show certain similarities in their linguistic behaviour. The only input to the program was *individual linguistic data,* and the procedure was particularly suitable in view of the difficulties in Sydney of grouping speakers according to class (see 2.5). Speaker variables were used to *interpret* the results of the analysis rather than as an input to it, and in fact speakers did fall into ethnic, status and age groups (cf. Le Page and Tabouret-Keller 1985: 127ff).

Figure 6.1 illustrates the type of patten revealed by PCA. Individual speakers are represented by dots, the only input to the program being a linguistic score on five vowel variables (see further Horvath 1985: 70). The programme plots speakers in terms of their scores on two principal components, represented as axes of the graph. These components are interpreted in social terms *after* the analysis by considering the social characteristics of the speakers who have been sorted on the basis of their linguistic behaviour into the two groups (periphery and core) which

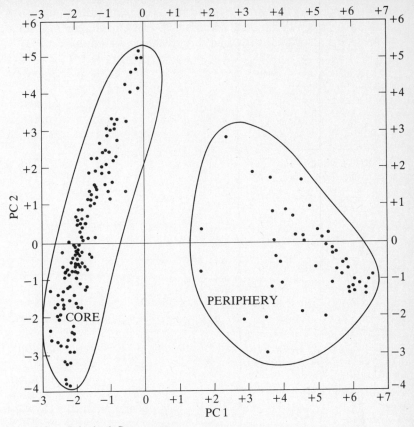

Key: PC = Principal Component

Figure 6.1   The Sydney speech community: core and periphery
(after Horvath 1985: 71)

emerge in Figure 6.1. In fact, Principal Component 1 divides speakers by ethnic group, distinguishing non-English accented from Australian English accented speakers. Principal Component 2, the vertical axis, distinguishes sociolects within the continuum of traditional Australian English accents.

The decision to use Principal Components Analysis in Sydney was related to an awareness of the problems of defining speaker variables (cf. chapter 5), and in fact the Sydney project is a particularly clear example of the interdependence between different stages of the research. The ultimate analytic method was chosen to take account both of sampling problems in the field and theoretical problems associated with speaker variables.

This discussion of quantification concludes our exploration in this chapter of a number of issues raised by a quantitative analysis of phonological variation in its social context. We focus in chapter 7 on some special problems associated with analysing *syntactic* variation.

7

Analysing Syntactic Variation

7.1 Introductory

For some years now, sociolinguists have attempted to extend quantitative methods to the study of syntactic variation, and have met with a number of problems which are both methodological and of a broader theoretical kind. Consequently, not all sociolinguistic studies of syntactic variation are quantitative, and not all take as their data base the corpora of naturally occurring speech preferred for phonological work; elicitation techniques of various kinds are sometimes used. Nor is it always illuminating (or even possible) in syntactic work to adopt the assumption which in quantitative phonological work is taken for granted: that the object of study is a set of surface variants expressing the same underlying *semantic* structure.

This chapter begins by examining some major fieldwork problems associated with the study of syntactic variation, going on to review in 7.3 some studies which have tackled them by means of various elicitation techniques. Section 7.4 reviews some quantitative studies which have attempted to take over directly from phonology the notion of the semantically neutral variable, and in subsequent sections analyses of variation which explicitly take into account *semantic* and *discourse* factors are discussed. However, since much published work combines various approaches, there will be a good deal of overlap between different parts of the discussion and it will be necessary throughout to refer to various theoretical and methodological issues which have received a good deal of attention in recent years.

7.2 Data Collection Problems

One characteristic difference between phonological and syntactic systems has far-reaching implications for the study of variation: although phonological systems change through time and so cannot be absolutely *closed* and *finite,* they are more closed and finite in character than syntactic systems. Speakers make use of a very sharply limited inventory of phonological contrasts, and realizations of any given unit are likely to crop up quite frequently in even a short piece of text. As we have seen, the difficulty often lies not in obtaining *tokens* of a variable, but in obtaining the *full range* of realizations associated with it. The position with syntax is however different, since it can never be guaranteed that a sufficient quantity of tokens of a given type of construction will ever appear in a piece of spontaneous discourse. This is partly a consequence of the non-finite or 'leaky' nature of syntactic systems, which in turn is associated with the relationship between syntax and speaker meaning (or intention). This relationship entails that speakers can exercise a great deal of choice in the way they encode their meanings; for example, even if questions (i.e. requests for information or for action) occur in a text, there is no guarantee that they will be realized syntactically as interrogatives; there is no simple isomorphic relationship between function and form.

Although these broader issues spill over into the whole question of extending the notion of the sociolinguistic variable into the domain of syntactic analysis, they are relevant to data collection because they often entail difficulties in obtaining sufficient quantities of a specific type of data. This problem emerges even where, intuitively, it seems likely that data will be plentiful, as can be demonstrated by the example of a study of variable subject/verb concord in Belfast vernacular speech (Policansky 1980; 1982). We find in that dialect alternation between standard and non-standard patterns of number agreement, so that a plural subject can co-occur with a singular verb:

1 Her sons was in the Orange Order
2 Them two fellows was hit

After listening to around 100 hours of the spontaneous peech of 48 inner-city speakers (see 4.3.1) the investigators received the impression that occurrences of examples such as (1) and (2) alternating with their standard counterparts were extremely frequent. However, this proved not to be the case, since even from such a large corpus, it was possible to extract only 560 utterance tokens - an average of less than 11.7 per speaker.

Investigators have tackled this kind of problem in a number of ways. Cheshire was able to collect enough data from Reading adolescents to carry out a quantitative analysis of the following: variation in the morphological structure of the third personal singular form of the verb; a separate study of the verbs HAVE, DO and BE; various aspects of the system of negation; the relative pronoun system. The large amounts of data needed for such an analysis were obtained by means of a participant observation method which allowed the investigator to record speakers over a long period, returning to collect more data if specific gaps emerged in the course of the analysis (cf. 3.1). Cheshire notes that even so a number of alternating items and structures did not occur frequently enough for a quantitative analysis, and some of the frequencies for the variables which *were* analysed are very low. The relative pronoun analysis, for example, distinguishes five variants, distributionally constrained by four different (linguistic) contextual factors; this complex analysis is based on only 82 occurrences (Cheshire 1982a: 73). As we shall see, much quantitative syntactic work shows a similar tendency to take account of (and indeed sometimes concentrate on) linguistic rather than social constraints on variation. This tends to compound problems caused by too few tokens (cf. 6.8.2).

A different approach to data collection may be found in Kallen's (1986) study of the co-occurrence of auxiliary *do* with main verb BE in Irish English:

3   These pancakes do be gorgeous
4   It doesn't be long coming

The *do be* construction does not correspond in any simple way to standard English forms of BE (as is clear if an attempt is made to 'translate' the second example), but encodes aspectual distinctions which are not always syntactically marked in standard English (Kallen 1986; J. Harris 1984). *Do be* constructions crop up relatively infrequently in spontaneous speech, a difficulty which Kallen addressed by obtaining the bulk of his data from rapid and anonymous observations (see 4.2.3). He wrote down instances of the construction immediately after hearing it, supplementing this data source with material from broadcast speech and a limited amount of tape-recorded data. This 'diary' method is sometimes suitable where the purpose is (as in Kallen's case) to examine linguistic constraints on variation. But it carries with it the usual problem associated with rapid and anonymous observations, *viz.* lack of information on the social identity of the speaker.

The occurrence of some kinds of construction is likely to be constrained by pragmatic factors – for example, interrogatives are not likely to crop up very often in the speech of a person who is being interviewed (cf. 3.3). Rather more subtly, J. Harris (1984) notes that tokens of the *hot news perfect* (see further 7.6), used to refer to events in the immediate past, were located in spontaneous, casual discourse rather than in the response speech found in interviews. This, like so many of the methodological issues which emerge in the study of syntactic variation, is part of a wider theoretical question, in this case the embedding of syntax in discourse and the close interrelationships between syntax, semantics and pragmatics (see 7.7). Some investigators have, however, used these pragmatic constraints on variation to help obtain, relatively reliably, tokens of a particular construction. Sometimes an extremely simple technique is sufficient - for example Coveney (1986) reports that he obtained enough data to allow him to study quantitatively different ways of expressing future time in the French verb, simply by asking speakers about their plans for the future. Similarly, in her study of variation between the conditional, imperfect subjunctive, present indicative and future indicative in the verbs of *si* clauses in Buenos Aires Spanish, Lavandera developed a set of interview questions (for example, 'Under what conditions would you feel happier than you presently are?') which succeeded in eliciting a high proportion of clauses expressing unreal conditions (Lavandera 1975; 1978a; 1982). She obtained 1,489 tokens of *si* clauses from 90 subjects, a body of data large enough to be analysed by the VARBRUL program (see 6.8.4).

Rather more elaborately, Sandra Harris (1984) collected *courtroom* data, using obvious situational constraints on discourse to enable to her to examine the form and functions of *questions* (cf. 3.2.1). This particular social context, in which the magistrate's role is that of questioner, ensures a high concentration of naturally occurring relevant data. Harris's method supplements the general approach used by Lavandera (of selectively directing the conversation) in that it raises the possibility of seeking out *situational contexts* which are likely to favour frequent occurrence of a given construction. We may conclude that although elicitation of syntactic data presents methodological problems, those problems are not insuperable and can often be solved by a little ingenuity.

7.3 The Use of Elicitation Techniques

7.3.1 Methods

One solution to the data-collection problems outlined in 7.2 is to supplement a corpus of naturally occurring speech with data gathered by some kind of experimental method. This involves accessing, directly or indirectly, the intuition of a native speaker (cf. 1.1). As part of an investigation of the Irish English perfect (see further 7.6), J. Harris (1983) used experimental techniques to help specify constraints on the Irish English *have-NP-V-en* type of perfect (P11), as exemplified in 5 and 6:

5   He has the course finished
6   She has the dress made

Examples of this construction were collected from 150 hours of recorded speech. Although on average it cropped up only once an hour, there appeared to be semantic restrictions on the type of verb with which it occurred; in the majority of cases it occurred with *dynamic verbs of activity,* the most frequent being *do, make, finish, write.* Supplementing the corpus with more recordings of naturally occurring speech would have been very time-consuming, so a questionnaire was designed in order to investigate (amongst other things) the possibility of such a constraint operating. If it operated absolutely, sentences like 7 and 8 ought to be judged unacceptable:

7 *He has his father relied on a lot
8 *He has two race-horses owned

To check this, 145 students were presented with twelve sentences, each containing the *have-NP-V-en* construction with a different verb, as shown in table 7.1. These verbs had been selected in groups of three from four categories: dynamic verbs of activity; dynamic momentary verbs; stative verbs of inert perception; and stative relational verbs. They were presented in random order, and the respondents were asked to judge the acceptability of the sentences. The results, presented in table 7.1, strikingly confirm the nature of the constraints suggested by the corpus data; the structure is very much more likely to occur with dynamic verbs, particularly verbs of activity. But significantly, table 7.1 also shows that it does not seem to be possible to elicit sharp judgements of acceptability which can be used to divide grammatical from ungrammatical sentences. We shall return to this point in 7.3.2.

Table 7.1 Judgements by 145 Irish English speakers on the acceptability of 12 verbs occurring with PII

Acceptable		Acceptable	
Dynamic verbs of activity		Stative verbs of perception	
BOOK	138	RECOGNIZE	17
WRITE	136	UNDERSTAND	11
MAKE	125	SEE	10
Dynamic momentary verbs		Stative relational verbs	
JUMP	39	OWN	13
HIT	28	RESEMBLE	12
KICK	20	RELY ON	7

Source: after J. Harris (1983: 36)

A number of similar experiments are described by Labov (1975); of particular interest is a series designed to investigate the failure of the negative attraction rule (i.e. the tendency to attach the negative marker to the quantifier) in some English dialects, in sentences of the following type:

9   All the men didn't arrive
10   Every man didn't arrive
11   Each of the men didn't arive
12   Anybody didn't arrive

Labov had hypothesized that there was 'a regular gradient of negative attraction to quantifiers, strongest to *any,* weaker for *each* and *every,* weakest for *all'* (1975: 19). This is parallel to the gradient of acceptability which emerged from Harris's results, and Labov attempted to accommodate the tendency of speakers to avoid making absolute judgements by asking them to assign to each sentence a score on a four-point scale, as follows:

4   =   No native speaker would say it

3   =   Other native speakers might conceivably say it

2   =   Awkward, but can conceive of saying it

1   =   Would say it without qualms

Table 7.2   The strength of negative attraction to quantifiers

	Grammaticality					
Quantifier	1	2	3	4	N	Mean
all	8	10	1		19	1.6
every	4	6	7	2	19	2.4
each	2	2	6	9	19	3.1
any	1	1	5	12	19	3.5

Source: adapted from Labov (1975: 20)

As table 7.2 shows, the results of the experiment confirm the original prediction of a gradient of acceptability. A number of other experimental studies, all using rather similar techniques, are described by Labov in two separate publications (Labov 1972d; 1975).

One well-known and very important point about experimental work which emerges clearly from the studies discussed in this section is that in order to frame a specific hypothesis the experimenter needs to have acquired in advance a good deal of detailed knowledge; Plutchik (1974) emphasizes this in his discussion of the applicability of experimental versus observational methods. Basic information about syntactic structure cannot be derived from experimentation in the absence of prior knowledge derived from observational methods. Both Labov and Harris had obtained this knowledge from analytic work on substantial bodies of data.

7.3.2 Some problems in the use of elicitation techniques

Although experimental methods provide a highly economical and efficient method of investigating a speaker's responses to particular items of structure, the main difficulty associated with them is the mismatch which sociolinguists have consistently found between what speakers *claim* when they are directly questioned, and what they actually *do,* as evidenced by their linguistic behaviour in naturally occurring conversation. A good example of this difficulty is provided by Davis (1984), who examined constraints on the *for to* complementizer in Belfast English, in sentences of the following type:

13   For to do that would be foolish
14   I got up early for to paint the kitchen
15   ?I want for to do that

Davis had suspected that *for to* could not introduce complements of the verb *want,* and one particular native speaker, when questioned, had confirmed this tentative hypothesis. However, a few minutes later in spontaneous conversation, he produced the following utterance:

16   I want for to be helpful

Difficulties in accessing the intuitions of linguistically naive informants are well known to field linguists generally, and have been reported from sources as diverse as the Soviet Union (Kibrik 1977) and Australia (Healey 1974; Dixon 1984). Dixon reports for example difficulties in obtaining the information he needed to write a grammar of Dyirbal. Many quite fluent Dyirbal speakers simply represented a dead end in that their intuitions could not be accessed. In practice, most information was obtained from a single highly intelligent, articulate and linguistically aware speaker, on whom Dixon relied almost totally; his procedure then was to check the data for idiolectal idiosyncrasies against the judgement of one other.

Labov's (1973) account of his investigation of various aspects of the negative attraction rule in Philadelphia demonstrates a further problem, associated with *attitudes* to particular varieties, characteristically encountered by researchers investigating a stigmatized language or dialect (cf. the discussion in 1.3 of Le Page's early work in the Caribbean). Both this difficulty and a more general difficulty of accessing intuitions are illustrated by Labov's experience in investigating constraints affecting so-called 'positive' *anymore* sentences such as 17 and 18:

17   We keep the beer here anymore
18   John's smoking anymore

The particular point at issue is that in standard English *anymore*, along with other items in the *any* series and a number of adverbials, is in main clauses usually restricted to interrogative or negative constructions; Labov (1973) cites the following dialogue to show the difficulty of investigating by direct questioning of a native speaker his hunch that this particular constraint was less binding in Philadelphia:

Interviewer: Can people say round here *We go to the movies anymore?*
Informant: We say *show,* not *movies*

The speaker's failure to comment overtly on syntactic structure here cannot of course be interpreted as reliable evidence that he habitually uses and understands the construction.

   The tendency for prescriptive ideologies to inhibit and distort responses in situations where informants are conscious of a competing set of standard norms became evident when Labov pressed his questions with people who had been heard using the construction in conversation. The usual reaction was confusion, followed by a claim that a 'mistake' had been made in not including a negative in the utterance. In general, responses to direct or indirect questioning about non-standard varieties are always conditioned by speakers' awareness of their social significance and usually reflect knowledge of the standard rules. Attempts in Belfast to investigate experimentally constraints on the highly stigmatized non-standard concord rule (see 7.4) ran up against these problems, and similar difficulties are encountered with bilingual speakers (8.3.2).

7.4 Syntactic Analysis and the Sociolinguistic Variable

7.4.1 The problem

When the data base for syntactic analysis is a body of naturally occurring speech rather than experimentally elicited material, *analysis* and *interpretation* of that data is liable to raise even more problems than finding a way to collect it in the first place (see 7.2). Labov's comments on the difficulty of applying the *principle of accountability* to the study of variable syntax suggest one reason for the problems. Recall the requirements of this principle (cf. 6.1) that 'all occurrences of a given variant are noted, and where it has been possible to define the variable as a closed set of variants, all non-occurrences of the variant in the relevant circumstances' (Labov 1982a: 30). Labov's rider to these conditions is however worth quoting in full:

> The requirement as stated is too strict. There are a number of variables that can be studied now by noting only each occurrence, but not each non-occurrence, *since it has not yet been possible to close the possible set of variants* [my emphasis]. Studies of the aspect markers of the Black English Vernacular, like invariant *be* are still at this stage. The same is true for the distribution of relative clauses, where we can't yet define the set of possible choices that the relative is selected from. Here, quantitative work is confined to tracing the relative frequency of occurrence in some globally defined section of speech, controlled for length by an independent measure like number of sentences, pages, or hours of speech. (Labov 1982a: 87)

There are a number of examples in the literature of the problem to which Labov is drawing attention here; certainly Kallen's *do be* variable falls into this category as do the perfective aspect markers discussed by J. Harris (1984). This seems to be the problem too with perfective *done*, a feature of Appalachian speech studied by Wolfram and Christian (1976). Examples of the usage are:

19   We thought he was done gone
20   The doctor done give him up
21   I done forgot when it opened

The authors report the number of occurrences of the surface form *done,* rather than presenting their information in terms of percentages which give a proportion of *possible* occurrences. Chambers and Trudgill (1980: 90) note that it is 'not possible to set up *done* as any kind of linguistic variable, since it is not a form which is involved in alternation with other forms that could be considered to be "equivalent ways of doing or saying the same thing"'. Sometimes, however, the difficulty to which Labov alludes in defining the set of possible choices is of a rather different kind, involving (linguistic) contextual constraints on possible variants.

Recall first the procedure which needs to be adopted in defining a *phonological* variable, of disregarding linguistic contexts which do not allow variation. Usually this presents no theoretical problem; for example in a certain range of phonetic environments in Belfast, back variants of (a) *never* occurred (see 6.2.2). Similar constraints, many of them much more obvious, are routinely specified for most phonological variables; for example /r/ is variably deleted in many dialects only pre-consonantally and word-finally. But what is routine in phonological analysis often presents problems in syntactic analysis. Consider again the example of subject/verb agreement in Belfast (cf.7.2).

Although sentences of the type illustrated by 1 and 2 occur sporadically throughout the data, a number of lexical and syntactic constraints seem to inhibit the co-occurrence of a singular verb with a plural subject. Particularly where the subject is a plural personal pronoun no variation seems to be permitted; but in our initial search for invariance (cf. 1.1), we still cannot specify this rule as categorical with the same confidence as we can define a constraint on a phonological variable. This became clear when, in an attempt to investigate further the nature of the personal pronoun constraint on the non-standard concord rule, all occurrences of *they* as subject in the speech of 12 speakers were collected (N=310), from which only one example was discovered of a singular verb:

22   He asked how many eggcups she had and what colour they was

Nor were any examples found of *we* or *you* co-occurring with a singular verb, and in a very real sense it is this constraint which distinguishes the Belfast vernacular concord system from that of other non-standard varieties. In London English, for example, singular forms of *be* (certainly past tense forms) seem to co-occur freely with *we* and *they* as subjects:

23   We was living in the other house then

It might be added that in the Belfast data no instances of *these* (in either its pronoun or determiner function) or of the related form *theseuns* were found as subjects of singular verbs. However, the semantically and syntactically equivalent item *them* (in both pronoun and determiner function) along with the related form *themuns* co-occurred freely with singular verbs, apparently favouring the application of the non-standard concord rule:

24   Them two fellows was hit
25   Them's the words he used to me
26   Themuns is thieves

Were it not for the single inconvenient occurrence in the data (example 22) of *they* as the subject of a singular verb, we could set up an initial list of 'invariant' environments, which themselves are characteristic of this vernacular system, prior to an investigation of patterns underlying the variability in the many environments which permitted it. But the problem which data of this kind present is whether or not contexts where the subject is realized by a personal pronoun or by *these* are possible 'variable' environments. It is possible to argue that the single occurrence of *they* in the data with a singular verb is accidental (a 'performance error') but equally possible to claim that the *non-occurrence* of *you, we* and *these* with a singular verb is the consequence of an accidental gap in the corpus; the line of reasoning characteristic of generative grammar is of little help to us here in choosing between these alternatives.

Nor are problems of this kind peculiar to the Belfast concord variable; similar indeterminacies are, for example, associated with attempts to specify the precise environments in which the zero form of the relative pronoun can occur. As in the case of the concord system, constraints seem to differ between one non-standard grammar and another. Miller (forthcoming) reports that Scottish English, unlike standard English, allows the omission of *subject* relative pronouns in sentence types where the subject of the main clause is realized as *there:*

27 There's not many people know of this law

However, constructions like 28, where the subject of the main clause is a 'heavy' NP, seem not to turn up in Scottish English, although they are usual in Somerset English:

28 The electrician came to mend the cooker couldn't find the fault (= The electrician who came. . .)

It is, however, not at all clear what the precise constraints on variable subject relative pronouns in these two vernacular systems might be.

These methodological difficulties are associated with a more general problem of deriving generalizations from corpuses. Defining relevant environments of a variable has been noted as a particularly serious obstacle to a satisfying analysis of syntactic variation by Lavandera (1978b), by G. Sankoff and Thibault (1980) and by Weiner and Labov (1983). Earlier versions of both Sankoff and Thibault's study of the French *avoir/être* variable and Weiner and Labov's study of the English agentless passive variable are discussed in some detail by Lavandera to demonstrate the nature of the difficulties, which in fact have not yet been satisfactorily resolved. Attempts to specify constraints on the application of the rule by appealing to the intuitions of the native speaker simply raise a fresh set of problems (see 7.3.2).

7.4.2 Quantitative studies of syntactic variation: some examples

Despite the difficulties of knowing what to count when the concept of the variable is applied to syntactic work, a large number of quantitative studies of syntactic variation are reported in the literature. To give some idea of their range and diversity, some of them are reviewed here.

G. Sankoff's (1980a) collection of papers on syntactic variation in both Montreal French and the Tok Pisin of Papua New Guinea employs a very wide range of approaches and includes at various points discussions of important theoretical and practical issues. Although versions of all the papers in the collection have been published elsewhere (but not always in English), they are cited here in these easily available versions except where the date or other details of the original publications are particularly relevant.

The syntactic work of Sankoff and her associates has always been influential. It was Sankoff's paper 'Above and beyond phonology in variable rules' (1973; 1980b) which first proposed extending the notion of the linguistic variable to syntax, demonstrating the methods and principles involved with three examples: variable placement of the future marker *bai* in Tok Pisin; variable deletion of the complementizer *que* in Montreal French; and variation in the use of French indefinite *on*. This discussion, along with Weiner and Labov's later study of the passive variable seems to have stimulated Lavandera's (1978b) critique of the use of the notion of the variable in syntactic studies (se further 7.5). By definition, of course, work employing the concept of the variable is quantitative; but as we shall see later in this chapter, much interesting work on syntactic variation (by Sankoff and others) is *qualitative,* or a mixture of qualitative and quantitative approaches.

Lavandera has pointed out that much work on syntactic variation tends to focus on syntactic rather than social constraints. Of the three variables discussed by G. Sankoff (1980b), only syntactic constraints on variation are reported for the *bai* and *que* variables, the *on* variable being the only one for which the influence of a speaker variable (age, in this case) is reported. It cannot of course be the case that syntactic variables do not pattern socially or stylistically; some of them plainly do, as the work of, for example, Cheshire has shown. But it is certainly true that many of the variables that have been studied do not show a clear effect of social constraints, and it seems reasonable to suggest (cf. Lavandera 1978b), that the concept of the linguistic variable is not applicable in these cases, since it was originally designed to examine apparently meaningless variation which is in fact of social and stylistic significance (Labov 1972b: 271).

One particularly interesting and detailed quantitative study in G. Sankoff (1980a) which so far in this chapter has received only passing mention is the English-language version of G. Sankoff and Thibault's (1977) substantial analysis of variation between the auxiliaries *avoir* and *être* in Montreal French, as in:

29   On est/a déménagé cinq six fois – 'we moved five or six times'

This substantial and carefully argued paper deals with a number of thorny methodological issues, such as defining the scope and relevant contexts of the syntactic variable (see 7.4.1) and problems associated with the low frequency of particular verbs. An important part of the discussion deals with the difficulty of deciding whether variation can be said to be between *semantically equivalent* forms which carry social meaning, or to encode an *aspectual* distinction; this latter issue is treated in the context of a (non-quantitative) analysis of the semantic distinctions underlying tense and aspect marking (see further 7.6 and 7.7). Finally, a number of quantitative analyses are carried out, including a variable rule analysis of the probability of speakers using one variant or the other, according to their *linguistic market* indices (cf. 5.3.2). The paper as a whole is an excellent scource of information on a range of relevant practical and theoretical issues.

Wolfram's (1980) account of variable constraints on prefixing *a-* to the present continuous form of the verb in Appalachian English (e.g. 'He got sick a'workin' so hard') is also a mixture of quantitative and non-quantitative analysis, the latter focusing on the now familiar problems of establishing relevant environments and possible semantic distinctions encoded in *a*-prefixing. A range of phonological and other constraints are then examined quantitatively.

Poplack (1980a) reports a VARBRUL analysis of the plural morpheme *-s*, which is variably realized as [s] and [ø] in Puerto Rican Spanish:

30   yo mi(s) hijo(s) le(s) digo – 'I tell my kids'

She is particularly interested in a possible relationship between choice of variant and communicative function, hypothesizing that the plural morpheme is less likely to be realized as [ø] when ambiguity results; compare for example 31 and 32:

31   los reyes – 'the kings'
32   las reinas – 'the queens'

Even if both plural markers in 31 are realized as [ø], the form of both the determiner and the noun adequately convey information about number (*pl.* [lo xeye], *sing.* [el xey]). However, if both plural markers in 32 are realized as [ø], ambiguity with the singular form [la xeina] may result (Poplack 1980a: 59). Interestingly, the results lead to a decisive rejection of a functionalist hypothesis; deletion rates are affected very little by the presence or absence of disambiguating information in the surface string. The factor which most powerfully predicts deletion is deletion of the first plural element in the string; if a plural in the phrase is going to be realized by [s], there is a strong tendency for it to be realized on this first element. Hence, strings of the form ⌀⌀s are rare or non-existent.

Quantitative syntactic studies do not necessarily take as their data base recordings of live conversation. Romaine's extension of the quantitative methods of sociolinguistics to the study of variation in relative clause marking in sixteenth-century written texts suggests an approach to the relationship between variation and change different from any we have discussed so far (Romaine 1982b). Interestingly, the ranking of stylistic and syntactic constraints on choice of relative pronoun variant appears to have changed little in 450 years; zero marking in subject position is preferred in written Scots in less formal styles. G. Sankoff and Vincent (1980) in a smaller historical investigation come to a parallel conclusion that stylistically stratified patterns of variable deletion of the negative particle *ne* in French have changed very little since the sixteenth century, when deletion was associated with informal styles. Nowadays, *ne* is used only rarely in conversational contexts, but is favoured in certain formal (particularly written) styles. Both of these studies show that variation does not lead inevitably to change. Stable variation can be maintained by speakers over many centuries as a stylistic and general sociolinguistic resource.

Kroch and Small (1978) extend the application of quantitative methods in quite a different way, taking as their data base several hours of talk-show (phone-in) conversation from a Philadelphia radio station. Two variables are investigated: presence versus absence of the complementizer *that*, and particle movement as exemplified in sentences of the following types:

33   John pointed out the mistake
34   John pointed the mistake out

Their main objective is to study the effect of *prescriptive ideologies* on listeners' attitudes to the alternating variants.

Also basing his work on media language, written as well as spoken, Bell (1985) studies in real time the spread of a process of determiner deletion in noun phrases which has become common in news reports, as demonstrated in 35 as opposed to 36:

35   fugitive financier Mr Robert Vesco
36   the fugitive financier Mr Robert Vesco

The pattern exemplified in 35 seems to have originated in the United States, with the high-prestige British media tending to favour the pattern typified by 36. Bell shows, however, that both the British media and the New Zealand media (which at one time followed the British norm) are gradually adopting the American norm. However, the change is taking place at a differential rate which seems to be related to the relative prestige of the various media.

Bell's application of the methodology of sociolinguistics in real time to an extensive body of written and broadcast data suggests an interesting and practicable way of studying the gradual diffusion of a linguistic change from an identifiable point of influence. It is clear that quantitative methodology can be applied, with interesting results, to data bases other than the bodies of naturally occurring spontaneous speech for which it was originally designed.

7.4.3 The role of the computer in syntactic analysis

The capacity of computers to handle *text* in various ways is particularly relevant to quantitative syntactic work; this is a function additional to their *sorting* and *counting* ('number-crunching') capacities which are useful in statistical analysis (cf. 6.8.4). One text-processing function is *parsing* (producing a syntactic analysis of stored data) using programs such as EYEBALL or, more recently, OXEYE (Butler 1985a). Another important aid to analysing syntactic variation is the production of a *concordance;* in addition to a reference location to word forms in a text which have been previously input, a concordance gives a certain amount of surrounding context. A very comprehensive and flexible concordance program widely used in Britain is The Oxford Concordance Program (see Butler 1985a for a description).

Analyses such as the Montreal *que* study which concentrates on specifying *syntactic* constraints on variation (cf. 7.4.2) will benefit greatly both from a parser and a concordance program – and in fact such a program was used to analyse the Montreal corpus. It is hard to see how some of this work could practicably have been carried out without computer aid; for example, the input to the analysis of *on* versus *tu/vous* realizations of the indefinite personal pronoun was '4,300 tokens, each one of which has been carefully studied as to its syntactic and discursive role. . .' (Laberge and Sankoff 1980: 287; see further 7.7). For such a massive study to be feasible, a concordance program which picks out tokens of the pronouns along with their surrounding context is probably a necessity.

Once the text has been accurately input to the computer, there are no particular practical problems associated with running a concordance program to study a wide range of syntactic variables; the major advantage of computer techniques is the ease with which repetitive processes can be carried out and large amounts of data stored which can later be added to. But the major obstacle to wider use of computers for textual processing is the time taken to input data. This is partly because of the size of the corpuses needed for syntactic analysis and partly because of the accuracy required in the transcript, which has to be input in computer-readable form. Since considerable resources of time are needed to input a large corpus successfully, textual processing by computer is impracticable for many researchers working on tight budgets. It might be added that when text is input for *phonological* analysis these problems are if anything magnified, and for these purely practical reasons it was possible in, for example, the Belfast project, to use computers only in a very limited way for text processing (as opposed to computation, where various statistical packages were extensively used).

There are several useful accounts of computer applications available. Butler (1985a) explains in detail their use in linguistic research generally, with a particular emphasis on textual processing. Leech and Beale (1984) provide an overview of their applications in English language research and of the computerized corpuses which are available. Johnson (1986) discusses the practicalities of using the textual processing capacities of computers for a specific research purpose, and Wells (1985) gives a useful (and rather sobering) account of the problems encountered by the Bristol Child Language Project in computer-processing a very large amount of socially and developmentally variable material. In general it is important for researchers who are seeking a model for their own projects to be aware of the extent to which much innovatory work in the analysis of variable syntax (such as Sankoff's) is computer-aided. Equally, one needs to be clear on the nature of the practical difficulties associated with computer-aided text-processing. It is of course perfectly possible in principle to carry out syntactic analysis of large corpuses manually; but the work of extracting tokens and identifying the surrounding environment is then very much more time-consuming. Some kinds of syntactic analysis require corpuses of data that in practice are probably too large to analyse by hand.

7.5 The Problem of Semantic Equivalence

There is one particular difficulty in extending the notion of the linguistic variable to the analysis of syntactic variation which has received extensive discussion in recent years (see for example Lavandera (1978b), Romaine (1984b) and Coveney (1986)). It was Lavandera who suggested that the concept of the linguistic variable could not usefully be applied to the analysis of syntactic variation because variants of so-called 'syntactic variables' were not semantically equivalent in the same way as pho-nological variables. Certainly it is clear that while phonological elements such as (t) or (a) are not in themselves bearers of meaning, syntactic or morphological elements often are. There is no real difficulty in accepting the functional equivalence of variants such as [t] and [ʔ] if they can occupy the same position in a set of words (such as the syllable final position in *bat, pit, hot*) without replacement of one by the other altering the semantic form of any item. But extending the notion of the variable to syntax suggests that we can show that syntactic variants are semantically equivalent in much the same way. As Lavandera remarks:

> *Laughing and laughin'* or [gɑːd] and [goːd] can more convincingly be shown to be used to say referentially the same thing than any pair of postulated synonymous syntactic constructions such as *the liquor store was broken into* versus *they broke into the liquor store.* Such a syntactic difference, as we can see in Labov and Weiner's study of this as a variable, requires quite an ingenious dismissal of possible differences in referential meaning. (Lavandera 1978b: 175).

Even in the revised version of their paper, which takes account of Lavandera's comments, Weiner and Labov are obliged to argue tortuously and not always convincingly that their alternants are semantically equivalent. They conclude: 'We therefore approach the passive with an eye to a bold simplification of the problems of meaning. We will treat active and passive as truth-conditionally equivalent and used on the whole to refer to the same state of affairs' (Weiner and Labov 1983: 32). The rather cautious tone of this statement of intent is not sufficient to resolve the conceptual difficulties presented by the notion of a syntactic (as opposed to phonological) variable. As Romaine (1984b) points out, the notion of semantic equivalence is difficult to work with in practice, even if we attempt, following Weiner and Labov, to limit it to truth-conditional equivalence. There are many reasons for this, which Romaine discusses at some length. Particularly, the notion of 'equivalent ways of doing or saying the same thing' to which Weiner and Labov obliquely refer (see above) is much less straightforward than it seems. Because syntax is embedded in discourse, entirely different forms might have similar functions (i.e. be used as equivalent ways of doing or saying the same thing); for this reason it is sometimes difficult to specify a principled way of knowing where to stop counting particular forms as variants of a variable. This problem may be seen as the converse of the one discussed at the beginning of this section – defining a complete set of alternants for a variable – and is best demonstrated by example.

It is well known that speakers of French have open to them a number of different ways of forming interrogatives; for example, Coveney (1986) has distinguished five different variants of the *wh* interrogative, two of which are [SVQ] and [QSV]. These may be exemplified as follows:

37   Mais vous êtes en France pour combien de temps?
38   Mais quelle heure est-il?

Coveney argues that evidence for viewing such examples as alternants might be adduced from the linguistic behaviour of speakers, citing as an example the following incident where he heard a Frenchwoman asking a younger man the following question, using an [SVQ] variant: 'Tu es d'où?' (*Where are you from*?). The addressee, however, failed to respond, even after repetition of the question (possibly, as Coveney suggests, being distracted by an alternative interpretation suggested by homophony with *tu es doux* ('you are sweet/gentle'). Finally, the problem was resolved by the speaker rephrasing the question as 'D'où tu es?' [QSV]. This may be said to constitute evidence that the speaker views [SVQ] and [QSV] as 'equivalent ways of doing or saying the same thing'.

Although it is certainly tempting to use reformulations of this kind as evidence that [VSQ] and [QSV] are variants of an underlying variable, used by speakers in spoken discourse much like successive realizations of *pit* as [pɪʔ] and [pʊt] when the first realization is not heard clearly, such evidence cannot consistently be relied upon without further qualification to define a set of syntactic variants. This is because analysis of *speaker* meaning (intention) and of *linguistic* meaning (the patterning of elements in the system) are different enterprises which need to be kept conceptually apart (see Hurford and Heasley 1983 for an elementary exposition of the issues). When speakers are looking for different ways of accomplishing the same goal (in Coveney's example, successfully requesting information) they are not limited to the various possibilities in the linguistic system for constructing formal interrogatives. Thus, as Romaine points out, the following utterances might be thought of as functionally equivalent, in that they have the same communicative purpose, even though the surface syntactic forms are not necessarily related:

It's cold in here
I'm cold
Are you cold?
Would you close the window?
Close the window

(Romaine 1984b: 422)

Certainly, speakers are free to select from a wide range of surface forms in order to achieve a particular communicative purpose, and it is quite likely that they will do so to attain appropriate levels of politeness, solidarity or social distance. Nor can we easily resolve this methodological problem by appealing to any clear theoretical definition of semantic equivalence based on formal syntactic relations between sentences, since even within generative syntax this is a highly unstable and controversial area of linguistic theory. Consider, for example, the criticisms of *transformations* by Bresnan (1982) as a means of handling the active/passive relationship and her alternative proposals; on the other hand, Gazdar and his colleagues (1985) have proposed a completely different framework for handling these relationships.

This lack of consensus on the way semantically and grammatically related sentences should be characterized is itself troublesome enough to a sociolinguist seeking guidance from syntactic theory; but to make things even more difficult, the very notion of semantic equivalence is a disputed one. Some linguists argue that such equivalence does not exist (Bolinger 1977) while others like Coveney argue that a weaker kind of equivalence (of a kind which cannot however easily be specified) is sufficient for identifying structures as variants of an underlying variable. To a number of theoretical linguists who have argued *against* a separation of syntax and discourse, the issue is irrelevant (Givón 1979a). Following their general line of reasoning sociolinguists like Dines (1980) have suggested that the notion of the variable should be extended into the domain of pragmatics (see further 7.7).

Despite the cluster of problems which emerges when the notion of the syntactic variable is extended beyond phonology, many investigators feel intuitively that some candidate 'syntactic variables' behave in a way more similar to phonological variables than others. Attempts have been made, presumably on the basis of this intuition, to formulate a taxonomy and a set of criteria for identifying 'genuine' variables (see Coveney 1986; Romaine 1984b). Romaine has concluded that the concept of the variable cannot usefully be applied to any but low-level morphological variation. Some of the work reviewed in 7.4.2 seems to fall into this category, such as the morpho-syntactic variation examined by Cheshire (1982a), or variation in Montreal French in the use of the negative particle *ne* (Sankoff and Vincent 1980). At the other end of the scale, alternations between the active and the agentless passive studied by Weiner and Labov do not seem to be candidate variables in any sense parallel to the concept of the phonological variable. Far from meeting the equivalence criterion, these alternations express differences in focus which can be explicated only with reference to the discourse matrix in which they are embedded; further-more, they do not have a systematic social distribution in the speech community. As Lavandera (1978b) has remarked, one paradoxical conse-quence of the 'sea-change' in the concept of the sociolinguistic variable evident in the Weiner and Labov paper is that the authors seem to be attempting to argue for a function of variation almost converse to that which emerged from Labov's earlier work. While a major contribution of this work was to show that apparently meaningless differences in form were in fact carriers of social and stylistic meaning, the 1983 paper attempts on the other hand to demonstrate that forms which are referentially equivalent carry neither social nor stylistic meaning, but are constrained almost entirely by their syntactic environment.

7.6 Semantic Equivalence between Standard and Non-standard Forms

The general issue of semantic equivalence is a complicated one which has been much discussed in the literature. But a different and less well-known set of problems emerges when attempts are made to examine alternation betwen *standard* and *non-standard* forms. In fact, a surprisingly small number of studies examine this dimension of syntactic variation; for example, many of the papers in Sankoff's 1980 collection concentrate on *grammatical* constraints, and the focus of Weiner and Labov (1983) is similar.

J. Harris (1984) points out that an assumption of direct semantic equivalence between standard and non-standard variants involves a further assumption that the variants are embedded in identical grammars and are simply different surface realizations of the same underlying syntactic (and ultimately semantic) structure. Cheshire's work shows that this assumption is too simple since, for example, main verb DO and auxiliary *do* behave quite differently in Reading vernacular and in standard English, the patterns of variation in Reading vernacular being quite different for each of the verb-form's two grammatical functions. A similar difference in underlying grammars is demonstrated by the non-standard concord rule in Belfast, which operates in accordance with certain constraints associated with the structure of the subject of the sentence (see 7.2). Since these particular constraints do not apparently operate upon variation in subject–verb agreement in standard English, which in turn is affected by a different set of constraints (see Huddleston 1984: 241), we must assume that the surface variants of the verb which occur in the two dialects are embedded in structurally different grammars.

So far, the problem as stated is parallel to the one encountered in Glasgow by Macaulay at the phonological level (se 6.3.1). The difficulty here in handling the (a) variable following Labov's model (which assumes an underlying structural identity) is that the (a) systems in RP and in Scottish English are embedded in structurally different phonologies; as a consequence the range of realizations in Glasgow does not correspond in any simple way to the range in RP, where there is a distinction at the phonemic level between front and back /a/ rather than at the subphonemic level as in Glasgow. But analysing *syntactic* variation in a situation of similar structural mismatch is even more difficult, largely as a natural consequence of the direct relationship between syntax and semantics.

Taking as our example the range of Irish English perfect constructions, we find an absence of semantic isomorphism between any set of Irish English sentences and any semantically related set of standard English sentences which exemplify the range of perfect constructions. For example, 39 to 44 below all have a present-tense marked form of *have* and are quite unremarkable examples of standard English present-perfect sentence types. However, all are quite anomalous even in educated varieties of Irish English, and would be 'translated' as shown below:

39   I've just seen my father = I'm after seeing my father
40   He has finished his course = He has his course finished
41   I've known him since he was a small boy = I know him from he was a wee fella
42   Have you ever been to Bellaghy? = Were you ever in Bellaghy?
43   I've been waiting here for ten minutes = I'm waiting here ten minutes
44   Have you sold your car? = Did you sell your car?

The striking lack of correspondence between the two sets of equivalents is, however, more than a simple difference in surface realization; the non-isomorphism is semantic as well as formal. We find, for example, that Irish English example 44 is not only equivalent to standard English example 44 but is also equivalent to the same standard English surface string. Thus, Irish English does not mark syntactically the semantic distinction expressed by the verb form in standard English between 'Have you sold your car?' and 'Did you sell your car?' However, an action completed in the recent past is expressed in Irish English by a construction of the type exemplified by 39, while standard English does not mark that semantic category (the *hot news* perfect) in the verb form at all (see Huddleston 1984: 143 for a summary of recent work on the semantics of tense and aspect in standard English).

Harris points out that the scope of temporal reference covered by the standard English present-perfect is covered in Irish English by no fewer than five forms, as exemplified above. To make matters worse, two of them, the present and preterite, overlap into other areas of temporal reference which are covered by identical forms in standard English (J. Harris 1984: 313, and cf. 43 and 44 above). Despite these methodological difficulties, Harris was to a limited extent able to analyse this variation quantitatively, collecting tokens from 15 hours of speech by 24 speakers. But his procedure was different in an important way from any we have examined so far; rather than counting the variants of a postulated underlying *syntactic* variable, he examined variation in the surface exponence of four *semantic* categories: *hot news, resultative, extended now* and *indefinite anterior*, exemplified by 39, 40, 43 and 44. These four distinctions are expressed by six different forms in Hiberno-English (see further J. Harris 1984), while standard English uses perfect forms in all cases.

Plainly, the additional methodological problems introduced by Harris's procedure are considerable. He comments:

In the initial stages of analysis the researcher is faced with the task of assigning the appropriate semantic category to each token. The onus on his/her ingenuity is reflected in the wide range of decisions that have to be made about the context in which tokens occur. For the purposes of quantifying phonological variation it is usually sufficient to take note of the immediate segmental or morphological context. However, when it comes to analysing higher-level syntactic variation, the scope of conditioning factors is greatly increased. Account may have to be taken not only of possible syntactic constraints at the level of clause structure, but also of much wider semantic, discourse and ultimately pragmatic considerations. (J. Harris 1984: 316)

The general conclusion is that problems associated with the semantic equivalence issue are compounded in an analysis of variation between standard and non-standard forms. Since standard English and Irish English syntactic forms do not mark the same temporal and aspectual distinctions, we cannot assume that they are embedded in the same underlying grammar. Some of the tense/aspect distinctions of American Black English which have attracted the attention of sociolinguists seem to introduce the same problems of underlying structural non-identity as the Irish English perfect – an example is perfective *done,* ilustrated by 19–21. However, differences between American Black English and standard American English, though acknowledged to be considerable, are usually discussed in syntactic terms rather in terms of an underlying semantic non-equivalence (see for example Labov 1973: 62). This preference is probably a consequence of the general orientation of American sociolinguistics to the theoretical assumptions of transformational-generative grammar (as implicit, for example, in Sankoff 1980b). But differences between dialects in underlying semantic structure are real enough, in the sense that they are sometimes reflected in speaker behaviour by cross-dialectal miscommunications and communicative breakdowns (Labov 1972d: 63; L. Milroy 1984).

7.7 Syntactic Variation: The Semantic and Discourse Contexts

Two different strategies seem to have been adopted by researchers in tackling the problems outlined in 7.5 and 7.6, which are associated with the relationship between syntax and various types of meaning. One is to minimize the significance of possible semantic differences between variants, and the other is to acknowledge and use as a foundation for the analysis the interrelationships betwen syntax, semantics and discourse. Investigators who opt for the first solution may seek out variable syntactic elements where meaning variation does not constitute a serious problem; this is the general approach taken by Cheshire. Weiner and Labov (1983) on the other hand attempt in a complicated chain of reasoning to argue that although there are indeed different stylistic and discourse meanings associated with the agentless passive and active alternants, and in some contexts different truth-conditional meanings, these differences might reasonably be disregarded.

The second type of solution, which acknowledges the association betwen syntax, pragmatics and discourse, is exemplified in John Harris's study of the Irish English tense/aspect system. But Beatriz Lavandera has adopted this approach to syntactic variation in a much more radical form, and argued for it in some detail. Her general approach is exemplified in this section with reference to two papers (Lavandera 1978a; 1982; see also Lavandera 1984). The first is a study of variation in *cocoliche,* the reduced form of Spanish spoken by Italian immigrants to Argentina; the second is a more general discussion of the appropriate way to study syntactic variation, which includes a re-analysis of the alternation between tenses of the subjunctive, the conditional and the indicative. These alternants, which are exemplified by 45 to 48 below, had originally been studied in Buenos Aires Spanish as semantically equivalent syntactic variants in *si* clauses, one of their possible environments (Lavandera 1975). All of them might be roughly translated as 'If I have time, I'll go.'

45 Si *tuviera* tiempo, iría (imperfect subjunctive)
46 Si *tendría* tiempo, iría (conditional)
47 Si *tengo* tiempo, iría (present indicative)
48 Si *tenía* tiempo, iría (imperfect indicative)

A quantitative analysis of these alternants, taken from 30 one-hour interviews of 15 men and 15 women, had revealed a preference for the indicative and conditional forms in lower-status groups and by all speakers in less careful styles. As a consequence, the overall frequency of subjunctive forms was relatively low. However, when she examined her *cocoliche* corpus (50 hours recorded from 50 speakers), Lavandera noted that the frequency of subjunctive forms in all environments was even lower than that observed in the Buenos Aires Spanish corpus; moreover there was independent evidence that this low frequency did not simply reflect a poor command of Spanish by the immigrants. A careful examination of the *cocoliche* corpus revealed not, as one might expect, a higher overall frequency of the *non-subjunctive* alternants, but rather at the *discourse level* an absence of *appropriate contexts* for the subjunctive. Lavandera illustrates this point, using as an example the tendency for *cocoliche* speakers to avoid *indirect speech,* which in certain types of Spanish clause is an obligatory environment for the subjunctive. Spanish speakers alternate between *present* and *imperfect* subjunctive in sentences of the following type:

49   Nos dijo que nos *quedemos/quedáramos* quietos hasta que el *vuelva/ volviera* – 'He told us to stay quiet until he came back'

Cocoliche speakers, however, despite showing an independently established ability to handle the subjunctive 'simply refrain from using indirect discourse, and use direct discourse instead, i.e. quotations preceded by a form of the performative 'to say' (*digo, dice*)' (Lavandera 1978a: 399). This is interpreted as a group specific discourse and stylistic preference, of the kind discussed by Gumperz (1982; see also 8.4.1).

Lavandera makes the point that the standard procedure in quantitative sociolinguistics would have been to start the analysis from *the forms themselves* rather than to examine initially the discourse contexts in which they were used. The procedure then would have been to express the frequency of the imperfect subjunctive in relation to all the contexts where its occurrence was possible. But such a procedure would simply have led to the conclusion that the investigator had failed to elicit environments where the variable could be studied, and would miss the point that speakers were in fact making use of an entirely different range of choices to express stylistic differences. The standard solution to this 'data-collecting problem' would be the one adopted by Lavandera herself in her 1975 study, of structuring interview questions so as to encourage the appearance of linguistic contexts which required the subjunctive (cf. 7.2). But this strategy, however successful, would not reveal the ability of *cocoliche* speakers to converse fluently and spontaneously without recourse to those contexts.

Lavandera's response to these difficulties is to propose an initial examination by the analyst of *discourse function* rather than of surface grammatical form, followed by consideration of the functions which are served by the form – the subjunctive in this case. Such an approach, as is demonstrated by the example of *cocoliche* speakers' avoidance of indirect speech, permits the important insight that the function fulfilled by the subjunctive in Spanish is fulfilled in *cocoliche* by quite other means. The enterprise of attempting to specify exhaustively the range of possible surface variants of a variable is thus argued to be irrelevant to a satisfying and explanatory account of syntactic variation.

In a more explicitly theoretical paper, Lavandera (1982) presents the general argument that syntactic variation can be studied only at a superficial level if the analytic method does not take account of the use which speakers make of variation for stylistic and discourse purposes; frequently they exploit subtle differences in meaning of the kind which (for example) Weiner and Labov deliberately simplify. This point is exemplified with reference to tense and mood variation in Spanish *si* clauses (see 50–52 above); Lavandera points out that although the alternants may be defined as variants of an underlying variable in the sense that they are *truth-conditional* semantic equivalents, and pattern according to external social factors, they differ in *modal* meaning (see Huddleston 1984: 165 for a discussion of these semantic issues). But in her earlier study where she had viewed the alternants as being 'equivalent ways of saying the same thing' she did not attempt to 'account for the interplay between the differences in modal meaning and the social conditioning in the use of these forms' (Lavandera 1982: 90 – her translation). In fact, although frequency of the forms correlated with age, sex and educational differences between speakers, different modal meanings appeared also to be associated with the verb forms a follows: imperfect subjunctive/ [UNREAL]; conditional/[POSSIBLE]; present indicative/[FACTUAL]. This correlation can be demonstrated by the following examples:

50 Si *pudiera* volver el tiempo atrás, me preocuparía más en eso [UNREAL] – 'If I could turn time back I'd worry more about that'
51 Si *tendría* que hacer una cosa como ésa, me gustaría [POSSIBLE] – 'If I had to do something like that, I'd like it'
52 Si él *tiene* un disgusto, no viene y me dice, mirá, me pasó esto y esto, nada, se lo calla [FACTUAL] – 'If he has a problem, he doesn't come and tell me, look here, such and such happened to me, nothing, he doesn't say anything, he keeps it to himself'

An examination of the Buenos Aires data reveals interesting interplays between variation of this kind in modal meaning and variation (associated with various extra-linguistic variables) in overall frequency of particular forms. The variables of age, sex and educational level interact in their influence on speaker choice of variant; for example sex of speaker emerges as influencing choice of variant in the less educated groups, but this difference dissappears in the highly educated groups. The patterns could be interpreted in different ways; one possibility is to argue that the correlation with extra-linguistic variables constitutes evidence that the forms are simply different ways of saying the same thing, that differences in modal meaning which do not affect truth-conditions are merely stylistic and so may be ignored. This is the type of argument proposed by Weiner and Labov (1983).

A second possibility, which Lavandera proposes, is that the analyst should account for, rather than ignore, the interplay between meaning differences and social distribution of variants. Such a position, however, involves accepting that the appropriate units of analysis are not surface forms, but higher-level semantic and discourse elements. The interplay between semantic and social conditioning factors may then be interpreted as reflecting differential preferences by social groups for certain communicative styles which involve different degrees of *assertiveness*. These differences in assertiveness (which, for example, contrast a speaker's stated commitment to the truth of a proposition with a tentative expression of opinion) are reflected in differences in modal meaning.

It is evident that Lavandera's arguments entail a very different conception from Labov's of the theoretical assumptions underlying the study of variation. Like Gumperz, she examines initially the use made by *speakers* of linguistic variation, rather than following Labov in examining, in terms of speaker characteristics, the patterning of variable elements in the *system* (cf. 1.2; 8.4.1). Furthermore, an analysis which attempts to account for the interrelationships between syntax, semantics and discourse involves quite a different relationship between sociolinguistic and syntactic theory than is implied by one which attempts to demonstrate that alternation takes place between semantically equivalent surface forms.

Although many of the studies collected in G. Sankoff (1980a) fall within Labov's standard quantitative paradigm (see 7.4.2), others resemble Lavandera's approach in focusing on the stylistic and discourse preferences of the speaker. Laberge and Sankoff's study of the indefinite pronoun in Montreal French (1980) and G. Sankoff and Brown's study of Tok Pisin (1980) examine the data from both perspectives.

Sankoff and Laberge are interested principally in the alternation between *on* on the one hand, and *tu/vous* on the other in their function as indefinite personal pronouns (cf. 7.4.3). However, since *on* can alternate also with first and third person pronouns, which like their second person counterparts can also have *definite* reference, it is not particularly easy to specify tokens of the alternating class (see Laberge and Sankoff 1980: 272ff for a large number of examples). An extended analysis of the functions of *on* with respect to all these alternating categories is an essential preliminary to the main (quantitative) analysis of syntactic variation.

The *discourse* constraints which favour indefinite reference are complex; the formulation of morals and truisms is one example discussed by the authors (cf. 53), and in this discourse function *on* is overwhelmingly preferred. Also considered are purely surface syntactic constraints, as in 54; it is noted that 'indefinite *tu* or *vous* cannot be used in contexts where there is a definite "you" immediately to the left, for fear of confusion with the latter' (p. 289):

53 Mais je me dis, des enfants c'est des enfants, *on* peut pas les faire penser comme des adultes, *on* peut pas – 'I tell myself, children are children; one can't make them think like adults – one just can't'
54 *Vous* [+def.] me demandez de vous raconter une partie de ma vie là, mais il y a des choses qu'*on* [-def.] peut pas expliquer pourtant – 'You (the interviewer) ask me to tell you part of my life, but there are things that one just can't explain'

The study takes into account constraints of the types exemplified in 53 and

54, assigning probabilistic weightings to characterize differences in their social distribution. The authors observe that analysis of this variable leads to a very broad consideration of the place of the constructions in discourse, of a large number of other constructions serving similar discourse functions and of speaker strategies similar to those considered by Lavandera. The study as a whole is an impressive combination of quantitative and non-quantitative types of reasoning.

Sankoff and Brown's study of relative clauses in Tok Pisin concentrates overwhelmingly on discourse function, syntactic structure being viewed as a 'component of, and derivative from, discourse structure' (Sankoff and Brown 1980: 211). One important issue illuminated by the analysis is the manner in which 'syntactic complexity' in a creole language develops in relation to the expanding discourse needs of its users. Like Lavandera's work, this long and complex paper demonstrates that an analysis sensitive to discourse and meaning illuminates patterns of variation which an analysis of surface syntactic variants cannot reveal. The particle *ia,* which functions as a relativizer, bracketing off relative from main clause, as in 55, is shown to have developed from an earlier deictic function, as in 56:

55   E, yupela lukim meri *ia bipo em istap ia?* – 'Hey, did you see the woman who used to live there?'
56   E! man *ia* toktok wantaim husat? – 'Hey! Who's this guy talking to?'

7.8 Conclusion

The work reviewed in 7.6 and 7.7 reveals a tendency to define the goals and methods of studying syntactic variation rather differently from those defined for the study of phonological variation. The relevance of the Principle of Accountability, the cornerstone of Labov's original quantitative method, is far from clear, and there is radical disagreement amongst investigators on even quite fundamental issues.

The entire field of syntactic analysis in sociolinguistics is characterized by diversity, and there are many important areas where agreement has not yet been reached on appropriate goals and methods. While we find as a consequence a range of possible approaches, there are also a number of theoretical and practical difficulties additional to those encountered in analysing phonological variation (cf. chapter 6). Many of these difficulties are related to the natural characteristics of syntactic systems – for example, their openness relative to phonological systems, and their inter-relationships with semantic and discourse patterns. Yet others are associated with the difficulties of accessing informants' intuitions; this particular difficulty of course surfaces in phonological work in a somewhat different form (see further 8.2.1). In phonological work, however, it is usually possible to obtain the material needed for a substantial and illuminating analysis of variation without being obliged to resort to direct elicitation. But in syntactic work it frequently is not.

8

Style-shifting and Code-switching

8.1 Introductory

This chapter shifts its focus away from variation between different speakers to look more carefully at ways of investigating variation in the language of a single speaker on different occasions. Although individual language behaviour apparently always varies in a patterned rather than a random way, some communities have access to linguistic repertoires which allow them to switch between codes which they (or others) perceive as different languages or different dialects of the same language. Where it does not seem feasible to separate out components of a repertoire in this way (as in monolingual and monodialectal communities) speakers are usually said to shift between 'styles'. For many years now investigators have accepted that although bilingual or bidialectal switching is a more clearly visible process than monolingual style-shifting, the psycho-social dynamics underlying these different kinds of intra-speaker variation are similar.

Because intra-speaker variation has been studied within frameworks associated with a number of different subject areas (particularly, monolingual style-shifting is often analysed quantitatively), it is practical to treat style-shifting and code-switching separately in this chapter. But such a separation has no *theoretical* justification. Speakers from monolingual and bilingual communities express by code-choice and code variation similar social meanings, and because terms like 'language', 'dialect' and 'style' are imprecise (if useful) labels, the superficially different types of intra-speaker variation which they describe frequently shade into each other, and cannot easily be separated. Moreover, speakers' *perceptions* of whether or not they have shifted languages, dialects or styles do not necessarily correspond in any direct way to the linguistic patterns which are revealed by standard methods of analysis. For this reason, evaluative reactions of persons to their own speech or that of others is of interest as a separate but related area of study.

A great many types of context-sensitive linguistic phenomena might be described as 'intra-speaker variation', ranging from the small-scale phonetic variables studied by Labov to large-scale discourse patterns (Stubbs 1983; see 3.2 above); address systems (Ervin-Tripp 1972); politeness strategies (Brown and Levinson 1978), and linguistic routines such as greetings, partings and phatic behaviour generally (Laver 1981). While acknowledging that other approaches are possible, we shall focus in this chapter mainly on two widely used methodological frameworks; these are Labov's quantitative paradigm and the ethnographic approach associated particularly with Dell Hymes (1972; 1974: see also Saville-Troike 1982).

The general purpose of ethnographic analysis is to investigate 'rules of speaking' – that is, the various situational factors which influence code choice. However, its tendency to operate with large taxonomies which are not derived from any clear theoretical framework makes evaluation and replication difficult; as Sherzer (1977) points out, investigators tend to study each reference group in terms peculiar to themselves, or their own society (see Baumann and Sherzer 1974 for examples). One particularly interesting and relatively recent development of the ethnographic tradition is Gumperz's 'interactional sociolinguistics', the name given to a set of methods for studying the ways speakers use linguistic variability to express various kinds of (often culture- or network-specific) social meaning (Gumperz 1982; see further 8.4.1 and 9.2 below).

A further framework to which some reference will be made in this chapter has been developed within social psychology (initially by Wallace Lambert but more recently by Howard Giles and his associates) for investigating patterns of evaluative reaction by listeners to a speaker's choice of code (Giles and Powesland 1975). I shall begin, however, by looking at Labov's model of stylistic variation, commenting also on difficulties encountered by investigators working within this framework.

8.2 The Quantitative Analysis of Stylistic Variation

We saw in 2.7 that Labov approached stylistic variation by placing two types of conversational style (casual and formal) and three types of reading style (elicited by a passage of continuous prose, a word-list, and a minimal pair list) along a unidimensional continuum from most casual to most careful speech. This procedure was motivated by the axiom that 'styles can be arranged along a single dimension, measured by the amount of attention paid to speech' (Labov 1972b: 208). Thus, casual style, or the style nearest to the vernacular, was said to be the product of the smallest amount of conscious self-monitoring, while minimal pair style, produced while speakers were reading pairs of words which were homophonous in the vernacular system, was the product of the maximum degree of self-monitoring. When this dimension of variation is considered with respect to speakers from a range of social classes, we find that *intra-speaker stylistic variation* can be said to reflect *inter-speaker social variation*, with speakers in their more careful styles approximating progressively to the norm of higher-status social groups (cf. tables 5.1 and 5.2). Because the same variables operate simultaneously on both of these dimensions, Labov suggested, in a memorable phrase, that it might be difficult to distinguish 'a casual salesman from a careful pipefitter' (Labov 1972b: 240).

Although he has more recently expressed reservations about the general theoretical validity of this continuum (Labov 1981), it was apparently intended originally to be a theoretically valid construct rather than simply a practical way of organizing stylistically variable data (see Labov 1972b: 99). There are, however, several difficulties of both a theoretical and a practical kind associated with the linear continuum model, which has been very widely applied. One cluster of problems derives from an implicit assumption that speech and reading are comparable types of behaviour which can rationally be located at different points along a single continuum; another is associated with using the variable of *amount of attention paid to speech* as a basis for explaining patterns of stylistic variation. These issues are interrelated in that the contrast between spontaneous speech and reading styles is a simulation, for experimental purposes, of differences in the amount of attention paid to speech which crop up in natural interaction. But since each of them presents a (partially) distinct set of problems, we shall approach them separately.

8.2.1 Conversational styles and reading styles: a continuum?

One particular difficulty which sometimes emerges in implementing Labov's procedure is of a general social or cultural kind, associated with levels of literacy or attitudes to the act of reading aloud. In Belfast, for example, many working-class speakers were illiterate or semiliterate, the latter group feeling comfortable with only three-letter words on the word-list. However, those who were confident in their ability to tackle the word-list often recited it at great speed, showing little sign of carefully monitoring their speech. On the contrary, stereotypical vernacular pronunciations such as [bɛ^{l}g] for the lexical item *bag* often occurred. But many of these same fluent word-list readers tackled the task of reading aloud a passage of continuous prose rather unhappily, in a halting, dysfluent manner. Certainly in these communities, where levels of literacy were relatively low and speakers were unfamiliar with the task of reading aloud, it was not possible to assume without further investigation that reading passage and word-list style simulated the attention factor in the rank-order proposed. In fact since so few speakers were able or willing to tackle the reading passage at all, quantitative comparison of word-list and reading passage style was not possible.

Further difficulties arise from an assumption that speakers will make strenuous attempts in *minimal pair style* to distinguish pairs of items which are homophonous in the vernacular system but differentiated in higher-status accents. It is true that they do so quite often; in Belfast the pairs *chop/chap : bag/beg* which merge or overlap in spontaneous conversation are regularly distinguished in word-list style (like the *god/guard* pair in New York City). Conversely, however, there are classes of phonological items which regularly contrast in conversational styles but not when elicited using controlled experimental techniques such as minimal pair tests. Nor can *judgements* of contrastivity (cf. Labov 1981) be reliably elicited by means of *commutation tests*. When questioned directly, speakers often claim that pairs of items are merged which can in conversational speech be heard as distinct or shown to be so by instrumental analysis. This general pattern of 'apparent merger' was observed in tokens of the MATE/MEAT class in Belfast (see 3.3.1) and in tokens of the *her/hair* pair, which speakers invariably read homophonously as [hør] but consistently distinguished in conversation as [hør]/[hɛ ə r]; indeed, one informant even commented on the mismatch between conversational and reading styles.

The phenomenon of falsely reported mergers is not confined to Belfast. Similar examples are *line/loin* in Essex, *full/fool* in Albuquerque, *hock/hawk* in Central Pennsylvania (Labov, Yaeger and Steiner 1972: 229–54). Trudgill also reports *fear/fair* and *too/toe* in Norwich (Trudgill 1974: 120–9). Although Labov's own work on sound change in progress firmly established that speakers did not always distinguish items presented as minimal pairs more reliably than in spontaneous speech, the impact of these findings has not (as far as I know) been discussed in the context of the stylistic continuum model. Certainly, we cannot automatically accept the assumption that speakers presented with minimal pairs will respond by making strenuous efforts to distinguish them; nor can minimal pair techniques (which involve experimental manipulation of the *speaker*) be assumed to yield reliable information about non-standard phonological *systems* (cf. 1.1).

Romaine (1980) has remarked that investigators who have worked on northern British dialects have found particular difficulty in implementing Labov's procedure of placing speech and reading styles along a single continuum. These difficulties, which are rather complex and of a different kind from any discussed so far in this section, have been noted by Romaine herself in Edinburgh (1978a), by Macaulay (1977) in Glasgow, and L. Milroy (1980) in Belfast. They seem to spring fundamentally from a relationship between the standard and the vernacular which differs from what Labov encountered in New York City. When standard and vernacular codes are widely separated, a radical switch between conversational and reading styles rather than a gradual shift of the kind observed by (for example) both Labov and Trudgill seems to take place. This pattern is demonstrated in table 8.1, which shows patterns of [ð] deletion intervocalically in items such as *mother* and *brother* in Belfast.

Tables 8.1 and 8.2   Frequency scores for two variables in three styles for thirteen Belfast speakers

| | (th) (% score)[a] | | | (a) (index score) | | |
	SS	IS	WLS	SS	IS	WLS
Donald B	56.25	90.00	0.00	3.00	2.66	3.00
George K	88.89	55.56	0.00	4.15	3.40	4.62
Mary T	50.00	7.14	0.00	2.05	1.40	1.00
Elsie D	25.00	33.33	0.00	2.65	1.60	2.31
Millie B	66.67	53.85	0.00	2.80	1.85	2.69
Brenda M	33.33	33.33	0.00	2.80	2.15	2.69
James H	100.00	100.00	0.00	3.30	2.75	2.92
Terence D	94.74	69.23	0.00	2.90	3.35	3.15
Brian B	93.75	75.00	75.00	3.65	2.65	3.00
Stewart M	75.00	66.67	0.00	4.05	2.80	3.00
Alice W	25.00	22.22	0.00	2.55	2.20	2.69
Lena S	20.00	0.00	0.00	2.40	1.92	2.46
Rose L	0.00	40.00	0.00	1.35	1.55	1.50

[a] Figures show percentage of zero variants

SS   = Spontaneous style
IS   = Interview style
WLS = Word-list style

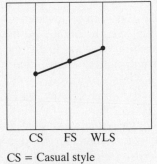

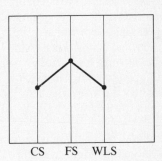

CS = Casual style
FS = Formal style
WLS = Word-list style

Figure 8.1   Patterns of stylistic variation
(adapted from Johnston 1983: 2)

Johnston (1983) has noted in connection with data collected in Edinburgh from 83 adults that irregular patterns of stylistic differentiation sometimes (but not always) emerge, with speakers adjusting their styles in an unexpected direction (see figure 8.1). One of the 'deviant' patterns which he lists emerged in Belfast in the (a) variable (table 8.2). The same pattern is shown diagrammatically in figure 8.1, contrasting with the one predicted by Labov's model (cf.5.1).

The patterns in tables 8.1 and 8.2 are not at all easily accounted for by the notion of a shift, correlating with amount of attention to speech, along a linear continuum towards a single norm; furthermore, since the two patterns are quite different, we need to argue that speaker strategies are much less uniform than this model implies.

The pattern emerging in table 8.1 suggests that many speakers have a near-categorical deletion rule in spontaneous conversation which *never* operates when they read aloud. In unscripted speech, however, this deletion rule operates more variably and gradually, subject to situational constraints of the general type suggested by Labov; speakers vary considerably in amount of deletion, but always tend to delete more frequently in conversation with peers than when they are being explicitly interviewed (i.e. responding to questions). However, as Brian B's behaviour shows, there is nothing to prevent them from using the vernacular form when reading in order to convey some kind of *social* meaning. It has been remarked in a number of domains (see Levinson 1983: 109 for an example) that speakers commonly extend their communicative resources by *violating* norms, and Brian, a particularly strong vernacular speaker with strong local network links, might be expected to do just that.

I would suggest that the striking *uniformity* evident in table 8.1 of (th) scores in word-list style (Brian being the only exception) can most plausibly be acounted for not by the attention factor, but by a low-level rule of the English spelling system which quite consistently uses *th* to correspond with [ð] in intervocalic positions. Although spelling clearly cannot be used generally to account for patterns of stylistic variation, it seems likely that a vernacular speaker who is aiming for a pronunciation appropriate to reading aloud (the one which he consciously views as 'correct') will be guided when possible by clearly rule-governed aspects of the spelling system.

Experimental psycholinguistic research suggests that this kind of grapheme to phoneme mapping is one of the strategies available to speakers in 'assembling' the phonological form of written words (another is what might be described as a lexical 'look up' procedure which generally makes use of semantic knowledge; see Kay 1985 for details and further references). Certainly, direct mapping of grapheme to phoneme helps in the case of (th) to give a speaker some idea of the higher-prestige pronunciation which speakers seem to consider appropriate for reading. Such an explanation accounts for the data in table 8.1 better than one which suggests that speakers approximate more closely to a prestige norm when they read because they are monitoring their speech more closely than in conversation; we simply cannot assume that setting up a speech/reading continuum to sample intra-speaker variation is an appropriate way of simulating 'attention to speech'. Furthermore, the notion of greater attention to the prestige pronunciation of a *single underlying norm* is unsatisfactory in that it does not account for the obvious fact that all but one of the speakers, whose scores in unscripted styles vary considerably, *consistently* pronounce [ð] when they read. The radical switch shown in table 8.1 suggests some kind of *dual* norm which has little to do with paying more attention to speech during reading.

Turning now to the data in table 8.2, we find that this type of argument cannot be advanced to account for the equally 'deviant' (a) pattern. Spelling is in general a poor guide to the prestige pronunciation of vowels, which at all social levels are subject to massive dialectal variation; speakers can know the prestige pronunciation of vowels only if they have some knowledge of the linguistic norms of the wider community. Labov of course sees this kind of shared knowledge of linguistic norms as the essential defining characteristic of the speech community (1966: 125), and the interrelationship of the social and stylistic dimensions of variation as evidence of the existence of such a speech community. But in divergent dialect communities like Belfast it is difficult to isolate one and only one high-prestige variety (cf. 6.3.1), and for this reason it is plausible to suggest that a vernacular speaker in such a community will not necessarily find it easy to identify a 'correct' variant appropriate for reading words in isolation. To support this view there is direct evidence on the Belfast tapes in the form of disputes between speakers about 'correct' pronunciations, and more general supporting evidence may be adduced from the widespread phenomenon of *hypercorrection* (J. Wells 1982: 113; see also 3.3.1). Hypercorrection amounts to a 'misfire' attempt at a prestige pronunciation which speakers have reconstructed by means of a linguistic schema fairly obviously derived by over-generalized analogical reasoning.

One strategy which a reader might adopt to deal with difficulty in identifying the 'correct' form is to resort to the spelling system (see above). But where this is unhelpful, as in the case of (a), s/he might resort to the vernacular norms with which s/he is familar. The shift in Interview Style relative to Spontaneous Speech which is evident in table 8.2 may then be interpreted not as an intermediate point on a continuum with a single prestige form at its further point, but as a modification of vernacular norms in response to the situational constraints to which conversation is subject. This modification takes place in accordance with the range-reduction principles discussed in 6.4.

Several more general conclusions might be drawn from the two Belfast examples shown in tables 8.1 and 8.2. First, it cannot always be assumed that people use a specially 'correct' kind of speech for reading. The phonological patterns of word-lists in relation to conversational styles will vary in a complicated way which cannot easily be explained, although an attempt has been made in this subsection to outline the complexities involved. The distance between vernacular and prestige forms seems to affect these patterns, and it is likely that a continuum model of the kind proposed by Labov is more reliably usable as a way of organizing variable data where speakers have a clear knowledge of wider community norms. Speakers who are embedded in tightknit networks such as those in working-class Belfast may not always have that knowledge.

Second, it is likely that speakers who place a high value on reading skills will respond differently from those who do not (but presumably place a high value on *conversational* skills: see L. Milroy 1980: 100). At the moment we just do not know enough to construct a satisfactory theory of socio-stylistic variation which embraces both speech and writing. Without taking into account the results of recent work on language processing, it is doubtful whether we can reasonably attempt it.

Third, it is clear from experimental work in that field that recognizing and producing words in conversation is a very different activity from recognizing and reading aloud written words (Garnham 1985; M. Harris and Coltheart 1986; Kay 1985). Furthermore, psycholinguists generally assume (reasonably, I think) that reading a passage of connected text involves rather different kinds of processing from reading isolated words on a word-list; additional factors such as *memory* and the influence of *context* are implicated in the former activity. At the moment we are not in a position to synthesize sociolinguistic and psycholinguistic approaches to speech production. But since the language processing involved in reading is complex and becoming increasingly well researched, it seems prudent for sociolinguists, until there is good reason to proceed otherwise, to analyse conversational and reading styles as separate areas of behaviour.

8.2.2 *Attention paid to speech: an alternative interpretation of the data*

Labov's analysis of regular stylistic variation in terms of the amount of attention paid to speech was intended to account for two interrelated patterns of variation. First, the speakers whom he studied in New York City used quantitatively more vernacular variants the further they moved to the left along a line upon which the styles were arranged in the order of Casual Style, Formal Style, Reading Passage Style, Word-List Style, Minimal Pair Style. Second, the distribution of most variables was influenced by an interaction effect between the *stylistic* and *social* dimensions, and it was for this reason that Labov distinguished between *markers*, which vary on both dimensions, and *indicators,* which vary on the social or regional dimension only (Labov 1972b: 179). Since speakers then seemed to be approximating in their careful styles to the speech of higher-status social groups, a consciousness of social stratification and its linguistic reflexes could be said to supply the motivation for them to pay more attention to speech in certain kinds of social context. We have already noted that from the point of view of sociological theory, a sociostylistic theory like this one which emphasizes the norms and values *shared* by speakers from different strata is highly controversial (see 5.3.2). It is, however, controversial for other reasons also, and Bell (1984b) has expounded in detail an alternative way of interpreting patterns of stylistic variation.

Bell's fundamental point is that 'at all levels of language variability, people are responding primarily to other people. Speakers are designing their style for their audience' (p.197). This view of *audience design* rather than *attention to speech* as the critical variable in accounting for stylistic variation can be justified on several counts. First, as the wording of Bell's comment suggests, the quantitative study of stylistic variation is brought into line with widely accepted approaches to bilingual code-switching (see further 8.4), where the identity of the addressee has generally been recognized as critically important. This gain in generality allows style-shifting and code-switching to be considered along with other kinds of interactive behaviour (such as politeness routines) which are best explained in terms of attention to the addressee. The comment might also be made that research from quite different traditions has also emphasized the care with which speakers design their speech styles in response to the needs of addressees; for example, Snow (1986: 80) points out that the care-takers of young children systematically grade the syntactic and phonological form and the semantic content of their speech in such a way as to communicate most efficiently and obtain a maximally compliant response from addressees.

Second, the capacity of speakers to use vernacular styles extremely carefully and self-consciously is more plausibly accounted for within a framework of audience design. Wolfson (1982) has criticized the attention to speech variable for its deficiency in this respect, and certainly many fieldworkers have had the experience of meeting 'experts' in the dialect who are routinely called upon to give special displays for outsiders; it is also intuitively obvious that an adequate theory of style needs to account for events such as vernacular poetry reading.

Third, our knowledge of the assiduity with which peer groups induce their members to maintain vernacular norms (see L. Milroy 1980: 28 for an example) does not square with a correlation between lack of attention and high levels of vernacular speech, but can be accommodated more readily within an audience design framework.

A fourth point is that there is very little *experimental* justification for the view that attention to speech is the critical factor in stylistic variation (cf. the comments in 8.2.1 on recent psycholinguistic research on reading). Noting that the main supporting empirical evidence cited is an experiment by the psychologist George Mahl (see Labov 1972b: 98 for details), Bell demonstrates that the results of Mahl's experiment can be interpreted at least equally plausibly as demonstrating the effect of the speaker's awareness of his or her addressee (Bell 1984b: 149).

Dressler and Wodak (1982) have discussed more recent experimental evidence which suggests that any relationship between attention and level of formality is a complicated and indirect one which cannot account satisfactorily for a large residue of observable (phonological) stylistic variation. Taking as an example speakers who are bidialectal in Viennese dialect and Standard Austrian German, they point out that one particular type of phonological variable which is affected by natural phonological processes in rapid speech might be analysed in terms of attention to speech (see also 6.6). They give as an example the alternation in intervocalic positions between [b] and [ß] in Austrian Standard German (as in *geben* 'give'). However, they note the existence of another type of stylistic variable which is not at all responsive to the attention factor, frequently exemplified by alternations between realizations characteristic of Standard Austrian German and of the local dialect (such as [œ]/[ø] alternating with [e:]/[e]/ as in *schön* 'beautiful'). It is argued that these switches represent realizations of two different underlying forms which cannot be accounted for in terms of attention to speech or viewed as coinciding with natural phonological processes. They do, however, respond to changes of various kinds in the *situational* context in much the same way as the variables which *can* be analysed in terms of attention to speech. Dressler and Wodak make the more general point that Labov's approach implicitly presents stylistic variation as relatively simple and uniform in character, whereas in reality it is a 'mixed bag of various factors' (p.351).

They go on to argue that a number of empirical findings can be accounted for in terms of attention to the *addressee* but not in terms of attention to *speech*. They cite a pilot study carried out by Leodolter and Stark (1972) of variation in the speech of a young upper-class Viennese man. Three different situations were compared; breakfast with wife and friends; tea with parents and wife and a birthday dinner with friends. The authors note the following differences in situation: the everyday routine type of event versus the formal invitation; the involvement of different participants; and variation in the interrelationships of the participants on the dimensions of intimacy, dominance and authority. These latter *participant-oriented* categories appeared to be more relevant to the young man's patterns of switching to Viennese dialect (two phonological variables were studied) than the formality of the situation. In this case variation is accounted for more satisfactorily by Bell's theory of audience design than by the attention variable, which is associated with formality.

Bell cites two sets of results which, rather more obviously and strikingly than Dressler and Wodak's data, can be best accounted for within his framework. The first is his own investigation in New Zealand into variation in amount of intervocalic /t/ voicing in the speech of four newscasters broadcasting from two different stations, A and B; A is of higher status than B, and /t/ voicing shows patterns of social and stylistic stratification in New Zealand. Since a considerable amount of attention is neccessarily paid to speech by *all* newscasters, it is hardly plausible to suggest that the exact amount depends on the station from which the news is being broadcast. However, as figure 8.2 shows, the style adopted by each of the four strikingly corresponds with the language patterns of the target audience, for whom they might be said to be designing a speech style (Bell 1984b: 171).

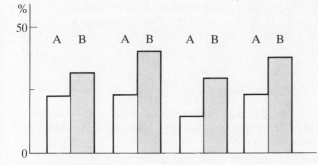

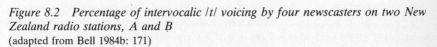

Figure 8.2   Percentage of intervocalic /t/ voicing by four newscasters on two New Zealand radio stations, A and B
(adapted from Bell 1984b: 171)

The second piece of evidence cited by Bell is Trudgill's finding from his analysis of patterns of /t/ glottalisation in his own interviewer speech, that variation in his own production correlated with his informants' levels of /t/ glottalization (1986b: 8). Again, this is difficult to explain in terms of the attention factor. But as Bell points out, these findings (and the audience design view of stylistic differentiation generally) are congruent with the accommodation theory of social psychology (Giles 1984; Thakerar et al 1982), which attempts a genuinely *explanatory* account of stylistic variation in terms of speaker response to the addressee.

There is further recent quantitative work which discusses stylistic differentiation in terms of response to different addressees, either ignoring or rejecting the attention variable. One example is the work of Coupland (1980; 1984), who measures against the speech of addressee clients variation in the speech of an assistant in a the travel agency. He finds that the shifts in the assistant's speech are parallel to differences between the clients, who are grouped according to occupation. Edwards's (1986) study of variation in the level of use of *patois* by British black adolescents finds considerable differences according to whether the addressee is black or white; in fact this is one of the situational variables which is systematically manipulated. Reid (1978) finds systematic differences in the speech of Edinburgh schoolboys, depending on whether they are talking to him or to their friends in the playground.

The general point might be made that the results of previous work examining stylistic variation in various languages, which have been interpreted implicitly or explicitly in terms of the attention variable, can equally well be interpreted in terms of audience design. Certainly variation in the Belfast variables (a) and (th) reported in 8.2.1 can be accounted for in this way; Spontaneous Speech scores are generally derived from utterances addressed to friends and intimates, while Interview Style is by definition produced in response to interview questions put by an outsider. Similar findings by Douglas-Cowie (1978) in Co. Derry, Northern Ireland; Thelander (1982) in Northern Sweden; Russell (1982) in Mombasa (analysing Swahili) may be cited.

8.2.3 Topic, setting and audience design

It has frequently been noted that various *situational* factors are associated with stylistic choice; large descriptive taxonomies which do not attempt an explanatory account may be found in D. Hymes (1974) and Brown and Fraser (1979). Of these, *participant, topic* and *setting* have generally been agreed to be critical, often under certain limited conditions, in triggering style-shifting. Examples of work where their effect is discussed in detail are Coupland (1984), Douglas-Cowie (1978) and Blom and Gumperz (1972). As Bell points out, the relationship between *topic* and style is exploited in sociolinguistic interviews by researchers who are seeking stylistically contrasting data; Trudgill (1974) subdivided his data according to topic, and Labov's danger of death question introduced a topic which for him at least reliably produced a high frequency of vernacular variants.

It might be objected that a theory of audience design does not account for all of these situationally triggered style-shifts, and that Labov's explanation of an attention lapse under emotional stress accounts at least for the danger of death data. But Bell suggests that the variables of topic and setting are in fact subservient to the addressee variable, in the sense that particular topics and settings are associated with specific types of addressee – let us say intimate as opposed to socially distant. Thus, a setting such as a workplace is often (but not always) associated with a more socially distant kind of addressee than a domestic setting, the danger of death question mentions a topic associated with an intimate addressee and so on. We might also speculate that in New York City emotional stress induced by the question results in *failure* to attend to the addressee; in Belfast on the other hand no style-shift is triggered because the question is of a type routinely asked by socially distant interlocutors such as journalists (cf. 3.1). Such a framework seems also to account for *metaphorical* shifting (Gumperz 1982: 61) where for example high-status speakers use vernacular forms associated with a different type of speaker to convey the flavour of an associated context.

An explanation based on audience design certainly seems capable of accounting for more than a simple stylistic shift towards norms appropriate to the addressee. Perhaps most importantly of all, it helps to explain why the interpersonal and intrapersonal dimensions of variation interact. Particular classes of speaker are associated with particular contexts and, as we have seen, a shift towards the standard in more 'formal' contexts is a very general finding of much quantitative work. But it is important to note that in different types of culture, different patterns of behaviour in face-to-face interaction may mean that the social and stylistic dimensions are not related in the same way. Unusual patterns are reported in Iran (Jahangiri and Hudson 1982), and in Scotland and other divergent dialect communities (Johnston 1983); Thelander (1982) reports a rather more complex set of configurations in northern Sweden. We still have some way to go in accounting for these patterns.

In conclusion, I should emphasize that the criticisms of Labov's original method reviewed in this section are not criticisms of the basic quantitative techniques, which have allowed great advances. Their use permits a comparison between the language behaviour of one individual on different occasions, or of different individuals on a single occasion, or an examination of the interrelationships between interpersonal and intrapersonal variation. Critics of Labovian theories of stylistic variation have used quantitative methods with great effect (but see Dressler and Wodak 1982 and Thelander 1982 for discussions of *qualitative* approaches); most objections have focused on the descriptive and theoretical framework within which Labov places his variable data.

I have relied heavily in this section on arguments developed by Bell, and to a lesser extent the findings of Dressler and Wodak, whose paper contains a useful discussion of the various psycho-social variables which mediate betwen linguistic choice and context of utterance. Although this issue will not be further explored here, it is worth commenting that to date the best attempt at an *explanatory* account of stylistic variation is probably social psychology's accommodation theory, of which Bell provides a critique. It seems clear that we need to add the broader insights of psychological theory to the careful analytic work of sociolinguistics if we are to understand style-shifting.

8.3 Code-switching and Code-mixing

8.3.1 Introductory

The point was made in 8.1 that similar (psycho-) social motives seemed to underlie language switching in bidialectal or bilingual communities, and style-shifting in monolingual communities. Although many researchers who have worked in bilingual and bidialectal communities are happy to use the insights derived from quantitative analysis, there is a strong tradition of obtaining naturally occurring variable data by ethnographic methods of observation (see 3.5) and of examining non-quantitatively the effects of various components of context. More recently, researchers have been concerned with discourse which is characterized by a mixture of codes *within* a single conversation, rather than discrete code choice which can be linked in any straightforward way to broad situational categories such as participant, setting or topic.

Attempts have been made to explain the motives underlying code-switching by examining the use made by speakers for rhetorical purposes of available linguistic resources (Lavandera 1978a; Gumperz 1982). There has also been a good deal of interest in specifying the linguistic (as opposed to situational) constraints on patterns of code-mixing, often with a view to contributing to current theoretical work on language universals (Poplack 1980b; Di Sciullo, Muysken and Singh 1986; Berk-Seligson 1986); some progress has been made towards formalizing these constraints (D. Sankoff and Poplack 1981). Although there is likely to be much in these approaches which illuminates the dynamics of monolingual style-switching, they have been developed mainly in bilingual communities.

In this section we shall look first at methods of obtaining variable data, and then at ways of presenting and interpreting results, taking into account the different theoretical interests which motivate investigators. More general accounts of research in this area may be found in Fasold (1984), Wardhaugh (1986) and Gumperz (1982).

8.3.2. Methods of data collection

Problems associated with the observer's paradox seem to be greatly increased in bilingual communities, fundamentally because the act of linguistic choice is very much more visible. This is not to say that speakers are always aware of code-switching behaviour; on the contrary, there is plenty of evidence to indicate that they are not (see Verma 1976 for a striking example). Rather more subtly, they have a *consciousness* of two or more named components in their repertoires which may be either structurally almost indistinguishable (like Panjabi and Urdu) or quite different typologically (like Irish and English). But each code is associated with different sets of social values (often particularly strongly associated with ethnicity – see 5.5) and so is appropriate for use with different interlocutors. Strong and explicit views of the appropriateness of using a given language with a particular type of conversational participant are commonly expressed; for example, in the West of Ireland, Irish/English bilinguals will switch to English not only in addressing an English-speaking monolingual, but in the presence of such a person who in Bell's terms is an *auditor* – that is, a person ratified as a participant in the interaction (Bell 1984b: 172). For example, two men amongst a group of bilingual customers who had been speaking to each other in Irish in a grocer's shop in Co. Donegal immediately switched to English and apologized when they noticed a monolingual auditor (myself). Despite my request that they continue their conversation in Irish, they apparently considered it impolite to do so. Similar incidents have been reported by Dorian in East Sutherland (1981: 79) and Gal in Oberwart (1979: 24), amongst bilingual speakers of Gaelic/English and Hungarian/German respectively. This kind of switching behaviour obviously creates difficulties for the fieldworker in addition to the more general ones outlined in chapter 3.

Examples of studies which have used very long-term participant observation methods are those of Blom and Gumperz in Hemnesberget and Gal in Oberwart. Observations are usually supplemented by some kind of elicitation or direct questioning on patterns of language use. The advantages of the participant observation method have already been assessed in some detail (see 4.3.2); its principal *disadvantage* is of course the length of time and the amount of energy and commitment necessary to carry out a long-term study. Furthermore, directly comparable and specific information cannot usually be gathered from different speakers and different communities.

The enhanced consciousness which bilinguals have of competence in two separate codes makes it feasible for researchers to ask speakers to *report* actual behaviour, in addition to observing it themselves. The choice then seems to be between questionnaires which attempt to discover situational factors controlling language choice, and the *language diary,* which is a record of a speaker's choices over a given period. Before looking at each in turn, we need to note a number of difficulties associated with both types of self-report method.

As Labov has always emphasized, speakers do not always report accurately on their own language behaviour. There are several reasons for this. First, reports are usually mediated through stereotypical views of language which reflect stereotypical attitudes to groups, including the speaker's own group (see Giles and Powesland 1975 for details). The expected pattern of response is that where a language or variety has high prestige speakers will often claim to use it, and where it is of low prestige they will deny knowledge of it. Thus, young men in Attica and Biotia deny their knowledge of Aranvitika because they want to be viewed as Greek-speaking (Trudgill 1983a: 140). Similarly, Le Page and Tabouret-Keller (1985) report that London Jamaican speakers deny any knowledge of creole, because they want to be considered English-speakers.

Mixed codes are particularly stigmatized, probably as a consequence of underlying ideologies of linguistic 'purity' (Milroy and Milroy 1985b; see also 1.3.2 and the comments of the Panjabi/English bilingual quoted below). 'Tex-Mex' is a derogatory term for the variety used by Spanish/English bilinguals in California. Similar terms are 'tuṭi fuṭi' (Panjabi and English); 'Joual' (Canadian French and English) and 'verbal salad' (Yoruba and English; reported by Amuda 1986). The nature of these language-mediated stereotypes can be investigated independently of patterns of language switching and mixing, by means of techniques such as semantic differential scales which ask judges to rate speakers of one or another language (or a mixture) on various types of ability or personal quality such as kindness, honesty or competence (Giles and Powesland 1975; Chana and Romaine 1984; Amuda 1986). Amuda has discussed a striking instance where such stereotypical perceptions of language use are particularly at variance with actual behaviour; amongst a group of educated speakers in Nigeria, the use of a mixed Yoruba/English code ('Switch') has in a number of communicative contexts increasingly become the norm. Yet, relative to both Yoruba and English it is consistently downgraded; when questioned directly, informants express the opinion that speakers should stop using 'Switch' (Amuda 1986: 142). The following example of a mixed Panjabi/English code illustrates vividly the same kind of mismatch between attitudes and behaviour:

> I mean. . .I'm guilty in that sense ke zIada esī English i bolde ɛ̃ fer ode nal edā honda ke to hadi jeṛi zoban ɛ, na? odec hər Ik sentence Ic je do tIn English de word honde ɛ . . . but I think that's wrong, I mean, mɛ̃ khod canā ke mɛ̃, na, jedo Panjabi bolda ɛ, pure Panjabi bolā esī mix kərde rɛne a, I mean, unconsciously, subconsciously, kəri jane ɛ, you know, pər I wish you know ke mɛ̃ pure Panjabi bol səkā

Translation:

> I mean. . .I'm guilty as well in the sense that we speak English more and then what happens is that when you speak your own language you get two or three English words in each sentence . . . but I think that's wrong, I mean, I myself would like to speak *pure* Panjab: Whenever I speak Panjabi. We keep mixing [Panjabi and English] I mean unconsciously, subconsciously, we keep doing it, you know, but I wish, you know, that I could speak *pure* Panjabi. (Chana and Romaine 1984: 450)

A further difficulty associated with any self-report method of data collection, quite distinct from the effect of stereotyping, is that people generally do not have a clear awareness of which aspects of their language use are of interest to linguists. Nor do they usually have access to a sufficiently precise vocabulary for reporting them. As Romaine has noted (1983), ethnic minorities may even lack a name for their language; in Britain, Panjabi-speakers have reported friends and family as using non-existent languages like 'African', 'Pakistani' and 'Indian'. Responses to direct questioning about specific details are frequently in terms of some stereotypical form which has risen to the surface of consciousness. Furthermore, bilinguals are not usually able to remember which language was used in any particular exchange; it has been suggested that asking them to report on incidence of switching is no more effective than asking a monolingual to report on incidence of future tenses (Gumperz 1982: 62). As a consequence of these difficulties of direct access to the speaker's knowledge of language use, much self-report by bilinguals is contradicted by observation of actual behaviour.

8.3.3 Questionnaire studies

A large number of questionnaire studies are reviewed by Fasold (1984), examples being Fishman, Cooper and Ma (1971), Barcelona (1977), Whitely (1974) and Parasher (1980). The main advantage of any kind of questionnaire study is of course that it is cheap and relatively quick to administer (cf. 1.2.2). Comparable and specific information about large-scale patterns of language choice can be obtained relatively quickly from very large numbers of speakers.

Recently, Amuda (1986) used questionnaires extensively to investigate patterns of Yoruba/English code-switching and code-mixing amongst a group of Nigerian bilinguals. While he was aware of the weakness of the method, he found for various reasons that it was for his purpose the most practical one and attempted to offset some of the disadvantages. For example, the accuracy of reported patterns was checked by observation of speakers in a number of speech situations; possible difficulties in labelling languages were dealt with by providing respondents with a structured set of options.

8.3.4 Language diaries

In Britain Romaine (1983) used a diary method as a supplement to participant observation methods for obtaining self-report data from Panjabi/English-speaking adolescents. More extensive and sophisticated use of the technique characterizes Gibbons's (1983) study of patterns of code-switching and code-mixing amongst Cantonese/English bilinguals in

Notes for filling up the language diary

Please note down each time you speak, even if it is only to ask for a bus ticket.

Time   Please indicate the hour, and length of the conversation, e.g. 12.45–1.05 p.m. If you can't remember, just indicate roughly how long – e.g. 10 mins.

Situation   Give the place and circumstance, e.g. Canteen – lunch
Knowles Room 5.40 – seminar
Home – playing mah-jhong

Style   The way you were talking, e.g. friendly, angry criticism, amusing chat, serious discussion.

Subject   What you talked about, e.g. politics, your lectures, academic work, poverty, Mary's morals, drugs, etc.

Principal speakers   Role – e.g. tutor, mother, stranger, fellow student, best friend, etc.
Education – please use the following codes:–

    1 primary   2C secondary Chinese only
    2E secondary English only   3 tertiary (Polytechnic, University, etc.)

Sex – M or F

Age – approximately, e.g. 35–40

Background – Chinese = C, or Western = W, Overseas Chinese = OC

Language   Please use the following codes:– 1 Cantonese   3 English
    2 Cantonese with English words   4 English with Cantonese words

Specify any other language, or mixture of languages, and give it a code number if you wish.

Figure 8.3 Language diary instructions
(adapted from Gibbons 1983: 55–6)

Table 8.3 Language diary: data obtained (see figure 8.3 above)

| Time | Situation | | | | Principal speakers | | | | | Language |
	Place	Circumstance	Style	Subject	Role	Education	Sex	Age	Background	(and comments)
5.00–5.15 p.m.	bus	way to City Hall	friendly	Eng. Drama & misc. chat	fellow student	3	M	20	C	1
5.15–5.30 p.m.	central district	way to City Hall	friendly	Eng. Dramatist: Osborne	fellow student	3	M	20	C	1
5.30–6.00 p.m.	City Hall Library	borrowing books	friendly	books	fellow student	3	M	20	C	1
6.10–6.17 p.m.	ferry	on the way home	friendly	our friends	friend	2E	M	23–25	C	1
6.40–7.00 p.m.	home	reading newspaper	amusing chat	news & TV prog.	aunt	–	F	63	C	Hakka
7.00–7.30 p.m.	home	dinner	amusing chat	news; TV prog.; work; family chat	aunt, sisters, nephews & nieces	–to 3	M&F	4–63	C	Hakka (with aunt & sisters)
8.30–8.37 p.m.	home	helping nephew to do his homework	discussion	homework	nephew	2E	M	13	C	1
9.40 p.m.	home	telling me to answer the phone	friendly	to answer the phone	aunt	–	F	63	C	Hakka

the University of Hong Kong. Over a 24 hour period 27 informants recorded code choices along with details of a range of factors which they considered might have led to these choices. An example of the form the instructions to the informants took, together with the type of response obtained, is shown in figure 8.3 and table 8.3 (after Gibbons 1983: 55–6).

Gibbons discusses the advantages and disadvantages of the technique in some detail. The general problem of lack of linguistic awareness (cf. 8.1 above) was overcome by laying out the type of information required in columns and specifying a number of well-defined factors likely to influence code choice. He attempted to ensure a reasonable level of accuracy by requiring informants to complete the diaries as soon after the event as possible, and checked accuracy more systematically by asking a small sample of three informants to tape-record all their verbal interactions. These recordings were then checked against the diary data, the three checked diaries compared with the remaining 24 with a view to assessing their probable level of accuracy and detecting systematic biases.

One advantage of the technique is that it by-passes problems associated with observation, since the observer is a genuine participant; it is unlikely in any case that Gibbons, an Englishman, could have carried out a successful participant observation study of the language behaviour of Hong Kong Chinese students. The major disadvantage is the high level of sophistication and effort needed to complete the diaries successfully, a problem which prevented Amuda from using the technique in Nigeria. We may conclude, as Gibbons does, that language diaries are capable of providing a great deal of useful and usable information. Problems associated with accuracy, comparability and lack of linguistic awareness, which Romaine encountered, can be dealt with fairly successfully by a more structured approach. Gibbons's work also illustrates the general principle (cf. 4.2) of using more than one investigative method in order to check possible biases. But since a high level of participant motivation is essential, it may not always be easy, particularly if financial resources are limited, to obtain co-operation from a sufficiently large number of informants.

8.4 Analysis and Interpretation of Variable Data

8.4.1 Observational data

People study code-switching for a number of different purposes. For example Gal (1978; 1979) is interested principally in patterns of language shift; Gumperz (1982) in the rhetorical and general communicative function of code-switching, and Poplack (1980b; 1981) in linguistic constraints on code-mixing. Where recordings are obtained using some kind of participant observation technique, the analytic approach is usually *post hoc* and interpretative – that is, the data are scrutinized for regularities that might give insight into the particular aspects of code-switching in which the investigator is interested. Where appropriate, this is done with benefit of insights from earlier work sometimes supplemented by responses to questionnaires.

Table 8.4 Implicational scale for language choice by speakers in Oberwart

Speaker's age	Interlocutor											
	1	2	3	4	5	6	7	8	9	10	11	12
14	H	GH		G	G	G	G			G		G
15	H	GH		G	G	G	G			G		G
25	H	GH	GH	GH	G	G	G	G	G	G		G
27	H	H		GH	G	G	G			G		G
17	H	H		H	GH	G	G			G		G
13	H	H		GH	GH	GH	GH			G		G
43	H	H		GH	GH		G	GH	GH	G		G
39	H	H		H	GH	GH	G	G	G	G		G
23	H	H		H	GH	H	G		GH	G		G
40	H	H		H	GH		GH	G	G	G		G
50	H	H		H	H	GH	GH	GH	G	G	G	G
52	H	H	H	GH	H		H	GH	G	G	G	G
60	H	H	H	H	H	H	H	GH	GH	G	G	H
40	H	H	H	H	H	H	H	GH	GH	GH		G
35	H	H		H	H	H	H	H	GH	H		G
61	H	H		H	H	H	H	H	GH	H		G
50	H	H	H	H	H	H	H	H	H	H		G
66	H	H		H	H	H	H	H	H	H	GH	G
60	H	H		H	H	H	H	H	H	H	GH	G
53	H	H		H	H	H	H	H	GH	H	GH	G
71	H	H		H	H	H	H	H	H	H	GH	G
54	H	H	H	H	H	H	H	H	H	H		G
69	H	H		H	H	H	H	H	H	H	GH	G
63	H	H		H	H	H	H	H	H	H	GH	H
59	H	H	H	H	H	H	H	H	H	H		H
60	H	H	H	H	H	H	H	H	H	H		H
64	H	H		H	H	H	H	H	H	H	H	H
71	H	H		H	H	H	H	H	H	H	H	H

Interlocutors: 1 = God; 2 = grandparents and their generation; 3 = black market clients; 4 = parents and their generations; 5 = age-mate pals, neighbours; 6 = brothers and sisters; 7 = salespeople; 8 = spouse; 9 = children and that generation; 10 = government. Languages: G = German; H = Hungarian.

Source: adapted from Gal (1979: 121)

Thus for example, following the general patterns suggested by D. Hymes (1974) and Blom and Gumperz (1972), Gal looked initially for the relevance of the situational variables of participant, setting and topic to code-switching. Concluding that *participant* was the critical variable to which the others were subservient (cf. 8.2.3), she was able to order her data implicationally (table 8.4). Such a scale shows that in Oberwart, some addressees are much more likely than others to be spoken to in German. Rank-ordering of informants according to age reveals further details of the manner in which the shift from Hungarian to German is taking place in an implicationally ordered set of conversational contexts. Gal's interpretation of the data enables her to formulate a coherent theory of the mechanism of *language shift* which integrates well with Labov's theory of the mechanism of *linguistic change*. As well as examining patterns of code-switching in terms of the speaker variable of age, she is able to use statistical techniques to compare the effects of the speaker variables of *sex, network* and *status*. (see further chapter 5).

We shall look in this section at two other reasons for studying code-switching, both of which involve an interpretative type of analysis similar to Gal's. John Gumperz has developed methods for studying the communicative functions of code-switching as part of a larger field of study which he describes as *interactional sociolinguistics*. Shana Poplack on the other hand is primarily interested in formulating (ultimately universal) *linguistic* constraints on patterns of code-switching. Both investigators focus on texts where the switch takes place within a single conversation or even within a single utterance; but despite using similar primary data, Poplack and Gumperz differ radically in their underlying theoretical orientation; following the general approach characteristic of most branches of linguistics, Poplack takes the *language* as a starting point, whereas Gumperz follows the ethnographic tradition of beginning with the *speaker* (see further 1.1).

Gumperz has discussed his interactional sociolinguistics in terms of a more general account of the relationship between data and theory, arguing for the development of 'a sociolinguistic theory which accounts for communicative functions of linguistic variability and for its relations to speakers' goals without reference to untestable functionalist assumptions about conformity or nonconformance to closed systems of norms' (gumperz 1982: 29). Thus, his focus is on the speaker's use of linguistic resources, rather than on patterns in a postulated abstract linguistic system which are then related to patterns in an equally abstract social system. This focus constitutes an attempt to escape from the indirect (and often problematic) relationship between theory and data which was discussed in 1.1; a comparison between the approaches of Gumperz and Labov in these terms reveals clearly the very abstract nature of Labov's models of sociolinguistic structure, despite their empirical basis. Gumperz begins not by identifying variable elements in a linguistic system, but by looking directly at interactions between speakers. Using a *post hoc* interpretative method (sometimes asking the participants themselves for interpretations), he examines the use to which they put the various available linguistic resources, and the inference which their conversational partners are able to draw from these 'discourse strategies'; conversational code-switching is one such strategy. This orientation towards speakers rather than linguistic forms is very different from that of most linguists, although as we have seen Lavandera has argued that it has a superior capacity to account for patterns of *syntactic* variation (Lavandera 1982; 1984: see also 7.7).

Gumperz gives numerous examples of the insights into conversational interaction provided by his methods. In the first of the two cited below, communication appears to be successful in that the addressee draws the intended inferences from a particular code-switching routine; in the other something goes wrong. The first involves a switch from English to Spanish in the conversation of two chicano professionals which serves to reiterate and emphasize a portion of the utterance; the second, an initial choice of American Black English by a householder who opened the door to a black interviewer who had made an appointment to interview the householder's wife:

1   The three old one spoke nothing but Spanish, nothing but Spanish. *No hablaban ingles* (they did not speak English).

[later in the same conversation]

A: I was . . . I got to thinking *vacilando el punto* (mulling over that point) you know?

2   Husband: So y're gonna check out ma ol lady, hah?
    Interviewer: Ah, no. I only came to get some information. They called from the office.

(Husband, dropping his smile, disappears without a word and calls his wife.)

(Gumperz 1982: 133)

Gumperz explains the linguistic source of the misunderstanding in 2 as follows:

The student reports that the interview that followed was stiff and quite unsatisfactory. Being black himself, he knew that he had 'blown it' by failing to recognize the significance of the husband's speech style in this particular case. The style is that of a formulaic opening gambit used to 'check out' strangers, to see whether or not they can come up with the appropriate formulaic reply. Intent on following the instructions he had received in his methodological training and doing well in what he saw as a formal interview, the interviewer failed to notice the husband's stylistic cues. Reflecting on the incident, he himself states that, in order to show that he was on the husband's wave-length, he should have replied with a typically black response like 'Yea, I'ma git some info' (I'm going to get some information) to prove his familiarity with and his ability to understand local verbal etiquette and values. Instead, his Standard English reply was taken by the husband as an indication that the interviewer was not one of them and, perhaps, not to be trusted.

Analyses similar to 1 and 2 have been carried out by Gal on her Oberwart data; for example she cites a fairly lengthy extract which demonstrates the way a participant in a mealtime dispute signals increasing anger by repeating a final, last-word comment in German (1979: 117). Although Gumperz appears to have developed his approach initially by examining the communicative functions of code-switching, the field of study which he describes as interactional sociolinguistics is somewhat broader than these examples imply. More broadly, he examines the various linguistic resources such as prosody, use of politeness and emphasis routines, and types of discourse pattern which speakers use to signal their orientation to each other. Often these are group-specific and are not

Table 8.5 Different types of code-switching (CS)

Type	Levels of integration into Base Language			CS?	Example
	Phon.	Morph.	Syn.		
1	✓	✓	✓	No	Es possible que te MOGUEEN (They might mug you)
2	–	–	✓	Yes	Las palabras HEAVY DUTY bien grandes, se me han olvidada. (I've forgotten the real big heavy duty words)
3	✓	–	–	Yes	[da' wari se] [That's what he said)
4	–	–	–	Yes	No creo que son FIFTY-DOLLAR SUEDE ONES (I don't think they're fifty-dollar suede ones)

Source: adapted from Poplack (1980b: 584)

understood by outsiders (cf. 2 above). Consequently, the approach can be used to examine situations of communicative breakdown in industrial and other workplace settings (see further 9.2). A theory of code-switching which resembles Gumperz's in that it focuses on *speaker motive* rather than *configurations in an abstract system* has been developed by Scotton (1982; 1983).

Poplack (1980b; 1981) has approached mixed-code data like 1, 2 and 3 via an initial examination of the linguistic system rather than the speaker. To help specify linguistic constraints on the points in an utterance at which switching can take place, she classifies code-switching as shown in table 8.5 according to degree of integration into the base language (i.e. the language in which the discourse seems generally to be proceeding).

Types of code-switching are also distinguished according to the point in structure where switching takes place; tag, intersentential and intrasentential switches reflect progressively increasing levels of structural embedding of the switched language into the base language (Poplack 1980b). The ultimate goal is to specify a set of universal linguistic constraints on code-switching; for example, Poplack suggests that there are restrictions on switching by Spanish/English bilinguals within noun phrases (see Gumperz 1982: 86; Poplack 1981). However, Berk-Seligson (1986) presents Spanish/Hebrew bilingual data which challenges claims of universality. Poplack has attempted to formalize her approach by developing with Sankoff an abstract grammar of code-switching (D. Sankoff and Poplack 1981). Parts of her analytic schema have been applied to Panjabi/English data (Chana and Romaine 1984) and Yoruba/English data (Amuda 1986).

8.4.2 Analysis and interpretation: self-report data

Since the aim of most questionnaire studies is to obtain information on the effect of large-scale situational categories on code choice, methods of analysing and presenting results tend to be a little more straightforward than those considered in 8.4.1. Unlike the language samples collected by participant observation methods, the data are usually comparable, so that quantitative techniques are often appropriate. Thus for example Parasher (1980) uses the familiar histogram, as shown in figure 8.4, to present information collected from 350 informants from two Indian cities on their language use in a number of different *domains* (or sets of similar situations). The methods used by Parasher and others who have carried out questionnaire studies are discussed by Fasold (1984: chapter 7).

Sometimes an attempt is made to use questionnaire data as a basis for a *predictive* model of language choice; i.e. one which states that, given certain situational conditions, a speaker will choose language X rather than language Y. These conditions can be presented graphically in the form of a

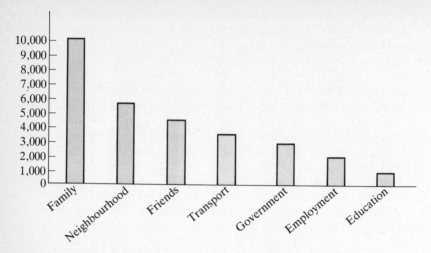

Figure 8.4   Use ratings for mother tongues in seven domains by educated Indians
(adapted from Parasher 1980)

tree diagram, which lays out situational constraints as a set of ordered, usually binary, choices. Clearly a model of this kind, as exemplified by figure 8.5, is rather more abstract than a simple quantitative presentation like figure 8.4. However, despite its aesthetic appeal and apparent advance over a simple descriptive presentation, it gives rise to certain difficulties. Particularly, switching rules tend not to be categorical, as Figure 8.5 suggests, but to be a matter of probabilities.

Gibbons's Hong Kong self-report data, collected by means of a language diary technique (see 8.3.4), is initially presented in the form of a tree diagram similar to figure 8.5. But he took the matter a good deal further, using computer-aided statistical procedures to carry out two types of analysis. The first was a series of cross-tabulations of the total number of 411 verbal exchanges reported in the language diaries (Gibbons 1983: 63). A predictive model like figure 8.5 underlay this analysis; factors such as the speaker's background and the interlocutor's background were related to language choice, the commonest choices being Cantonese, English, and a mixture of English and Cantonese on a Cantonese base which Gibbons described as MIX.

Gibbons's second type of analysis examined the *linguistic composition* of MIX, using as the data base a collection of student conversations collected by the students themselves. Situational factors such as topic, and a number of social characteristics of the speaker were related to variation in the

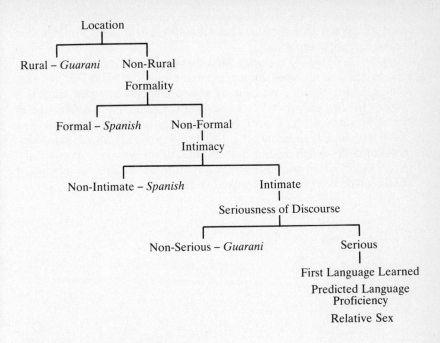

Figure 8.5   Factors affecting code choice
(adapted from Rubin 1968: 109)

linguistic composition of MIX (Gibbons 1983: 154). The procedure then was to assign to each *syllable* one of three values, depending on whether it was Cantonese, English, or of English origin but heavily modified towards the norms of MIX. The numbers obtained in this way provided the input for a computer-aided statistical program of the same general type as VARBRUL, which was designed to pick out the situational factors corresponding best with variation in syllable count.

8.5 Conclusion

Because intra-speaker variation is of interest to investigators from a number of disciplines, this chapter has covered a great deal of varied material; social psychologists have been particularly active in developing explanatory theories to account for the regularities underlying style-shifting and code-switching. Style-shifting has most often been studied quantitatively within the Labovian paradigm, while other investigative traditions and theoretical goals are associated with the study of code-switching. Because of the effect of the interlocutor on language choice, data-collection problems are generally acute in studies of intra-personal variation; this is particularly true where the object of study is a bilingual or bidialectal linguistic repertoire.

Following Bell (1984b) it is suggested that *audience design* is the critical variable underlying all types of intra-personal linguistic variation, and that monolingual style-shifting can be more coherently characterized using this model than the one elaborated by Labov where *attention to speech* is said to be the important variable. Currently, various approaches to code-switching are being developed; some investigators focus primarily on the *pragmatic* functions of code-switching and code-mixing, or on *situational* constraints, while others are more concerned with *linguistic* constraints on mixing, or on the linguistic composition of mixed codes.

9

Sociolinguistics: Some Practical Applications

9.1 Introductory

The purpose of this book has been to explore methods and problems associated with the enterprise of *obtaining, analysing* and *interpreting* language samples of a kind which allow the inevitably variable language behaviour of real speakers to be modelled as realistically as possible. We do not want our model to show the linguistic world as flat, inhabited by people who do not use the resources of variability which are the property of every known community. Most contemporary models of language, whatever their achievements in illuminating the nature of language structure or linguistic ability, are however of a type very different from any discussed here.

The generative model particularly has been criticized for equating *structure* with *homogeneity* (see particularly Labov 1975). It is not surprising that linguists who accept the major principle underlying most sociolinguistic models that *heterogeneity* is a patterned and important aspect of normal human linguistic ability should find this model unilliminating in studying (for example) non-standard syntactic systems (7.3.2; 7.5: see also L. Milroy 1985). Nor have current *psycholinguistic* models yet considered systematically the effect of situational and wider linguistic context upon the language production and comprehension abilities of speakers; although considerable advances have been made in this field in recent years, experimental work usually focuses on the subject's ability to handle single, decontextualized lexical items (for a recent overview see M. Harris and Coltheart 1986).

Popular conceptions are no more likely than these formal models to view structured heterogeneity as an essential property of human language. A common belief in the western world, where nation states have generally developed highly focused linguistic standards, is that there is one and only one 'correct' way of using the language. As a consequence of this belief, varieties other than those accepted as standard are held to be inferior; one might say that the standard language is *legitimized* and structures different from it which are characteristic of other varieties are thought of as corruptions of the standard and as illegitimate. These widely held and deeply entrenched views appear to be highly resistant to conscious reflection, and resemble the formal models discussed above in their implicit acceptance of an equation between homogeneity and orderliness (or structure). They partly account for difficulties in accessing the intuitions of speakers of non-standard dialects and in obtaining reliable self-reports on patterns of variation (cf. 8.3.2).

In general, sociolinguists are well aware of the mismatch between widely accepted popular and academic linguistic models on the one hand, and a more realistic variation-sensitive account of contemporary language use on the other. But there is one particular associated difficulty which needs to be faced if sociolinguistic methods are to be applied more routinely than at present to the solution of sociolinguistic problems. The popular model of language outlined above, which I shall refer to as 'the standard ideology', often influences judgements of speakers' language abilities even in *professional* contexts where language is the explicit focus of attention and where a realistic concept of its variable and patterned nature is a matter of practical importance. The characteristics and practical implications of this ideology are explored in detail elsewhere (Milroy and Milroy 1985a).

The wider social and political significance of matters related to language and language use has been touched on at various points in this book; consider for example the work of the Linguistic Minorities Project (2.2.4), which was originally set up under the auspices of a government department to obtain systematic information for a number of practical purposes on the range of languages in use in contemporary Britain. There are certainly a large number of quite varied contexts where sociolinguistic methods might be applied, some better explored than others. For example, a recent volume entitled *Applied Sociolinguistics* (Trudgill 1984a) includes an account of the use of quantitative method in a legal context (J. Milroy 1984) and a study of the news-editing process (Bell 1984a). Neither of these applied areas is yet as well developed as the various educational topics addressed by the majority of the contributions.

In the remainder of this chapter, we shall look briefly at recent work in three areas where sociolinguistic methods have been applied fairly extensively. The first is the *interactional sociolinguistics* developed over the last ten years or so by John Gumperz. The other two, *the educational system* and *formal language assessment* procedures, have been a focus of interest from the time that Labov first developed quantitative methods for handling urban dialects (see particularly Labov 1972a).

9.2 Interactional Sociolinguistics

The main interest of this work is in the field of intergroup (particularly interethnic) communication. One publication, *Crosstalk,* is designed as a training manual for those involved in interethnic communication in British industrial contexts. Unsatisfactory conversational exchanges, which are held to contribute to general problems of interethnic conflict, are analysed under three main headings. These are: (1) different cultural assumptions underlying communicative acts; (2) different ways of structuring inform-ation; and (3) different 'ways of speaking'. Item (3) deals particularly with language-specific differences in the conventional use of prosodic features to structure discourse and signal meaning (Gumperz, Jupp and Roberts 1979).

The theoretical principles underlying *Crosstalk* are set out clearly by Gumperz, whose general method involves the *post hoc* analysis and interpretation of selected conversational exchanges (see Gumperz 1982 and 8.4.1 above). But because *Crosstalk* is designed as a training manual, it makes extensive use of constructed data, and more recently Thorpe (1983) has taken this applied area further with a fully accountable analysis of an applied area further with a fully accountable analysis of an interview of an Asian trainee on a skillcentre course by an English skillcentre instructor.

Although communication appears on the surface to be proceeding smoothly, Thorpe shows that as a result of differences in communicative norms of the kind specified in *Crosstalk,* the interview was unsatisfactory. Despite the fact that he was well intentioned, sympathetic and carefully trained in handling the specific difficulties of ethnic minority trainees, the interviewer (who was attempting to find a way to break a piece of bad news) did not manage to engage the trainee in any kind of collaborative discussion of his performance; neither did the trainee succeed in taking the floor so that he could discuss his problems. The analysis of this unsuccessful encounter focuses mainly on turntaking patterns and on the way the interlocutors introduce and discuss topics.

Clearly, the methods of applied interactional sociolinguistics are of some social and political significance. In fact they focus chiefly on communi-cation problems in various 'gatekeeping' contexts which are of critical importance to those who, like the trainee discussed by Thorpe, are attempting to gain access to goods, services and opportunities (see also Furnborough, Jupp, Munns and Roberts 1982). Readers are referred to Gumperz's own work for a more detailed account of methods and principles.

9.3 The Educational System

No attempt can be made in this section to deal comprehensively with the many complex sociolinguistic issues relevant to eduction. But I shall attempt to illustrate, with reference to recent work, some advances in the application of sociolinguistic methods.

In recent years, the suggestion that the language of non-standard speakers should be recognized in classrooms as linguistically valid and standard English taught without any implication of disrespect for other varieties has been the source of a great deal of debate amongst linguists, parents and others. However, the counterproductive effects in the classroom of attitudes deriving from the standard ideology both on relationships with pupils and on good, systematic teaching are acknowledged by many teachers. The general problem was discussed from a sociolinguistic perspective more than twenty years ago by Halliday, McIntosh and Strevens (1964: 75–111, 232–52) and more recently by (amongst many others) Trudgill (1975), Cheshire (1982b; 1984) and Stubbs (1986). A number of general issues relating to the socially patterned nature of variation and the undesirable implications and counterproductive effects of prescriptive attitudes have been raised. Sociolinguists have also pointed out that an awareness of the socially patterned nature of linguistic variation and the linguistically valid nature of non-standard varieties does not amount to the abandonment of any attempt to teach standard English. On the contrary, a number of the contributions to a collection of papers on educational linguistics edited by Carter (1982) argue for a careful analytic approach to English language teaching based on the insights and findings of sociolinguistics. Generally speaking, there is a tendency for recent work to go beyond the discussion of general principle characteristic of earlier writing in this area, and to engage in a more immediately practical way with details of pedagogical practice.

Cheshire's study of the strategies adopted by teachers for correcting the written work of non-standard speakers is a particularly interesting example of a rather specific application of sociolinguistic method. By analysing samples of speech and writing by young non-standard speakers in the town of Reading, Cheshire shows, contrary to popular assumption, that the children do not in any sense lack knowledge of standard forms; rather, frequencies of non-standard morphological variants (for example, inflectional *s* on present tense first person verb forms such as *I sing*) are, as one might predict on the basis of knowledge of likely patterns of variation, lower in written work than in speech). Her analysis suggests that standard English cannot be taught efficiently unless the teacher has a clear understanding of the small but systematic differences between standard English norms and local dialect norms. If expressions such as *I sings* which do not correspond to standard English are counted as 'mistakes' and if such non-standard constructions which have a regular distribution in the spoken language of the community are not differentiated from other kinds of developmental difficulty in writing (as discussed by Perera (1984)), pupils become unnecessarily confused and may respond by using standard features hypercorrectly. Cheshire cites the following data from the work of Reading children who seem to have got the idea that *s* should *never* be attached to a verb stem:

1   It taste all rich and creamy
2   A hedgehog live in a hole

(Cheshire 1984: 552)

The same kind of hypercorrection in the written work of speakers of British Black English is noted by V. Edwards (1984: 567), who cites the following examples:

3   They picked up the sacks of golds
4   Some of her friends had a fights

The issue here is that many varieties of British Black English, like creolized Englishes generally, do not mark the third person singular form of the verb and the plural form of the noun by the form *s*, as in the following examples:

5   It look very good
6   The headlight are thing that you put on at night

Children who are corrected without further comment for using perfectly normal Black English expressions like 5 and 6 become understandably confused as to exactly when *s* *should* appear, and respond by over-generalizing its use. The problem arises because the teacher does not take account of systematic differences in morphological structure between standard English and Black English.

   Such examples show the relevance to classroom practice of sociolinguistic analytic method and of some of the more detailed findings of recent research. Although the work of Cheshire on a non-standard indigenous dialect and of Edwards on Black English exemplifies the same general principle, it is important to point out that problems of British Black English speakers in the educational system are particularly severe. The educational underachievement of this group relative to both indigenous British children and other groups of immigrant origin is well known, and probably springs from a number of social, historical and attitudinal as well as linguistic factors. However, British Black English is characterized by a number of creole features which differentiate the underlying system sharply from that of standard English (see Sutcliffe 1982 and V. Edwards

1986 for a description). A recent report on educational underachievement in the black community has identified these linguistic differences and lack of public and professional awareness of their character and extent as the most important contributory factor to this underachievement (Gibson and Barrow 1986).

In the United States, where the educational problems of the black community have been recognized for many years now as an important social and political issue, difficulties similar to those encountered in Britain gave rise in Ann Arbor, Michigan in 1979 to the so-called 'Black English Trial'. Expert evidence given in this trial is a further example of a rather detailed and technical application of sociolinguistic methods and findings to what is essentially an educational issue. The plaintiffs – parents of children whose progress at school had been poor – argued that the authorities had failed to take account of social, cultural and economic factors which impaired normal progress. In fact, the case was ultimately argued on whether the authorities had taken action to overcome the *linguistic* barriers which might impede the children's progress. Labov (1982b) has described the case in detail, and discussed some associated ethical issues (cf. 4.4.3).

The plaintiffs presented rather detailed technical evidence, derived from a number of sociolinguistic accounts of Black English. One of their specific points was that because assessment methods (in this case the Wepman Auditory Discrimination Test) did not take account of the structural characteristics of the Black English phonological system, the children were wrongly diagnosed as having language and auditory perception problems. Since the Wepman requires testees to distinguish between minimal pairs like *reef/wreath, pin/pen*, it was said to be biased against Black English and southern dialect speakers who often pronounced these pairs the same. As the children were required to make distinctions not present in their dialect, it was argued that their auditory and perceptual skills were likely to be underestimated with the consequence that they were inappropriately placed in remedial classes where learning opportunities were limited. Examination of the Wepman scores as entered in the children's school records showed that this had actually happened. The judge ruled that the failure of the authorities to recognize Black English as a separate language system meant that the children were handicapped in learning to read and write standard English and their social mobility ultimately blocked. The authorities were ordered to take steps to remedy the situation.

9.4 Formal Language Assessment

9.4.1 Some general issues

The complaints against the Wepman Auditory Discrimination Test in the Black English Trial illustrate the importance of systematic knowledge of the variable patterns of non-standard dialects in constructing and inter- preting language assessment procedures. But the applications of sociol- inguistic method to such procedures are very much more extensive than this example suggests.

In the past, sociolinguists have not been slow to spell out the relevance of their work to language assessment. The best-known contribution to this applied area is probably Labov's influential polemic 'The logic of nonstan- dard English' (in Labov 1972a), where he pointed out that many language tests widely used by educational psychologists were constructed on the basis of a set of invalid assumptions about the nature of language. Particularly, they ignored the influence of social context on language behaviour, and their design was in general strongly influenced by the complex of popular attitudes to language which I have referred to in this chapter as 'the standard ideology'. Since this article first appeared (1969), language testing has come under fire from a number of quarters, concern generally being expressed about its validity if a number of sociolinguistic factors are not taken into account in test design, implementation and interpretation.

In Britain, language testing has not generally been a focus of social and political concern as it has in the United States. This is largely because in the United States tests are very widely used to measure linguistic ability and to determine the kind of education most appropriate to the child who has encountered learning problems. Thus, a poorly designed language test is likely to have rather serious practical consequences. Social legislation concerned with improving the opportunities of ethnic minorities has made testing a particularly important practical issue, and much recent work by sociolinguists has examined bias against ethnic minorities of the same general type as the Ann Arbor plaintiffs found in the Wepman.

A good example of this work is Wolfram's (1974) analysis of the widely used Illinois Test of Psycholinguistic Ability (see also Wolfram and Christian 1980). ITPA contains a battery of subtests designed to measure grammatical ability, one of which is the Grammatical Closure Subtest. The procedure here is for the child to supply a missing word when the tester points to a stimulus picture, as for example when he shows a picture of two beds, points to one and says 'Here is a bed'. Next, he points to both and says 'Here are two —'. The purpose of this test item is to assess whether the child can produce plurals correctly; all items in the subtest require him or her to supply a morphological element of some kind. Since the test rubric requires responses to be in standard English in order to be considered correct, the child who,responds with *hisself* for *himself*, *mans* or *man* for *men* or *hanged up* for *hung up* is scored as incorrect. Wolfram calculates that out of a total of 33 items in the subtest, 27 may legitimately have different dialect forms, and while it is not to be expected that a given speaker will use non-standard forms for all 27 items, non-standard responses to even a fraction of these will systematically depress the scores of non-standard speakers. Problems arise because the results of tests like these are often still used to support arguments that non-standard speaking testees lack language ability in some unspecified way.

The criticisms of Wolfram and others of ITPA are fundamentally concerned with structural differences between dialects, and in recent years a start has been made on constructing tests which are not systematically biased against non-standard speakers (see for example Weiner, Lewnau and Erway 1983). But a different criticism has been made, which questions the assumption that all social groups have a similar orientation towards the task of testing. This point follows from an understanding of the notion of communicative competence, the main issue being that a test is a highly specialized event with specific rules for testees which are in fact never made explicit. For this reason, tests should not automatically be considered neutral with respect to social group of testee (see J. Edwards 1979; Taylor 1977; Taylor and Peters 1982; Wald 1981).

An important characteristic of test questions is that they are not genuine requests for information; the testee may have to give obvious information already accessible to the tester in identifying a picture, an activity or an object. Labov made the point that children often respond to conditions like this with silence, which may then be taken as an inability to encode a verbal response to the question. In fact, since test questions function as requests for a display of knowledge, it is probably understanding of this function rather than general language ability which is being tested.

Bridges (1985) has recently argued that variation in children's interpretation of test questions can often be attributed to variation in the method of presenting the task. But the social dimension is also relevant, in that even at the preschool stage middle-class socialization patterns seem to encourage children to respond to questions by displaying knowledge. The preschoolers studied by Wells in Bristol already showed variation according to class in their ability to handle test questions appropriately, a difference not found in spontaneous speech (G. Wells 1985: 333). Parallel to these findings, the work of Tizard and Hughes (1984) suggests that even at this early age middle-class children are better able than their working-class counterparts to handle public and formal interaction in the manner expected by teachers and other professionals. Their participant observation study of a small number of working- and middle-class children in both domestic and nursery school environments found that while there was little difference *at home* between the groups with respect to either maternal linguistic input or type or quantity of language produced, the difference *at nursery school* was dramatic. In response to various questions (relating, for example, to story books or activities) the middle-class children were more voluble and forthcoming than the working-class children, who then tended to be seen by the staff as less able and in need of some kind of compensatory input. The authors conclude that 'judgements on children's language abilities should be very tentative until a context is found where they talk freely and spontaneously' (Tizard and Hughes 1984: 258).

Citing Labov's early work, they point out that this essentially socio-linguistic issue is now understood by academic psychologists. One such psychologist is Carroll, who notes that 'some of the more important language abilities can be established only through studies of language performances in realistic, non-testing situations' (1979: 22). The difficulty then is not simple lack of knowledge, but that practical implications are rarely followed through: 'Teachers continue to make judgements of children on the basis of their classroom behaviour alone, doctors and psychologists on the basis of a clinic interview and test, perhaps supplemented by observations at school' (Tizard and Hughes 1984: 257). What seems to be required now is the construction of systematic means of language assessment which take into account the sensitivity of language context; and in fact techniques have been developed for assessing children's language in naturalistic situations (Lund and Duchan 1983). Similar procedures for assessing the communicative ability and potential of adult aphasics are beginning to appear (Green 1984: Lesser and Milroy 1987).

One particularly thorough piece of sociolinguistic work in this applied area is Wald's (1981) study of ten- to twelve-year-old Spanish bilingual children in California. With the explicit purpose of developing fairer and more efficient language assessment instruments, Wald systematically investigates the relationship between language performance and context. A sharp distinction is drawn between *language proficiency* as measured by standardized tests and *language ability*, 'the actual knowledge a speaker has of a language which is made use of in a variety of situations' (1981: 2). Given the fact that language proficiency measures which are intended to indicate *educational potential* succeed in eliciting only a tiny proportion of the linguistic structures of which a child is capable, Wald argues that language ability is the more relevant concept. Ideally, a language ability assessment instrument should pinpoint specific areas of difficulty, thereby suggesting guidelines for remedial action. Wald's procedure for investigating language ability follows standard sociolinguistic methodological principles, taking as the data base samples of language collected in three situations:

1   A *group interview* where an adult attempts to encourage conversation among peers.
2   A *peer conference* where children are left alone with a school-like task for about ten minutes; they are asked to construct a story to match comic strip pictures.
3   A *test interview*, where a standardized test is administered.

The similarities and differences between the language behaviour which emerged in session 3 and in the other sessions form the basis of Wald's distinction between language ability and language proficiency. His findings demonstrate in some detail potential applications of sociolinguistic methods and principles to the task of constructing language assessment procedures.

First, a similar pattern of *morphological* development emerges in all three situations, except (as one might expect) when the child's vernacular forms of the morphological elements measured in the test situation are non-standard and stigmatized. In that case the test tends to *underestimate* ability.

Second, *syntactic development* cannot be adequately sampled in test situations, information about specific constructions (such as relative clauses) emerging only in the group interview and the peer conference. The reason for this is the familiar one (to sociolinguists at least: cf. 3.2.2.) that extended stretches of speech emerge only occasionally in response to questions. One important practical point which Wald makes is that even a ten-minute corpus of spontaneous speech, if skilfully elicited, can yield concrete information about quite specific strengths and weaknesses.

Third, Wald makes the crucial point, which we shall go on to consider in 9.4.2, that formal test procedures generally cannot discriminate between *vernacular* and *under-developed* (or pathological) forms. We have already seen an example of this problem in the systematic bias of the Illinois Test of Psycholinguistic Ability against non-standard speakers; inevitably it will also fail to identify children with genuine developmental problems. But the distinction emerges clearly if the norms of the *group* are compared with the language behaviour of the individual.

9.4.2 Language assessment in clinical settings

It is worth elaborating on Wald's third point a little with particular reference to language assessment procedures in Britain. Wald's work is concerned principally with the use of language tests in the American educational system. In Britain they appear to be used less systematically and routinely in this domain, but very extensively in the speech therapy service where, as might be expected, the problems outlined in this section commonly emerge. But although the same principles hold, differences between Britain and the United States in the *application* of language testing procedures give rise to different practical outcomes. While inadequate tests in America may result directly in loss of educational opportunity, in British speech therapy clinics they result chiefly in inefficient and time-consuming assessment and remediation procedures. But it is obviously particularly important in clinical contexts to keep in mind the distinction drawn by Wald between pathological forms and non-standard or colloquial forms; language deficit theories which are intended to explain educational underachievement by children from low-status groups are particularly unhelpful in their tendency to blur this distinction.

In an extended critique of assessment procedures used in British speech therapy clinics, Crystal, Fletcher and Garman (1976) note that the conception of grammar embodied there is frequently similar to that current in society generally. They find that this results in a confusion between pathological and colloquial forms which seems to spring from a tendency to think of the norms of written language as characterizing 'normal' language and of speech as having 'little', or 'no' or 'debased' grammar. They cite one test in current use which describes the forms 'gonna', 'wanna' and 'gotta' as 'articulatory errors' (Crystal, Fletcher and Garman 1976: 12).

Although the distinction between pathological forms and virtually pan-lectal colloquial forms such as these should not present too many difficulties, distinguishing pathological forms from the vernacular forms of small or localized communities is sometimes less straightforward. The following examples, transcribed from the speech of a twelve-year-old girl in a Northern Ireland speech therapy clinic, should make the problem clear:

7   Therapist: Is he writing a letter?
    Girl: No. He writing the homework
8   She my best friend

These utterances illustrate difficulty with both the auxiliary verb system and the copula. This is a very widespread and specific linguistic problem amongst language disordered English-speaking children. It has severe functional consequences in that it affects their ability to cope with *negatives* and *interrogatives*, both of which require operations involving an auxiliary verb. The forms used by the girl might be said to be pathological forms in Northern Ireland, because they are not systematically distributed in the local speech community. However, one community where forms similar to 7 and 8 have a regular distribution is the Black English-speaking community in both Britain and the United States; *be* deletion is a characteristic of *creoles* generally (Sutcliffe 1984).

The distinction between pathological and vernacular forms needs to be made not in absolute terms, but in the terms familiar to a sociolinguist; the individual speaker's language is examined in relation to the *community norm*. As Wald points out, one way to clarify the distinction if local vernacular forms are not already known is to identify forms with a regular social distribution by sampling the language of *groups* of speakers.

9.4.3 Language assessment and bilingualism

The problem of defining what is normal in terms of patterns of community behaviour is a rather general one for speech therapists. Nowhere is the difficulty more acute than with respect to the bilingual population, where code-switching and code-mixing is the norm. Generally speaking, the patterns underlying this behaviour are quite well known to sociolinguists (see for example Chana and Romaine 1984) but have not yet become well known to professionals in the social, educational and health services who deal with young bilingual children. The difficulties which may consequently arise are illustrated by the following incident reported in a case study of a Panjabi/English-speaking bilingual child in Newcastle upon Tyne (Finnie 1985).

The child was referred to a speech therapist because it was suspected that his language was delayed. Having noticed that the child's mother sometimes used Panjabi, sometimes English, and sometimes a mixture, the therapist advised her not to mix languages when she spoke to the child. Given the systematic and largely unconscious nature of code choice and code-switching, (cf. 8.3.2), it is unlikely that this advice would be either appropriate or useful, and may even have been positively unhelpful; the following data taken from Scothern's study of Tariq, a three-year old from a Newcastle family bilingual in Panjabi and English, shows clearly that one function of code-switching is emphatic admonition of the child. Similar examples from a number of different communities are cited by Fasold (1984: 204). Here, Tariq's mother and elder sister are trying to make him climb down from the table:

Sister:	Get down off there (Tariq remains on table)
Sister:	(more loudly) [he toŋɔ tə] (Tariq remains on table)
Mother:	he [toŋɔtə] (Tariq remains on table)
Mother:	Come down you, come down (Tariq climbs down)

(Scothern 1985: 24)

This mismatch between actual patterns of bilingual language use and the proposed strategy for dealing with the language difficulties of a child from the same community as Tariq seems to stem from an inaccurate conception of what constitutes 'normal' language behaviour.

The notion of *communicative competence* is not generally well understood; academics who have worked with the concept have not so far succeeded in communicating its significance to interested professionals. Particularly, the implications of the point that bilinguals select one or another language (or a mixture) according to situation in much the same way as monolinguals select different styles are not usually followed through. Moreover, language use by bilinguals (like language use generally) needs to be understood in terms of *community* norms rather than some idealized notion of a perfect bilingual speaker. Conceptual confusions concerning the nature of societal bilingualism may, as we have seen, result in inappropriate (although usually well-intentioned) educational and remedial initiatives; they may also result in unsatisfactory theories which attempt to explain low educational achievement.

The notion of *semilingualism,* developed by educational psychologists such as Cummins in Canada and Skutnabb-Kangas in Sweden (see Cummins 1983 and Skutnabb-Kangas 1983) is apparently rapidly gaining currency in Britain and is an example of just such a theory. Semilingualism is a term used to describe a condition where bilingual children are said to know neither of their two languages well enough to sustain the advanced cognitive processes which enable them to benefit from mainstream education. As Martin-Jones and Romaine point out (1985), this line of reasoning is suspiciously like a new version of language deficit theory and, like the original deficit theories criticized by Labov, cannot easily be sustained in the face of sociolinguistic evidence. This becomes clear if we examine Cummins's (1979) definition of bilingual competence in terms of some ideal bilingual speaker with perfect knowledge of both languages; in fact bilingual speakers characteristically use each of their languages in *different* social contexts and would not be expected to use either of them in all contexts. In response to the need for a more realistic concept of normal linguistic behaviour in bilingual communities, language assessment procedures based on community norms and constructed on sounder sociolinguistic principles have recently begun to appear (Rivera 1983). But much more work is needed in this applied area.

An additional problem in assessing young bilingual children is that at present it is hard to specify what is *developmentally* normal, since very little is known about bilingual language acquisition and development patterns. For example, it is not at all clear whether a young British-born Panjabi/English bilingual child will acquire the syntactic patterns of English in the same form or the same order as his or her monolingual counterpart, and speech therapists in Britain are unable to follow their standard practice of assessing the language abilities of young children against both a developmental and a community norm (see Crystal et al 1976 for details of the procedure).

9.5 Concluding Remarks

For several reasons it seems particularly appropriate to focus in the final chapter of this book on applications of sociolinguistic methods. First, most sociolinguists are acutely aware of the relevance of their work to a range of social problems. Second, from the earliest days of the development of the field a high standard has been set, particularly by William Labov, in exploring major applications. Although the discussion in this chapter shows that there is little room for complacency, it is fair to say that over the last twenty years this standard has been maintained. Sociolinguists have continued to meet the challenge of working in communities of many types with real speakers, and of involving themselves in applied areas which often require substantial effort in mastering various theoretical and practical *non-linguistic* issues.

In recent years, sociolinguistic method has been applied at a very much more detailed level than in the past; at this earlier phase of development, scholars anxious to communicate the significance of their findings mustered considerable rhetorical and polemic skills to construct convincing arguments capable of changing professional practice. This shift in orientation may be illustrated by comparing Wald's work on language assessment with Labov's original polemic contribution to the same field. 'The logic on nonstandard English' (see p.205 above). Simply *because* many of Labov's criticisms of language assessment procedures are now generally accepted, it has become possible for scholars like Wald to work in a more focused way and produce more specific recommendations. But in many applied areas there exists (for various social, political, ideological and occasionally purely practical reasons) a yawning gap between what is accepted in principle and what is carried out in practice.

The final reason for concluding this book with a chapter on applications of sociolinguistic methodology is perhaps also the most important. Although I have dealt in several places with some quite difficult intellectual issues and indeed throughout the book stressed the need to specify underlying theoretical goals and assumptions, I hope to have demonstrated also that not all aspects of sociolinguistic method need be the exclusive property of specialists. It is there to be used, as relevant and appropriate, by anyone who wishes for whatever purpose to find a way of compiling an honest and accountable description of the way ordinary people use language in their daily lives. I hope that this book will help those who want to embark upon this task.

References

Adams, B. (ed.) (1964) *Ulster dialects: a symposium.* Hollywood, Co. Down: Ulster Folk Museum.

Ahlqvist, A. (ed.) (1982) *Papers from the 5th international conference on historical linguistics* (Current Issues in Linguistic Theory, 21). Amsterdam: John Benjamins.

Alatis, J. (ed.) (1978) *International dimensions of bilingual education* Washington DC: Georgetown University Press.

Albó, A. (1970) Social constraints on Cochabamba Quechua. Unpublished Ph.D. dissertation, University of Cornell.

Amuda, A. (1986) Language mixing by Yoruba speakers of English. Unpublished PhD thesis, University of Reading.

Australian Institute of Aboriginal Studies (1980) Research grants: information and conditions for applicants. Canberra: AIAS.

Barcelona, H. M. (1977) Language usage and preference patterns of Philipino bilinguals. In E. M. Pascasio (ed.), 64–71.

Baumann, R. and Sherzer, J. (eds) (1974) *Explorations in the ethnography of speaking.* Cambridge: CUP.

Bell, A. (1984a) Good copy – bad news: the syntax and semantics of news editing. In Trudgill (ed;) (1984a), 73–116.

Bell, A. (1984b) Language style as audience design. *Language in Society* 13, 2, 145–204.

Bell, A. (1985) One rule of news English: geographical, social and historical spread. *Te Reo* 28, 95–117.

Berk-Seligson, S. (1986) Linguistic constraints on intra-sentential code-switching: a study of Spanish/Hebrew bilingualism. *Language in Society* 15, 3, 313–48.

Bloomfield, L. (1926) A set of postulates for the study of language. *Language* 2. 153–64.

Bloomfield L. (1935) *Language.* London; Allen and Unwin.

Blom, J.-P. and Gumperz, J. J. (1972) Social meaning in linguistic structures: code-switching in Norway. In Gumperz and Hymes (eds), 407–34.

Boal, F. W. and Poole, M. A. (1976) Religious residential segregation and residential decision making in the Belfast urban area. Unpublished report to the Social Science Research Council, London.

Boissevain, J. (1974) *Friends of friends: networks, manipulators and coalitions.* Oxford: Blackwell.

Bolinger, D. (1977) *Meaning and form*, London: Longman.

Bolinger, D. (1980) *Language: the loaded weapon*. London: Longman.

Bortoni-Ricardo, S. M. (1985) *The urbanisation of rural dialect speakers: a sociolinguistic study in Brazil*. Cambridge: CUP.

Bowman, E. (1959) An attempt at an analysis of modern Yucatec from a small corpus of recorded speech. *Anthropological Linguistic* 1, 4. 43–86.

Bresnan, J. (1982) *The mental representation of grammatical relations*. Cambridge, Mass.: MIT Press.

Bridges, A (1985) 'Ask a silly question. . .': some of what goes on in language comprehension tests. *Language Teaching and Therapy*. 1, 3. 135–48.

Bright, W. (1964) Social dialect and linguistic history. In D. Hymes (ed.) 469–72.

Briggs, C. L. (1984) Learning how to ask: native meta-communicative competence and the incompetence of fieldworkers. *Language in Society* 13, 1, 1–28.

Brown, P. and Fraser, C. (1979) Speech as a marker of situation. In Scherer and Giles (eds), 33–62.

Brown, P. and Levinson, S. C.(1978). Universals in language usage: politeness phenomena. In Goody (ed.), 56–289.

Burton, F. (1978) *The politics of legitimacy - struggles in a Belfast community*. (Appendix entitled 'Theory and methodology in participant observation'). London: Routledge.

Butler, C. (1985a) *Computers in linguistics*. Oxford: Blackwell.

Butler, C. (1985b) *Statistics in linguistics*. Oxford: Blackwell.

Cameron, D. and Coates, J. (1985) Some problems in the sociolinguistic explanation of sex differences. *Language and communication* 5, 3. 143–51.

Carroll, J. B. (1979) Psychometric approaches to the study of language abilities. In Fillmore et al. (eds), 13–31.

Carter, R. (ed.) (1982) *Linguistics and the teacher*. London: Routledge.

Chambers, J. K. and Trudgill, P. (1980) *Dialectology*. Cambridge: CUP.

Chambers, J. M., Cleveland, W. S., Kleiner, B. and Tukey, P. A. (1983) *Graphical methods for data analysis*. Belmont, Calif.: Wadsworth.

Chana, V. and Romaine, S., (1984) Evaluative reactions to Panjabi–English code-switching. *Journal of Multilingual and Multicultural Development* 5. 447–53.

Chen, M. Y. (1976) Relative chronology: three methods of reconstruction. *Journal of Linguistics* 12, 209–58.

Cheshire, J. (1982a) *Variation in an English dialect: a sociolinguistic study*. Cambridge: CUP.

Cheshire, J. (1982b) Dialect features and linguistic conflict in schools. *Educational Review* 34, 1. 53–67.

Cheshire, J. (1984) Indigenous non-standard varieties and education. In Trudgill (ed.) (1984b), 564–58.

Chomsky, N. (1957) *Syntactic structures*. The Hague: Mouton.

Chomsky, N. (1965) *Aspects of the theory of syntax*. Cambridge, Mass.: MIT Press.

Chomsky, N. (1980) *Rules and representations*. Oxford: Blackwell.

Clyne, M. (1982) *Multilingual Australia*. Melbourne: River Seine Publications.

Coates, J. (1986) *Women, men and language*. London: Longman.

Cohen A. (ed.) (1982) *Belonging*. Manchester: MUP.

Congalton, A. A. (1962) *Social standings of occupations in Sydney*. Sydney: School of Sociology, University of New South Wales.

Congalton, A. A. (1969) *Status and prestige in Australia*. Melbourne: Cheshire.

Coulthard, M. (1977) *An introduction to discourse analysis*. London: Longman.

Coulmas, F. (ed.) (1981) *Conversational routines*. The Hague: Mouton.

Coupland, N. (1980) Style-shifting in a Cardiff work-setting. *Language in Society*, 9, 1–12.

Coupland, N. (1984) Accommodation at work: some phonological data and their applications. *International Journal of the Sociology of Language* 46, 49–70.

Coveney, A. (1986) Grammatical variability in French. Paper presented at a seminar in the Dept. of English Language, University of Newcastle upon Tyne.

Crystal, D. and Davy, D. (1969) *Investigating English style*. London: Longman.

Crystal, D., Fletcher, P. and Garman, M. (1976) *The grammatical analysis of language disability*. London: Arnold.

Cummins, J. (1979) Linguistic interdependence and the educational development of bilingual children. *Review of Educational Research* 49, 222–51.

Cummins, J. (1983) *Bilingualism and social education: issues in assessment and pedagogy*. Clevedon, Avon: Multilingual Matters.

Davis, A. (1984) Behind the *for–to* filter: *for–to* infinitives in Belfast and the theory of government. *Sheffield Working Papers in Language and Linguistics* 1, 56–71.

De Camp, D. (1961) Social and geographical factors in Jamaican dialects. In Le Page (ed.), 61–84.

De Camp, D. (1971) Implicational scales and sociolinguistic linearity. *Linguistics* 71, 30–43.

Dines, E. (1980) Variation in discourse – 'and stuff like that'. *Language in Society* 9, 13–33.

Di Sciullo, A. M., Muysken, P. and Singh, R. (1986) Government and code-mixing. *Journal of Linguistics* 22. 1–24.

Dixon, R. M. W. (1971) *The Dyirbal language of North Queensland*. Cambridge: CUP.

Dixon, R. M. W. (1980) *The languages of Australia*. Cambridge: CUP.

Dixon, R. M. W. (1984) *Searching for Aboriginal languages*. St Lucia: University of Queensland Press.

Dixon, R. M. W. and Blake, B. J. (eds) (1979) *Handbook of Australian languages* (Vol.1). Canberra: ANU Press, and Amsterdam: John Benjamins.

Dorian, N. (1981) *Language death*. Philadelphia: University of Pennsylvania Press.

Douglas-Cowie, E. (1978) Linguistic code-switching in a Northern Irish village: social interaction and social ambition. In Trudgill (ed.), 37–51.

Downes, W. (1984) *Language and society*. London: Fontana.

Dressler, W. U. and Wodak, R. (1982) Sociophonological methods in the study of sociolinguistic variation in Viennese German. *Language in society* 11, 1, 339–70.

Duran, R. P. (ed.) (1981) *Latino language and communicative behavior*. New Jersey: Ablex.

Eades, D. (1982) You gotta know how to talk: information-seeking in South-east Queensland Aboriginal society. *Australian Journal of Linguistics* 2. 61–83.

Edwards, J. (1979) *Language and disadvantage*. London: Arnold.

Edwards, V. (1984) British Black English and education. In Trudgill (ed.) (1984b), 559–72.

Edwards, V. (1986) *Language in a black community*. Clevedon, Avon: Multilingual Matters.

Ellis, A. W. (ed.) (1985) *Progress in the psychology of language* (Vol. 2). New York: Lawrence Erlbaum Associates.

Erickson, B. H. and Nosanchuk, T. A. (1977) *Understanding data*. Toronto: McGraw-Hill Ryerson.

Ervin-Tripp, S. (1972) Sociolinguistic rules of address. In Pride and Holmes (eds), 225–40.

Fasold, R. (1978) Language variation and linguistic competence. In D. Sankoff (ed.), 85–96.

Fasold, R. (1984) *The sociolinguistics of society*. Oxford: Blackwell.

Fillmore, C. J., Kempler, D. and Wang, S. -Y, (eds) (1979) *Individual differences in language ability and language behavior*. New York: Academic Press.

Filstead, W. (ed.) (1971) *Qualitative methodology*. Chicago: Free Press.

Finnie, K. (1985) A case study of a language disordered child. MS, Department of Speech, University of Newcastle upon Tyne.

Fishman, J., Cooper, R. and Ma, R. (1971) *Bilingualism in the Barrio*. Bloomington: Indiana UP, and The Hague: Mouton.

Fraser, C. and Scherer, K. R. (eds) (1982) *Advances in the social psychology of language*. Cambridge: CUP.

Furnborough, P., Jupp, T., Munns, R. and Roberts, C. (1982) Language disadvantage and discrimination: breaking the cycle of majority group perception. *Journal of Multilingual and Multicultural Development* 3,3. 247–66.

Gal, S. (1978) Variation and change in patterns of speaking: language shift in Austria. In D. Sankoff (ed.), 227–38.

Gal, S. (1979) *Language shift: social determinants of linguistic change in bilingual Austria*. New York: Academic Press.

Garnham, A. (1985) *Psycholinguistics: central topics*. London: Methuen.

Gazdar, G., Klein, E., Pullum. G. and Sag, I. (1985) *Generalized phrase structure grammar*. Oxford: Blackwell.

Gibbons, J. P. (1983) Code choice and code mixing in the speech of students at the University of Hong Kong. Unpublished PhD thesis, University of Reading.

Gibson, A. and Barrow, J. (1986) *The unequal struggle*. London: Centre for Caribbean studies.

Giles, H. (ed.) (1984) The dynamics of speech accommodation. *International Journal of the Sociology of Language 46* (Special issue).

Giles, H. and Powesland. P. F. (1975) *Speech style and social evaluation*. London: Academic Press.

Givón, T. (1979a) *On understanding grammar*. New York: Academic Press.

Givón T. (ed.) (1979b) *Syntax and semantics* (Vol. 12). New York: Academic Press.

Goldthorpe, J. E. (1985) *An introduction to sociology* (3rd edn). Cambridge: CUP.

Good, C. (1979) Language as social activity: negotiating conversation. *Journal of Pragmatics, 3*, 151–67.

Goody, E. N. (ed.) (1978) *Questions and politeness*. Cambridge: CUP.

Granovetter, M. (1973) The strength of weak ties. *American Journal of Sociology* 78, 1360–80.

Green, G. (1984) Communication in aphasia therapy: some of the procedures and issues involved. *British Journal of Disorders of Communication* 20, 2. 35–46.

Greenbaum, S. and Quirk, R. (1970) *Elicitation experiments in English: linguistic studies in use and attitude*. London: Longman.

Greenhill, R., Murray, M. and Spence, J. (1977) *Photography*. London: Macdonald.

Gregg R. J. (1964) Scotch-Irish urban speech in Ulster. In Adams (ed.), 163–91.

Gumperz, J. J. (1971) *Language in social groups*. Stanford: Stanford UP.

Gumperz, J. J. (1982) *Discourse strategies*. Cambridge: CUP.

Gumperz, J. J. and Hymes, D. (eds). (1972) *Directions in sociolinguistics*. New York: Holt, Rinehart and Winston.

Gumperz, J. J., Jupp, T. C. and Roberts, C. (1979) *Crosstalk: a study of cross-cultural communication*. Southall: National Centre for Industrial Language Training.

Gunn, B. (1983) Aspects of intonation in the speech of the Cork urban area. Unpublished MA thesis, University College, Cork.

Guy, G. (1980) Variation in the group and the individual: the case of final stop deletion. In Labov (ed.) 1–36.

Halliday, M. A. K., McIntosh, A. and Strevens, P. (1964) *The linguistic sciences and language teaching*. London: Longman.

Halsey, A. H. (1978) *Change in British society*. Oxford: OUP.

Hammond, D. (ed.) (1978) *Songs of Belfast*. Dublin: Gilbert Dalton.

Harris, J. (1983) The Hiberno-English 'I've it eaten' construction; what is it and where does it come from? *Teanga* (Journal for the Irish Association of Applied Linguistics) 3. 30–43.

Harris, J. (1984) Syntactic variation and dialect divergence. *Journal of Linguistics* 20, 2. 303–27.

Harris, J. (1985) *Phonological variation and change*. Cambridge; CUP.

Harris, J., Little, D. and Singleton, D. (eds) (1986) *Perspectives on the English language in Ireland*. Dublin: Trinity College.

Harris, M. and Coltheart, M. (1986) *Language processing in adults and children*. London: Routledge.

Harris, R. (1972) *Prejudice and tolerance in Ulster*. Manchester: MUP.

Harris, S. (1984) Questions as a mode of control in magistrates' courts. *International Journal of the Sociology of Language*. 49, 5–27.

Harris, Z. S. (1951) *Methods in structural linguistics*. Chicago: University of Chicago Press.

Hartford, B., Valdman, A. and Foster, C. (eds). (1982) *Issues in international bilingual education: the role of the vernacular*. New York: Plenum Press.

Healey, A. (1974) *Handling unsophisticated linguistic informants*. Canberra: ANU, Research School of Pacific Studies.

Heath, C. D. (1980) *The pronunciation of English in Cannock, Staffordshire*. Oxford: Blackwell.

Hewitt, R. (1982) White adolescent creole users and the politics of friendship. *Journal of Multilingual and Multicultural Development* 3, 217–32.

Hoaglin, D., Mosteller, M. and Tukey, J. (eds.) (1983) *Understanding robust and exploratory data analysis.* New York: Wiley.

Hoaglin, D., Mosteller, M. and Tukey, J. (eds.) (1985) *Exploring data tables, trends and shapes.* New York: Wiley.

Holmquist, J. C. (1985) Social correlates of a linguistic variable: a study in a Spanish village. *Language in Society* 14, 2. 191–204.

Horvath, B. (1985) *Variation in Australian English.* Cambridge: CUP.

Houck, C. L. (1968) Methodology of an urban speech survey. *Leeds Studies in English*, NS II, 115–28.

Huddleston, R. (1984) *Introduction to the grammar of English.* Cambridge: CUP.

Hudson, R. A. (1980) *Sociolinguistics.* Cambridge: CUP.

Hudson, R. A. and Holloway, A. F. (1977) Variation in London English, Report to the Social Science Research Council.

Hurford, J. R. (1967) The speech of one family. Unpublished PhD thesis, University of London.

Hurford, J. and Heasley, B. (1983) *Semantics: a course book.* Cambridge: CUP.

Hymes, D. (ed.) (1964) *Language in culture and society.* New York: Harper and Row.

Hymes, D. (1972) On communicative competence. In Pride and Holmes (eds), 269–93.

Hymes, D. (1974) *Foundations in sociolinguistics: an ethnographic approach.* Philadelphia: University of Pennsylvania Press.

Hymes, D. and Fought, J. (1980) *Amercian structuralism.* The Hague: Mouton.

Hymes, V. (1975) The ethnography of linguistic intuitions at Warm Springs. In Reich (ed.), 29–36.

Jahangiri, N. (1980) A sociolinguistic study of Tehrani Persian. PhD thesis, University of London.

Jahangiri, N. and Hudson, R. A.. (1982) Patterns of variation in Tehrani Persian. In Romaine (ed.), 49–63.

Johnson, M. (1986) Transcription and computer analysis of child language. Paper presented at the Child Language Seminar, University of Durham.

Johnston, P. (1983) Irregular style variation patterns in Edinburgh speech. *Scottish Language* 2, 1–19.

Kallen, J. (1986) The co-occurrence of *do* and *be* in Hiberno-English. In Harris et al. (eds.), 133–48.

Kay, J. (1985) Mechanisms of oral reading: a critical appraisal of cognitive models. In Ellis (ed.), 73–105.

Kerswill, P. (1984) Levels of linguistic variation in Durham. In *Cambridge Papers in Phonetics and Experimental Linguistics* 3. Department of Linguistics, University of Cambridge.

Kibrik, A. E. (1977) *The methodology of field investigations in linguistics.* Janua Linguarum, Series Minor. The Hague: Mouton.

Klein, W. and Dittmar, N. (1979) *Developing grammars.* Berlin: Springer.

Knowles, G. (1978) The nature of phonological variables in Scouse. In Trudgill (ed.) 80–90.

Kroch, A. and Small, C. (1978) Grammatical ideology and its effect on speech. In D. Sankoff (ed.), 45–56.

Kurath, H. (1972) *Studies in area linguistics.* Bloomington: Indiana UP.

Laberge, S. and Sankoff, G. (1980) Anything *you* can do. In G. Sankoff (1980a), 271–93.

Labov, W. (1966) *The social stratification of English in New York City.* Washingotn, DC: Center for Applied Linguistics.

Labov, W. (1972a) *Language in the inner city.* Philadelphia: Pennsylvania University Press.

Labov. W. (1972b) *Sociolinguistic patterns.* Philadelphia: Pennsylvania University Press.

Labov, W. (1972c) Some principles of linguistic methodology. *Language in Society* 1, 97–120.

Labov, W. (1973) Where do grammars stop? In Shuy (ed.), 43–88.

Labov, W. (1975) *What is a linguistic fact?* Lisse: Peter de Ridder Press.

Labov, W. (ed.) (1980) *Locating language in time and space.* New York: Academic Press.

Labov, W. (1981) Field methods used by the project on linguistic change and variation. *Sociolinguistic Working Paper* 81. Austin, Texas: South Western Educational Development Laboratory.

Labov, W. (1982a) Building on empirical foundations. In Lehmann and Malkiel (eds.), 79–92.

Labov, W. (1982b) Objectivity and commitment in linguistic science: the case of the Black English trial in Ann Arbor. *Language in Society* 11, 165–201.

Labov, W., Cohen, P., Robins, C. and Lewis, J. (1968) A study of the non-standard English of Negro and Puerto-Rican speakers in New York City. Report on Co-operative Research Project 3288. Washington D.C.: Office of Education.

Labov, W. and Fanshel, D. (1977) *Therapeutic discourse.* New York: Academic Press.

Labov, W. and Sankoff, D. (1980) Preface to Labov (ed.).

Labov, W., Yaeger, M. and Steiner, R. (1972) A quantitative study of sound change in progress. Report on NSF Project no. GS-3287. University of Pennsylvania: US Regional Survey.

Larson, S. S. (1982) The two sides of the house: identity and social organisation in Kilbroney, Northern Ireland. In Cohen (ed.), 131–64.

Lass, N., McReynolds, N.V., Northern, J.L. and Yoder, D.E. et al. (eds) (1982) *Speech, Language, and hearing: normal processes and clinical disorders* (3 vols). Philadelphia: Saunders.

Lass, R. (1984) *Phonology: an introduction to basic concepts.* Cambridge: CUP.

Lavandera, B. (1975) Linguistic structure and sociolinguistic conditioning in the use of verbal endings in *si* clauses (Buenos Aires Spanish). Unpublishied PhD dissertation, University of Pennsylvania.

Lavandera, B. (1978a) The variable component in bilingual performance. In Alatis (ed.), 391–411.

Lavandera, B. (1978b) Where does the sociolinguistic variable stop? *Language in Society*, 7. 171–82.

Lavandera, B. (1982) Le principe de réinterpretation dans la théorie de la variation. In Dittmar, N. and Schlieben-Lange, B (eds.), *Die Soziolinguistik in romanischsprachigen Ländern,* 87–96. Narr: Tübingen.

Lavandera B, (1984) *Variación y significado.* Buenos Aires: Hachette.

Laver, J. (1981) Linguistic routines and politeness in greeting and parting. In Coulmas (ed.), 289–318.

Leech, G. and Beale, A. (1984) Computers in English language research. *Language Teaching* 17, 3. 216–29.

Lehmann, W. P. and Malkiel, Y. (eds) (1982) *Perspectives on historical linguistics*. Amsterdam and Philadelphia: Benjamins.

Leodolter, R. and Stark, H. (1972) Soziolinguistische Interpretation der 'Schnells-prechregeln'. In Dressler, W. et al. (1972) Phonologische Schnellsprechregeln in der Wiener Umgangsprache. *Wiener Linguistische Gazette*, 1–29. Cited by Dressler and Wodak (1982).

Le Page, R. B. (1954) Linguistic survey of the British Caribbean: Questionnaire A. Jamaicia: University College of the West Indies.

Le Page, R. B. (1957/8) General outlines of creole English dialects in the Caribbean. *Orbis* 6, 373–91, and 7, 54–64.

Le Page, R. B. (ed.) (1961) *Creole language studies II*. London: Macmillan.

Le Page, R. B. and Tabouret-Keller, A. (1985) *Acts of identity*. Cambridge: CUP.

Lepschy, G. (1982) *A survey of structural linguistics* (2nd edn). Oxford: Blackwell.

Lesser, R. and Milroy, L. (1987) Two frontiers in aphasia therapy. *Bulletin of the College of Speech Therapists*. London: CST.

Levinson, S. (1983) *Pragmatics*. Cambridge: CUP.

Linguistic Minorities Project (1985) *The other languages of England*. London: Routledge.

Lloyd, P. (1979) *Slums of hope?* Harmondsworth: Penguin.

Longacre, R. E. (1964) *Grammar discovery procedures*. The Hague: Mouton.

Lovie, A. (1985) *New developments in statistics for psychology and the social sciences*. London: British Psychological Society and Methuen.

Lund, N. J. and Duchan, J. F. (1983) *Assessing children's language in naturalistic contexts*. Englewood Cliffs: Prentice-Hall.

Macaulay, R. K. S. (1977) *Language, social class, and education*. Edinburgh: Edinburgh UP.

Macaulay, R. K. S. (1978) Variation and consistency in Glaswegian English. In Trudgill (ed.) 132–43.

MacAfee, C. (1983) *Glasgow*. Amsterdam: Benjamins.

McCawley, J. D. (1971) Tense and time reference in English. In Filmore, C. J. and Langedoen, D. T. (eds) *Studies in linguistic semantics*. New York: Holt, Rinehart and Winston. 96–103.

McEntegart, D. and Le Page, R. B. (1982) An appraisal of the statistical techniques used in the Sociolinguistic Survey of Multilingual Communities. In Romaine (ed.) 105–24.

McIntosh, A. (1952) *An introduction to a survey of Scottish dialects*. Edinburgh: Nelson.

Martin-Jones, M. and Romaine, S. (1985) Semilingualism: a half-baked theory of communicative competence. *Applied Linguistics* 7, 26–38.

Mewett, P. (1982) Associational categories and the social location of relationships in a Lewis crofting community. In Cohen (ed.), 101–130.

Miller, J. (1986) *That:* a relative pronoun? Sociolinguistics and syntactic analysis. Presented at the 6th Sociolinguistics Symposium, University of Newcastle upon Tyne.

Miller J. (forthcoming) The grammar of Scottish English. Pamphlet written for the Economic and Social Research Council.

Milroy, J. (1976) Length and height variation in the vowels of Belfast vernacular. *Belfast Working Papers in Language and Linguistics* 1. 3.

Milroy, J. (1981a) *Regional accents of English: Belfast*. Belfast: Blackstaff.

Milroy, J. (1981b) Review of D. Sankoff (ed.) (1978). *Language in Society* 10. 104–11.

Milroy, J. (1982) Probing under the tip of the iceberg: phonological normalization and the shape of speech communities. In Romaine (ed.) 35–47.

Milroy, J. (1984) Sociolinguistic methodology and the identification of speakers' voices in legal proceedings. In Trudgill (ed.) (1984a), 51–72.

Milroy, J. (1985) The methodology of urban language studies: the example of Belfast. In J. Harris et al (ed.), 31–48.

Milroy, J. (forthcoming) *Society and language change*. To be published by Basil Blackwell.

Milroy, J. and Harris, J. (1980) When is a merger not a merger? The MEAT/ MATE problem in a present-day English vernacular. *English world wide* 1,2, 199–210.

Milroy, J., Milroy, L., Gunn, B., Harris, J., Pitts, A. and Policansky, L. (1983) Sociolinguistic variation and linguistic change in Belfast. Report to the Social Science Research Council. (Grant no. HR 5777.)

Milroy, J. and Milroy, L. (1978) Belfast; change and variation in an urban vernacular. In Trudgill (ed.), 19–36.

Milroy, J. and Milroy, L. (1985a) *Authority in language*. London: Routledge.

Milroy, J. and Milroy, L. (1985b) Linguistic change. Social network and speaker innovation. *Journal of Linguistics*. 21. 339–84.

Milroy, L. (1980) *Language and social networks*. Oxford: Blackwell.

Milroy, L. (1985) What a performance! Some problems with the competence– performance distinction. *Australian Journal of Linguistics* 51, 1–17.

Milroy, L. (in press) Review of Horvath, 1985. To appear in *Language and Society*.

Moore, T. and Carling, C. (1982) *Understanding language: towards a post-Chomskyan linguistics*. London: Macmillan.

Morawska, A. and Smith, G. (1984) The adult language use survey of the Linguistic Minorities Project. *LMP Working Paper* 9. London: University of London Institute of Education.

Moser, C. A. and Kalton, G. (1971) *Survey methods in social investigation*. London: Heinemann.

Neu, H. (1980) Ranking of constraints on /t,d/ deletion in American English: a statistical analysis. In Labov (ed.), 37–54.

Nordberg, B. (1980) Sociolinguistic fieldwork experiences of the unit for advanced studies in modern Swedish. FUMS Report no. 90. Uppsala: FUMS.

Ochs, E. (1979) Transcription as theory. In Ochs and Schieffelin (eds.), 43–72.

Ochs, E. and Schieffelin, B. B. (eds) (1979) *Developmental pragmatics*. New York: Academic Press.

Orton, H. (1962) *Survey of English dialects: introduction*. Leeds: E. J. Arnold.

Pascasio, E. M. (ed.) (1977) *The Filipino bilingual: studies on Philipine bilingualism and bilingual education*. Quezon City: Ateneo de Manila University Press.

Parasher, S. N. (1980) Mother-tongue-English diglossia: a case-study of educated Indian bilinguals' language use. *Anthropological Linguistics*. 22, 4. 151–68.

Patterson, D. (1860) *Provincialisms of Belfast*. Belfast: Mayne Boyd.

Payne, A. C. (1980) Factors controlling the acquisition of the Philadelphia dialect by out-of-state children. In Labov (ed.), 143–78.

Perera, K. (1984) *Children's writing and reading*. Oxford: Blackwell.

Petyt, M. (1980) *The study of dialect: an introduction to dialectology*. London: Deutsch.

Pitts, A. (1982) The elusive vernacular: an account of fieldwork techniques in urban sociolinguistic studies in Northern Ireland. *Belfast Working Papers in Language and Linguistics* 6. 104–21.

Pitts, A. (1983) Urban speech in Ulster: a comparative study of two communities. Unpublished PhD dissertation, University of Michigan.

Pitts, A. (1985) Urban influence on phonological variation in a Northern Irish speech community. *English World Wide* 6, 1. 59–85.

Plutchik, R. (1974) *Foundations of experimental research* (2nd edn). New York: Harper and Row.

Policansky, L. (1980) Belfast verb concord variation. Paper presented at the Third Sociolinguistics Symposium, West Midlands College of Education, Walsall.

Policansky, L. (1982) Grammatical variation in Belfast English. *Belfast Working Papers in Language and Linguistics* 6. 37–66.

Poplack, S. (1980a) The notion of the plural in Puerto Rican Spanish: competing constraints on (s) deletion. In Labov (ed.), 55–68.

Poplack, S. (1980b) Sometimes I'll start a sentence in English Y TERMINO EN ESPANOL: towards a typology of codeswitching. *Linguistics* 18, 561–618.

Poplack, S. (1981) Syntactic structures and social functions of codeswitching. In Duran (ed.), 169–84.

Poplack. S. (1982) Bilingualism and the vernacular. In Hartford et al. (eds), 1–24.

Pride, J. B. and Holmes, J. (eds) (1972) *Sociolinguistics*. Harmondsworth: Penguin.

Quirk, R., Greenbaum, S., Leech, G. and Svartvik, J. ((1972) *A grammar of contemporary English*. London: Longman.

Reich, P. A. (ed.) (1975) *Proceedings of the second LACUS Forum*. Columbia and South Carolina: Hornbeam Press.

Reid, E. (1978) Social and stylistic variation in the speech of children: some evidence from Edinburgh. In Trudgill (ed.), 158–72.

Reid, I. (1977) *Social class differences in Britain*. London: Open Books.

Rimmer, S. (1982) On variability in Birmingham speech. MALS Journal 7. 1–16.

Rivera, C. (ed.) (1983) *An ethnographic/sociolinguistic approach to language proficiency assessment*. Clevedon, Avon: Multilingual Matters.

Romaine, S. (1978a) Post-vocalic /r/ in Scottish English: sound change in progress. In Trudgill (ed.), 144–57.

Romaine, S. (1978b) Problems in the investigation of linguistic attitudes in *Work in Progress*, 11–29. Dept. of Linguistics, University of Edinburgh.

Romaine, S. (1980) A critical overview of the methodology of urban British sociolinguistics. *English World Wide* 1, 2. 163–98.

Romaine, S. (ed.) (1982a) *Sociolinguistic variation in speech communities*. London: Arnold.

Romaine, S. (1982b) The reconstruction of language in its social context: methodology for a socio-historical linguistic theory. In Ahlqvist (ed.), 293–303.

Romaine, S. (1983) Collecting and interpreting self-reported data on the language of linguistic minorities by means of 'language diaries'. MALS Journal 8, 3–30.

Romaine, S. (1984a) *The language of children and adolescents.* Oxford: Blackwell.

Romaine, S. (1984b) On the problem of syntactic variation and pragmatic meaning in sociolinguistic theory. *Folia linguistica* 18, 3–4, 409–437.

Rubin, J. (1968) *National bilingualism in Paraguay.* The Hague: Mouton.

Russell, J. (1982) Networks and sociolinguistic variation in an African urban setting. In Romaine (ed.), 125–40.

Rynkiewich, M. A. and Spradley, J. P. (1971) *Ethnics and anthropology: dilemmas in fieldwork.* New York: Wiley.

Sacks, H., Schegloff, E. and Jefferson, G. (1974) A simplest systematics for the organisation of turn-taking in conversation. *Language* 50, 696–735.

Samarin, W. J. (1967) *Field linguistics.* New York: Holt, Rinehart, and Winston.

Sankoff, D. (ed.) (1978) *Linguistic variation: models and methods.* New York: Academic Press.

Sankoff, D. and Laberge, S. (1978) The linguistic market and the statistical explanation of variability. In D. Sankoff (ed), 239–50.

Sankoff, D. and Poplack, S. (1981) A formal grammar for codeswitching. *Papers in Linguistics: International Journal of Human Communication* 14, 1. 3–45.

Sankoff, G. (1980a) *The social life of language.* Philadelphia, University of Pennsylvania Press.

Sankoff, G. (1980b) Above and beyond phonology in variable rules. In G. Sankoff (1980a), 81–93.

Sankoff, G. (1980c) A quantitative paradigm for the study of communicative competence. In G. Sankoff (1980a), 47–79.

Sankoff, G. and Brown, P. (1980) The origins of syntax in discourse. A case study of Tok Pisin relatives. In G. Sankoff (1980a), 211–55.

Sankoff, G. and Laberge, S, (1980) On the acquisition of native speakers by a language. In Sankoff (1980a), 195–209.

Sankoff, G. and Thibault, P. (1980) The alternation between the auxiliaries *avoir* and *être* in Montreal French. In G. Sankoff (1980a), 295–309.

Sankoff, G. ad Vincent, D. (1980) The productive use of *ne* in spoken Montreal French. In G. Sankoff (1980a), 295–310.

Saville-Troike, M. (ed.) (1977) *Linguistics and anthropology.* Washington, D.C.: Georgetown University Press.

Saville-Troike, M. (1982) *The ethnography of communication.* Oxford: Blackwell.

Schegloff, E. (1979) The relevance of repair to syntax for conversation. In Givón (ed.) 261–86.

Scherer, K. R. and Giles, H. (eds.), (1979) *Social markers in speech.* Cambridge: CUP.

Schmidt, A. (1985) *Young people's Dyirbal.* Cambridge: CUP.

Scothern, J. (1985) A case-study of a bilingual child in his family environment. Unpublished undergraduate dissertation, Department of Speech, University of Newcastle upon Tyne.

Scotton, C. M. (1982) The possibility of codeswitching; motivation for maintaining multilingualism. *Anthropological Linguistics* 24, 4. 432–44.

Scotton, C. M. (1983) The negotiation of identities in conversations: a theory of markedness and code choice. *International Journal of the Sociology of Language* 44, 115–36.

Sherzer, J. (1977) The ethnography of speaking: a critical appraisal. In Saville-Troike (ed.), 43–57.

Shopen, T. and Williams, J. M. (eds) (1980) *Standards and dialects in English*. Cambridge, Mass.: Winthrop.

Shuy, R. W. (ed.) (1973) *Sociolinguistics, current trends and prospects*. Georgetown University Round Table: Georgetown.

Shuy, R. W., Wolfram, W. A. and Riley, W. K. (1968) *Field techniques in an urban language study*. Washington, DC: Center for Applied Linguistics.

Singh, R. (1983) We, they and us: a note on code-switching and stratification in North India. *Language in Society* 12, 71–73.

Singh, R. (1985) Grammatical constraints on code-mixing: evidence from Hindi-English. *Canadian Journal of Linguistics* 30, 1. 33–45.

Sivertsen, E. (1960) *Cockney phonology*. Oslo: Oslo UP.

Skutnabb-Kangas, T. (1983) *Bilingualism or not: the education of minorities*. Clevedon, Avon: Multilingual Matters.

Smith, G. (1984) Sampling linguistic minorities: a technical report on the adult language use survey. *LMP Working Paper* 4. London: University of London Institute of Education.

Smith, G. (1985) Language, ethnicity, employment, education and research: the struggle of the Sylheti-speaking people in London, *CLE/LMP Working Paper* 13. London: University of London Institute of Education.

Snow, C. (1986) Conversations with children. In Fletcher, P. and Garman, M. (eds), *Language acquisition* (2nd edn). Cambridge: CUP 69–88.

Snow, C. and Ferguson C. (eds) (1979) *Talking to children: language input and acquisition*. Cambridge: CUP.

Stubbs, M. (1983) *Discourse analysis*. Oxford: Blackwell.

Stubbs, M. (1986) *Educational linguistics*. Oxford: Blackwell.

Sutcliffe, D. (1982) *British Black English,* Oxford: Blackwell.

Sutcliffe, D. (1984) British Black English and West Indian Creoles, In Trudgill (ed.) (1984b), 219–37.

Sutton, P. and Walsh, M. (1979) *Revised sociolinguistic fieldwork manual for Australia*. Canberra: Inst. of Aboriginal Studies.

Taylor, O. (1977) The sociolinguistic dimension in standardised testing. In Saville-Troike (ed.), 257–66.

Taylor, O. and Peters, C. (1982) Sociolinguistics and communication disorders. In Lass et al. (eds), Vol. 2, 802–818.

Thakerar, J. N. Giles, H. and Cheshire, J. (1982) Psychological and linguistic parameters of speech accommodation theory. In Fraser and Scherer (eds.), 205–55.

Thelander, Mats (1982) A qualitative approach to the quantitative data of speech variation. In Romaine (ed.), 65–83.

Tizard, B. and Hughes, M. (1984) *Young children learning*. London: Fontana.

Thompson, E. P. (1963) *The making of the English working class*. London: Gollancz.

Thorpe, D. (1983) 'Letting him down lightly'. A training appraisal interview.

NCILT Working Paper 37, London: National Centre for Industrial Language Training.

Trudgill, P. (1974) *The social differentiation of English in Norwich*. Cambridge: CUP.

Trudgill, P. (ed.) (1978) *Sociolinguistic patterns in British English*. London, Arnold.

Trudgill, P. (1983a) *On dialect*. Oxford: Blackwell.

Trudgill, P. (1983b) *Sociolinguistics* (2nd edn). Harmondsworth: Penguin.

Trudgill, P. (ed.) (1984a) *Language in the British Isles*. London: Academic Press.

Trudgill, P. (ed.) (1984b) *Applied Sociolinguistics*. London: Academic Press.

Trudgill, P. (1985) *Accent, dialect and the school*. London: Arnold,

Trudgill, P. (1986a) The apparent time paradigm: Norwich revisited. Paper presented at the 6th Sociolinguistics Symposium, University of Newcastle upon Tyne.

Trudgill, P. (1986b) *Dialects in contact*. Oxford: Blackwell.

Tukey, J. (1977) *Exploratory data analysis*. Reading, Mass.,: Addison Wesley.

Verma, S. K. (1976) Code-switching: Hindi-English. *Lingua,* 38, 2. 153–65.

Vidich, A. (1971) Participant observation and the collection and interpretation of data. In Filstead (ed.), 164–73.

Viereck, W. (1966) *Phonematische analyse des Dialekts von Gateshead-upon-Tyne, Co. Durham*. Hamburg: Cram, de Gruyter.

Wakelin, M. (1972) *Patterns in the folk speech of the British Isles*. London: Athlone.

Wald, B. (1981) Topic and situation as factors in language performance. *NCBR Working Paper*. California: National Center for Bilingual Research.

Wang, W. S. -Y, (1969) Competing changes as a cause of residue. *Language* 45, 9–25.

Wardhaugh, R. (1986) *An introduction to sociolinguistics*. Oxford: Blackwell.

Weiner, E. J. and Labov, W. (1983) Constraints on the agentless passive. *Journal of Linguistics*, 19. 29–58.

Weissmann, E. (1970) Phonematische analyse des Stadtdialects von Bristol. *Phonetica* 21, 151–81; 211–40.

Wells, G. (1985) *Language development in the preschool years*. Cambridge: CUP.

Wells, J. C. (1982) *Accents of English: an introduction*. Cambridge: CUP.

Whitely, W. H. (ed.) (1974) *Language in Kenya*. Nairobi: OUP.

Weiner, F. D., Lewnau, N. E. and Erway, E. (1983) Measuring language competency in speakers of black American English. *Journal of Speech and Hearing Disorders* 48, 76–84.

Wilson, J. (1981) Come on now, answer the question: an analysis of constraints on answers. *Belfast Working Papers in Language and Linguistics* 5. 93–121.

Wolfram, W. (1974) Levels of sociolinguistic bias in testing. Mimeo. Washington DC: Center for Applied Linguistics.

Wolfram, W. (1980) *a*-Prefixing in Appalachian English. In Labov (ed.), 107–42.

Wolfram, W, and Christian, D. (1976) *Appalachian speech*. Washington DC: Center for Applied Linguistics.

Wolfram, W. and Christian, D. (1980) On the application of Sociolinguistic information: test evaluation and dialect differences in Appalachia. In Shopen and Williams (eds), 177–209.

Wolfson, N. (1982) *CHP: the conversational historic present in American English narrative*. Dordrecht: Foris.

Woolford, E. (1982) Bilingual code-switching and syntactic theory. *Linguistic Inquiry* 13, 519–35.

Index